The 12th Disciple
Book One
By Scott Peters

Cover Artwork
Illustrated Covers by Maya Ritchie
Graphic Design Cover by Crystal Peak Design
www.crystalpeak.com

Copyright Information

The 12ᵗʰ Disciple

Acknowledgements

To my family, thank you. To my friends, thank you. I am truly blessed. Thank you Gretchen, Heather, and Emily for editing much of the material. For our brave American soldiers and first responders to tragedies of unimaginable magnitude, thank you. For the people of Egypt, Libya, and other countries fighting for personal freedoms and a better way of life, thanks for your inspiration. To those people in the Holy Land, may peace be with you.

www.12thdisciple.com

Twitter: 12DiscipleBook

To contact the author: scott@gigs-n-rigs.com

Preface
From the author...

First and foremost, the 12th Disciple is fiction, religious fiction. When I told some people that I was writing religious fiction, some commented that the Bible was a great place to start. I wasn't bothered by the comments because I believe in religious freedoms and expression. Life is a journey, and many people will experience God at different intersections in their own life. My life has experienced God at different intersections and I don't believe my experience is unique.

I was baptized Presbyterian and became a practicing Catholic. The Presbyterian Church was free flowing filled with great choirs and less kneeling. The Catholic Church provides more consistency in their approach to mass and reading scriptures, and the familiarity of mass becomes comfortable to many members. I have found that there is no right or wrong way to worship a creator, just as long as the worship serves to better humanity...all of humanity.

The 12th Disciple is my second publication in five years. I learned much from the first writing experience (mostly, what not to do). The 12th Disciple has no curse words. I wanted to write a book devoid of bad language to maintain the integrity of what the Bible and religious leaders have taught me over the years. The concepts of virginity and Immaculate Conception are maintained throughout the narrative also. In fact, there are several Biblical concepts promoted in the 12th Disciple. For me, the Bible contains the greatest stories ever told...period.

Rarely do we see a sequel (The New Testament) completely blow away a first book (The Old Testament).

The concept of evil is written differently in The 12th Disciple. I refer to evil people as **Samil**. Evil people can be American, Muslim, Russian, Christian, Iranian or any nationality and culture for that matter. I believe humanity should begin to separate evil from nationality and culture. Evil Americans are really no different than evil people everywhere else. Whether people are blowing up Federal Buildings in Oklahoma City, flying planes into buildings in New York City, shooting children on Utoya Island, blowing up a disco in Germany or Israel, or poisoning hundreds of people in Guyana, the result is the same...pure evil.

I hope you enjoy reading The 12th Disciple. Two years was spent writing, researching, and putting together a story of modern day heroes. The story is about a period leading up to Revelation. The modern day Disciples are made up of men and women from all over the world. They begin to understand their calling when they locate the 12th Disciple.

****

Matt lunged forward into darkness. His body was wet with sweat as he contemplated his surroundings. Soft surface beneath him, covers below his waist, and mattress to each side of him. He was in bed and beginning to process reality. Matt reached tentatively to his right fumbling for the lamp on a cluttered end table with a sports drink, book, and phone. Matt was careful not to knock anything off or spill the drink.

The light illuminated the room of a 25 year old. A flat screen TV was mounted above a dresser at the foot of the bed, crooked. A dirty clothes hamper draped with work out clothes, button down dress shirts, and socks rolled into balls littered the top of the hamper and the floor. An inspirational picture with the definition of "Courage" reflected an activity during September 11th, 2001 when three firemen placed an American flag at ground zero, eerily similar to World War 2 and the positioning of an American Flag at Iwo Jima. The picture rested above Matt's computer desk. In the corner of the room there was a computer desk with a laptop, printer, and pictures of Matt's family, a family not extended, but limited to an older sister. Mary was a beautiful 29-year-old woman with her own family. Her children, John age 3 and Rebecca age 1, were good kids and had the look of joy in a holiday photograph. Michael, Mary's husband, was a 32 year-old owner of a pizza joint that featured Chicago style pies and a massive game room for kids to remain occupied and away from their parents. Michael was also a veteran of the second Gulf War under the leadership of George W Bush. Serving as a Marine, Michael had seen plenty of action and scored many confirmed kills of the enemy in Iraq and abroad. Michael was good to Matt.

Reaching under the bed, Matt found his journal and turned to a page with a folded corner. Still writing in cursive, Matt began to document the dream that had just unfolded. There was a wall, a massive wall in a plaza that had been built brick by brick. The bricks were large and made of sandstone; their yellowish hue gave way to red liquid oozing from the pores of rock. Matt paused to think for a couple seconds, and then documented his thoughts in the journal. Was the liquid blood? As he thought about the question he began to think of its rhetorical nature. What did the liquid represent? Whose blood and why was it coming from a wall? Matt searched his mind once again and thought back to Iraq and Afghanistan. Had he seen anything similar to these surroundings while serving in both countries? Not that he could remember.

The plaza was empty in the dream except for a scattering of black birds that perched atop the wall. The wall was large and as Matt remembered looking up at the birds, the sun burned bright in the background. The black birds almost eclipsed the sun and cast shadows over the plaza and elongated silhouettes along on the wall. The thought of birds at the wall seemed odd to Matt as the location didn't seem like a natural habitat for big, black birds. It was almost as if the birds had found their way to the wall by traveling a great distance.

Pausing for a moment, Matt thought hard about what happened next in his dream. As his attention was drawn from the black birds and sun, Matt gazed to his left along the wall. Several yards down the wall stood a woman, maybe 19 or 20 with her head hung low looking down at the ground. Both her arms were outstretched leaning against the wall with palms flat against the stone. Because the woman's head was down, Matt couldn't get a good look at her initially. She was obviously in distress and tears were dropping from her cheeks to the stone floor. Matt's first feeling was an air of shame emanating from her emotional demeanor. She wasn't Western; she was shifting her weight back and forth from left to right as she peered at the ground. Matt could remember wanting to help the woman, but felt cautious about invading her space along the wall. After spending time fighting wars in the Middle East, Matt was hesitant to involve himself in something that appeared to be an invitation.

As the lady stood there, rhythmically rocking back and forth, blood began to run from the wall down her arms. Matt noticed the lady didn't appear to be alarmed by the viscous material trickling down her hands, covering her forearms, and retreating into her garments where it blotted her clothing. Was this woman someone he had killed in a military deployment overseas? Matt paused for a moment and closed his eyes, he couldn't remember killing any women, at least not deliberately. He closed his eyes; he played out the remainder of his dream. The woman noticed Matt nearby and slowly brought her arms down from the wall. She turned to face him and he noticed her beauty beneath the circumstance. She had long dark hair that ran flat to her scalp and down along her shoulders and back. The hair seemed to terminate around the region of her waist. At her waistline, there was a rope tied around the garment that ran from her shoulders to a length below the knees. The garment was woven and made to fit this woman, not sexy, but made for durability. Her eyes were blue in a sea of olive colored skin and her features were soft with delicate lines around the cheekbones and jaw line. Matt turned a few pages back in the journal to find the same woman in a different setting. He flipped a few more pages back and studied a paragraph intensely. After a couple seconds, he found the same description of the woman standing along the shoreline of a river. The woman didn't have blood on her arms or garments, but she cupped her hands and took water from the rivulet. Matt had noted that she turned in his direction, and he had awakened from the dream in a similar fashion to this morning's encounter.

Matt chuckled to himself as he pictured something while reading the woman's description. He thought that his description reflected the physical traits of Pocahontas in the Disney films and that maybe he was watching too much senseless TV with his nephew. Matt continued to look over the past entries of his journal to find clues and patterns. Not noticing much right away, he returned to continue his current entry. As the woman turned toward him, she rolled her hands over to expose her palms. They were covered in blood that dripped at the fingertips. After examining her hands, Matt stole a glance back at her face and her lips began to move. In English, and without an accent, she spoke to him,

"Please help me."

Her request was without desperation or emotion. Matt viewed the request as more matter of fact than, "Hey buddy, hurry it up, I'm bleeding to death." At that point, the woman formed two creases on each side of her lips and forced a little smile. The last thing Matt remembered was waking up in terror and not knowing where he was.

Matt bought the journal seven months earlier after returning with his Special Operation's unit from Afghanistan. Initially he wanted to document some of his thoughts about war and recall fond memories of fallen friends, but his writing quickly turned to the chronicling of dreams and vivid encounters with this ubiquitous woman. Matt turned his arm over to read his watch.

1:40 am

Matt welcomed the idea of more sleep before his 5:00 am wake up call. As he turned to the end table to extinguish the lamp, a cat jumped from the floor directly to his lap.

"Hey Scratches."

Scratches returned the greeting with a meow.

"Lights Out."

Scratches began to purr. Matt moved the cat to his left and rolled toward her. He was happy to have Scratches as company; she was a good cat.

****

Mornings came early for Matt. After traveling half the world with the military, Matt understood the importance of being up early. Many times he would lay awake in bed and think about things. Things that took him back to his time as a child when life seemed more innocent. Things that took him overseas to fight an enemy that he didn't know or understand very well. Things that reminded him of his parents and how good they were to him and Mary.

His room was pitch black. He had learned to sleep in total darkness as a soldier in Special Operations. While serving with his Special Ops Division, he would always find an area that was completely dark to sleep in for the night. He didn't want any surprises while he drifted off to rest his body and recharge his batteries. Matt also slept with a flashlight and a 1911 .45 semi automatic handgun that was modified with a laser sight. He slept with both companions every night since returning home from the Middle East. As Matt lay in complete darkness, he thought about the woman in his dream. There may have been a number of connections with the woman in the dream and experiences in his real life. Matt spent some time in Littleton during the late 1990's and his dad was stationed at Lowry Air Force Base. His dad was working with the Air Force to test satellite recognition systems for Missile Defense. With Norad, the Air Force Academy, and several Air Force bases within driving distance, Matt's dad was busy winding down his career. His dad had flown F-15s up until the point his rank relegated him to training and earned him an office with a nameplate on the door. His dad was respected.

Mom stayed at home for much of Matt's childhood. She found it easier to raise him and Mary instead of focus on a career with multiple military moves. She was smart and had graduated from Texas Tech with honors. Mom and Dad had met while he was stationed at Reese Air Force Base for a brief period of time. She was contracted with the military during her graduate studies as an engineer and met his father on base. She was working on drag coefficents of Air Force jets and his father took an interest in her schoolwork. They waited a few years and married after she finished graduate school. His mom was revered.

Many moves brought them to Littleton and dad's duties with the Air Force were a main reason. Matt enjoyed Littleton and the bedroom community close to Denver. However, there was one incident emblazoned in his mind that set a course for the rest of his life. April 20th, 1999 was the day that Matt had almost lost his older sister and remembers burying a few friends. Columbine had become recognized as one of the greatest school tragedies in recent history and was an anniversary of the Waco siege and bombing of the Alfred P. Murrah building in Oklahoma City. Matt had no idea that April 20th would become such an important date in the course of his history. Mary had been in the library when the massacre began at Columbine. After distressed teachers informed the students to get down, Mary took refuge in a closet and cracked the door for viewing. Barely able to see activity from the door, Mary watched as the belligerents went from table to table and executed students. She was horrified and blocked out much of the memory that took place in the library. His sister had been courageous.

Matt's mom had received a phone call from a friend at about 11:40 am on April 20th and she immediately went into action. She stopped by a nearby elementary school and grabbed Matt out of class and headed for Columbine. Matt and his mom were met with mass panic and chaos at Columbine. Police had set up barriers well in advance of the high school entrances by the time they arrived onsite. They were instructed to rendezvous at Clement Park. It was at that point Matt noticed his sister being escorted by two policemen. Mary had blood all over her upper torso and arms, much like the woman in his dream. Matt didn't know if there was a connection between the woman in the dream and the attack on Columbine that left his sister scarred. As Matt was completing his work at elementary school, he anticipated that he would carry on his school career at Columbine, which he did. However the tragedy didn't end there in 1999...

Mary was a very strong person and her life changed after April 20th, 1999. She was more reserved around people and became obsessive about how to exit a room, a building, or even her own house. She was very protective of Matt, and even though she graduated from Columbine following the tragedy, she didn't want her brother to attend the high school. She was concerned about copycat incidents and the stigma surrounding the school. Matt's parents didn't feel the same way as Mary. They felt Columbine had been a good school for Mary and would be equally beneficial to Matt's education. He would attend Columbine as well. Matt's first year was wonderful as he played football, baseball, and wrestled. His wrestling skills took him to the state championship where he was beaten by a junior wrestler in the same weight class. Even though Matt was good enough to compete with the junior, he lacked the experience in a wrestling tournament to win the title. He shot for the other wrestler's legs and missed his mark, only to find himself in a reversal and losing more points. Matt didn't get pinned, but he lost the match by 2 points. Matt began to understand the importance of minimizing mistakes in life.

His freshman year at Columbine was great and he enjoyed the social circles and athletic activities of high school. Matt had also begun martial arts and training in mixed martial arts competition during his freshman year. He enjoyed fighting and beating an opponent. Submission was the clearest form of defeat, and he enjoyed when opponents were knocked or tapped out. Much of his sophomore year was shaping up to be better than his freshman year. Matt had trained all summer long for football, baseball, and wrestling. When he wasn't scooping ice cream at a locally owned parlor, he was running, punching bags, or catching passes from his teammates. Matt had become part of the 200 lb. club and was bench-pressing in excess of 200 lbs. at the weight room. All of his coaches had taken notice and Matt was destined to excel academically and athletically. John Lennon wrote about life happening while we make other plans, the same was true with Mary and Matt.

****

Mary was enjoying her sophomore year at The University of Colorado when the Dean of Business called her cell phone. Mary was glued to the TV in the commons of the Business School when she received the call. Classes had been cancelled because two planes slammed into The World Trade Center buildings, a plane had flown into the Pentagon, and another plane erratically crashed into a Pennsylvanian field. Students were huddled, for hours, around any news source that provided information of an apparent terrorist attack on the United States.

The Dean instructed Mary to come to her office immediately; Mary informed the Dean that she was already in the building watching news of the attack.

The Dean emphasized, "Please come quickly to my office on the 2nd floor," before she hung up the phone.

Mary knew that emotions were running high for everyone on this fateful Tuesday and didn't think much of the Dean's urgency. She headed towards the office. The Dean bypassed her Administrative Assistant and walked right to Mary. Mary had never met Dean Phillips before, but knew of her success inside the university and outside in a civilian world. She was very gracious and polite as she offered Mary a seat near her desk.

Dean Phillips was not watching the news in her office, but Mary could hear a TV with news on just outside the door.

"Please forgive me for the abruptness and our meeting like this."

Mary nodded in affirmation and remained silent.

"The tragic events of today have undoubtedly changed the history of our nation and untold families throughout the world. The CIA was called in to work with the airlines to scrutinize the flight manifests and each of the passengers that perished."

Because Mary felt a little uncomfortable and had been through the tragedy of Columbine two years prior, she wanted to connect with the Dean on some level.

Mary interjected, "I have seen the horrors of terror and live with the consequences of Columbine every day. I held dying friends in my arms that were buried 3 days later. What happened today will have lingering effects forever. I still fight with the guilt of surviving in the library that day."

Dean Phillips knew that Mary attended Columbine. She was a very special student that had overcome tragedy and death once before, the Dean would share Mary's newest trial with her face-to-face.

Dean Phillips hesitated and folded her hands together resting her elbows on the desk.

"Mary, you're a very special woman and I'm aware of your resolve and bravery at Columbine. I'm here to share some more tragic news with you today."

Mary leaned forward on the chair and became completely focused on Dean Phillips' lips.

"Mary, one of the flights was in route from Washington to Los Angeles. According to the manifest, Mr. & Mrs. Hiatt from Littleton, Colorado were on the plane bound for Los Angeles. I received a call from the CIA to inform me that your parents have perished in the plane that struck the Pentagon. Because your father is active in the military and working with the Air Force on classified programs, the CIA has confirmed that both of your parents made the flight and perished upon impact. I'm truly sorry for your loss."

Mary was still recovering from the bloodshed of Columbine. Her parents had been a wonderful support system through her graduation and placement at The University of Colorado. The University of Colorado had shown their support to Mary by offering her a full scholarship as reward for an academic performance that placed her in the top 15% of her graduating class. Without hesitation, Mary bolted from the office. As Dean Phillips exited her chair and made it to the office door, she witnessed Mary vanish through the oversized double doors that separated the atrium from the rest of the Business School. Dean Phillips would give Mary time to connect with her surviving family and friends before she would follow up with her later that evening.

Mary frantically dialed her parents' cell phones repeatedly. All she received was voice mail when she was successful making it through an overloaded circuit board. Anybody and everybody were calling friends, family, airlines, the White House, Governor's offices, and military bases throughout the world. Each of Mary's attempts to call had a one in three hundred million chance to get through.

She crossed the street from the campus to the apartment she shared with another student. Sarah, her roommate, wasn't there. Mary tossed her backpack down on the couch and hit power on the TV remote. She surfed the channels to CNN and tossed the remote on the love seat. Mary had thought about Matt on her walk from the Business School to her apartment. She didn't want to call him and alarm him of the news of their parents; she wanted to see Matt in person. Before that, she had to find out for herself. After the computer was powered up, she used the search engine for American Airlines. She clicked on the link and looked for numbers. American Airlines had already posted a hotline for inquiries of family members that had questions about relatives. Mary began to dial the number listed. Failed attempt after failed attempt with her cell phone; she needed her charger. While retrieving her charger she grabbed the cordless phone. Mary was now dialing with two phones to reach the hotline for American Airlines. A representative came on the phone.

"This is American Airlines, Richard speaking, how may I help you?"

Mary didn't hesitate

"I believe my parents may have been on the flight from Washington Dulles to Los Angeles. I need you to confirm that they were on the flight."

"May I have your first and last name and the first and last names of your parents?"

"Mary Hiatt and my parents' names are Robert and Dorothy Hiatt. Can you please check your records and see if they boarded the plane?"

Richard was excellent at speaking with people and had been assigned by management to answer emergency phone calls shortly after American Airlines learned of two planes being hijacked and crashed into the World Trade Center and Pentagon.

"Mary, how did you discover that your parents might have been on this flight?"

"I go to school at The University of Colorado and the Dean of Business called me into her office about 15 minutes ago to inform me about my parents. I left her office and came home to phone American Airlines directly. Is it true?"

Richard had been searching his database. The CIA shared information with the airlines about next of kin, notification procedures, and very general protocol. Mary Hiatt checked out as next of kin and notes were listed by her name that Dean Phillips had been notified to deliver the news. Richard typed 4:17 pm in his log as the time Mary Hiatt phoned.

"Mary, as I search my database for manifests and information, can you take a couple deep breaths and possibly get something to drink?" Mary was anxious and breathing heavily, she thought that might be a good idea as she waited. Richard stated,

"Let me know when you're back on the phone."

Mary got a soda from the fridge and dampened a washcloth. She placed the cloth at the base of her neck and returned to the phone.

"I'm back."

"Mary, I have the manifest for the flight from Dulles to Los Angeles and I show that a Robert and Dorothy Hiatt boarded the plane this morning at Dulles and are presumed deceased with all others aboard the aircraft."

Mary tilted her head back. The soda remained unopened and she closed her eyes. The wash towel went from the base of her neck to her face and eyes. She began to weep for the loss of her parents.

"Mary, are you with someone or by yourself?"

Her eyes remained closed, "I'm by myself."

She thought of Matt at Columbine.

"I want you to know that I'm here to remain on the line with you for as long as you wish and I'll dispatch someone to your home for assistance."

Little did Richard know that Robert's Air Force squadron had already been alerted and an agent had been assigned to look over the interests of Mary and Matt.

Mary removed the washcloth from her face and spoke softly to Richard,

"I need to go find my younger brother, I appreciate the offer, but I must find Matt right now."

Richard reiterated he would help by dispatching assistance from American Airlines or the Littleton police.

"No thanks, I'll find my brother and we'll manage."

Mary hung up the phone and turned her attention to the TV. CNN was interviewing people in New York that were located at the newly termed "Ground Zero" in New York City. Mary dialed Matt's cell number; she figured he'd be staying with a friend.

****

Matt's alarm clock went off at 5:00 am as scheduled. He was still thinking about his sister and how strong she had been for him after his parents' passing. The alarm reminded Matt of his days in Special Operations training. Matt had downloaded the sound of an LWRC M6A2 automatic weapon and programmed his iPod to play the firing for his alarm. The sound was amplified through a docking station that had speakers. The instructor for Matt's division used to scare the troops by waking them up to the sound of an automatic weapon. By using blanks, the instructor would sneak into the barracks and begin to fire the weapon. At first, the gunfire scared Matt speechless, elevating his heart rate to dangerously high levels. After several weeks of being roused by the fire of an automatic weapon, he became used to the sound and even anticipated it. Scratches, on the other hand, had never gotten used to the sound of an automatic weapon early in the morning. She scurried to the kitchen to wait for breakfast.

Matt rolled out of bed and went to his dresser. He threw on a shirt, socks, and grabbed his windbreaker. On the top of the dresser was a harness for his .45. He put his arms through the harness and tugged the straps to secure the belt. Matt retrieved the firearm and tucked it under his left pectoral muscle. With his right hand, Matt could arm himself from the holster on the harness in about one second. He had practiced while being stationed overseas for months at a time. Not only could he arm himself in a second, but he could also hit a target within a few inches at one hundred yards. Firing a round took only ½ second. Matt had timed himself on the range discharging round after round until he was satisfied that he could take out an objective in less than two seconds.

As Matt headed for the door to his townhome, he called Scratches to her dish. Scratches had shown up 7 months ago after Matt's return from the Middle East. Scratches would paw at Matt's front door until he opened it. She was emaciated, homeless, and losing fur when he first discovered her. The idea of a cat for a companion appealed to him, and he spoiled her with toys, a cat tree, and catnip. Matt was amused by Scratches reaction to catnip and enjoyed watching her tear up the house after exposure to the herb.

Matt turned the knob and began his jog from the front of his porch. Los Angeles had become an interesting city during the past 7 months. The city and the state of California were out of money and cutting budgets to unreasonable levels for teachers, police, and firemen. Matt understood the impact of cutting budgets for the military. Training was cut first and the bar was lowered for many applicants coming into the military to serve their country. This put them and veterans at great risk when they went into battle. Matt depressed the button on his watch to start the stopwatch. He was off into the darkness of LA.

He pushed himself to run 5 minute 30 second miles for a five-mile stretch. His course involved some hills and a stroll through the campus of UCLA. There wasn't much to see on a run this early in the morning and Matt remained focused on his watch. Summer in Los Angeles was a great place to stay in shape and train for his next assignment with the Marines. Even though Matt was stationed at Pendleton for briefings and some training, the military allowed him to work as a civilian and maintain status as a reservist; this was one of the perks of being in Special Operations. Down time was important to those involved with Special Operations.

5 minutes and 23 seconds in the first mile. Matt was now on the terrain of UCLA. Well lit and covered with canopy, Matt

loved the campus. His times would slough off while on campus because he liked looking around and taking in the university. The guards knew Matt and let him roam the campus freely. He could be trusted and his presence made the guards feel like the campus was a little safer with Matt there. As he cut through the campus he looked at his watch, 5 minutes and 41 seconds, pretty normal for this stretch. Matt saluted the guard as he exited the gate; the guard was a veteran of Desert Storm and permanently disabled with a knee replacement. Matt found himself back in the darkness of the city.

He was on Sunset Boulevard and picking up steam. Approaching a bridge he noticed a stranger peering through a chain link fence looking down on Sunset Boulevard. Matt did a quick assessment. Man of large stature, probably 6'4 or 6'5, with leather pants and combat boots. The man wore a leather vest and his arms were exposed to the shoulder; tattoos on both arms. He was black and wore a beret. His arms were crossed and Matt could make out sizable biceps, triceps, and deltoids. Matt noticed that the man was staring right at him and Matt returned the stare as he went under the bridge. He reached into his windbreaker and switched the safety on his .45 to the off position. As he came through the bridge, Matt heard a chopper fire up and ride the acccelerator. The chopper took off and switched gears rapidly as it disappeared down a suburban street. Matt realized that the encounter was not by chance, and that someone was watching him; watching him to track the route of his run and where to make contact. Matt did not view the encounter as hostile because he didn't have to shoot anybody or interrogate someone. Maybe the encounter was nothing. Matt looked down at his watch, 5 minutes and 17 seconds. He left the .45 ready to fire.

Matt veered off his course before he reached the townhouse. He knew that if somebody were stalking his townhome they would be surveying from a car, nearby home or apartment, or in shrubbery adjacent to his home. Matt went from prey to predator. He peeled off his route ½ mile from his home. Matt drew his .45 and began to hug a fence line down an alley. He had canvassed many alleys before and fleshed out places to hide: driveways, open gates, oversized posts, open vehicles, boats, and trashcans. If something looked disturbed, Matt did a quick assessment and moved on. He understood the importance of maintaining a fast pace through the alley; as stalkers were likely to be alarmed and make mistakes when they were surprised. Matt knew the well-lit streets and ones left pitch. He chose to move down the streets that were left pitch. Anything that didn't look familiar, Matt gravitated toward. He checked out vans and cars that he didn't recognize, any suspicious activity in both houses and apartments on the way back to his townhome; lights on, curtains drawn back, or movement on the 2nd floor drew his suspicion. Matt was an expert at clearing homes, streets, and vehicles left empty on the side of a road. Too many of his brothers and sisters in the military had been picked off by snipers and improvised explosive devices on the roads of Iraq and Afghanistan. Matt knew what he was looking for.

Arrival at his townhome was met without incident and Matt chose to clear it before entering. He scaled the fence that bordered his property and a neighbor to the north. In a matter of seconds he was on the roof and climbing the eave quietly. Matt knew the eave would be less noisy than the main roof of the house. As he climbed the eave, Matt would kneel down and peer into each window from above. The gables peaked at 24 feet above the ground and Matt utilized the ridge to cross from the north side of the townhome to the south. He scaled down both gable ends and looked for signs of movement or entry in his home; nothing seemed out of the ordinary. That's when he caught something out of the corner of his eye. Up the street under a lamppost was the same man he had seen on the bridge. This time he was seated on the motorcycle with both arms outstretched on the bars. Matt and the stranger were involved in an awkward stare again. Matt raised his .45 and engaged the trigger to spot the laser. The laser was aimed right at the stranger's upper chest around the proximity of his aorta. The man on the motorcycle looked down at his chest and back up at Matt; he started the motorcycle and revved the engine a few times. He drove by Matt's townhome and up the street. Matt kept the laser sight locked on the stranger's temple as he passed the townhome; he didn't seem concerned that Matt had a lock on him.

Matt turned his attention back to the townhome and clearing his windows and doors. Back door clear, garage door clear, side door clear, front door clear, the windows appeared to be locked and undisturbed. He went in through the front door and saw Scratches waiting for him. She was licking the upper portion of her paws and grooming her face.

"Anybody here Scratches?"

Scratches meowed.

Matt went through each room methodically with the .45 outstretched and arms running parallel to the laser site. The townhouse was clear. Matt went to his security system at the computer desk and ran back digital data on each one of his rooms simultaneously on the laptop with split screen. Nobody had entered the townhome. Matt hit a few keys on the keyboard and sent the security feed over the Internet. Matt reached into his windbreaker and grabbed his Smartphone. He punched the Internet button, went to favorites, and brought up SECURITY. He placed his index finger over the SECURITY button. The Smartphone prompted Matt to accept a live feed. He accepted the live feed. He was now looking at Scratches near the front door of his townhome on his Smartphone. Matt had the option to toggle from room to room on the phone. He checked each of the rooms until he saw himself in the bedroom looking at the phone. By then, Scratches was sneaking up on Matt and he took the laser site from the gun and began to move it erratically on the carpet. Scratches chased the laser in all directions. Matt moved the laser up the wall and Scratches jumped to reach the red dot on the wall. Matt began laughing as Scratches chased the laser site frantically around the room.

A quick shower, energy drink, and a bowl of cereal prepared Matt for the day. Although he was concerned about the stranger stalking him, Matt wasn't convinced the man was hostile; the stranger seemed more of a pest than anything else. As Matt looked in the mirror of the bathroom, he saw his computer desk with his sister's family in the reflection. He wondered if his strange dream had something to do with his sister Mary, or if this random woman was more of an allegory representing something deeper in Matt's psyche. He buttoned down his shirt, pulled on his dress slacks, threw a tie around his neck, and was out the door to his garage. In the garage waiting was Matt's 2011 Mustang; one thing he didn't skimp on was the horsepower of an American made classic. Matt was extra careful as he backed out, gun in its holster ready to fire. Nothing seemed out of the ordinary in the neighborhood. Matt kept his right arm close to his chest as he moved out of the driveway and down the street. He was leaving for work at 6:40 am

****

Matt enjoyed his job working for a defense contractor servicing Pendleton. Delta Defense Corporation had relied heavily on Matt's consulting to develop weapons, gear, and provisions for all divisions of the military. Matt had worn the heavy packs, eaten the MREs, slept in tents and bags sold to the Marines, and more importantly, engaged the enemy and scored kills during his campaigns. Matt provided critical information to the development of products and their usefulness to troops fighting abroad. He was somewhat of a hero around the office. 7:05 am was a typical time for Matt to arrive at the office. Delta Defense had about 290 people working in offices throughout the world. Matt had been assigned to work with Delta Defense during his time between deployments. The pay was good and the work was interesting. Glass double doors with DD on the front met Matt as he entered.

"Good morning Mr. Hiatt," Matt heard the greeting from his left as he entered the building.

"And a great morning to you too Ms. Hannah," Matt gestured toward the reception desk.

Matt carried himself well and was usually noticed by the opposite sex. At 6'2 and 215 lbs., Matt had the physique of a decathlete with larger biceps. The buttoned down dress shirt and tie made Matt's appearance bigger and more sophisticated. A harness with a gun in tow made Matt seem invincible. His dark hair was combed neatly and semi-parted to the right. The light blue button down shirt he chose earlier that morning accentuated his light blue eyes. Ms. Hannah kept her eyes on Matt as he whisked by and pushed the "up" elevator button.

"Ms. Hannah," Matt caught Susan off guard in a stare.

"Yes Mr. Hiatt," Less confidence in Susan's voice was apparent after being discovered.

"Have a great birthday." The arrow lit up and the doors opened for Matt.

"Thank you Mr. Hiatt." Susan was pleased Matt remembered her birthday.

Matt entered the elevator and pushed seven. The seventh floor required a special key for access. Matt took his card and inserted it into the slot. The doors began to close and he adjusted his tie. A quick trip to the seventh floor and the elevator doors opened. There was an atrium and security tables on each side of a hallway upon exiting the elevator.

"Hey Matt, good morning." One of the security officers moved toward him.

Matt raised his arms and allowed the officers to do a quick search

"As usual, we'll check your weapon and leave it up here."

The officer disarmed Matt and the wand waved over his upper torso.

"Any other weapons Matt?" One of the officers inquired as he waved the wand from top to bottom.

Without stopping, the wand buzzed and the officer checked Matt's sternum area. He pulled out a gold cross and waved the wand back over the area, the wand went silent.

"I've got a KT around my ankle," Matt motioned to his left ankle.

"You haven't worn the KT since starting here, something different?" Another officer began to disarm the KT around Matt's ankle while the wand continued to work its way down.

"Just a gut feeling I have, thought wearing it today might be a good idea."

"All clear Matt, have a good morning."

"As always gentlemen, at ease and carry on." Matt continued down the corridor and the hallway opened up into half-wall cubicles bordered by full offices on the perimeter. Research and design accounted for a lion's share of work that took place on the 7th floor of Delta. Top graduates in engineering, science, math, and psychology found their way to the seventh floor of Delta through hard work and innovation. Over the years, Matt felt like Corporate America had given up its place as a great manufacturer; Delta allowed him to see a small segment of people still committed to design and manufacturing of products in the United States. All of the products Delta offered had to be manufactured in the United States and split between two independent contractors. Delta employees, civilian and military, had to be cleared by the CIA and carried security clearance at high levels. The subcontractors underwent more stringent scrutinizing, as they possessed the engineering, design, and raw materials to manufacture new products. Even a backpack for the military was classified and given the highest priority of security. Delta Defense had begun work on large-scale interceptors for intercontinental ballistic missiles. The threat of nuclear weapons being launched from multiple hostile countries had become very real over the past decade. Protection of the US was not only paramount, but key to the success of allied nations too. The divide between good and evil had grown wider in recent years; Matt had seen this first hand in the Middle East. The irony with the Holy Land and chaos in and around Jerusalem bothered Matt. He felt most religions in the area were missing the point of calling such an area a Holy Land and maintaining peace. The United States hadn't helped the situation in the Holy Land with its backdoor policies and inconsistencies with support over the years.

The 7th floor was relatively empty at this hour, but Matt knew Noah would be in his office. He headed for offices on the left side of the building.

Noah was huddled over his computer and whacking the keys on the keyboard. He was one of the hardest working employees at Delta and Matt had worked closely with him on some major projects. Matt stopped at Noah's door.

"You get any closer to that screen and you'll glow in the dark."

Noah turned slightly, "Now that's something the military can utilize, I think I'll get a little closer."

Noah turned all the way around in his wheelchair to face Matt.

"How have you been?"

"Great. How was vacation?" Matt took a few steps into the office and sat down across from Noah's desk. Noah rolled the wheelchair to an oversized desk.

"Vacation was great. Cabo San Lucas is home to some of the best beaches, postcard sunsets, and more importantly, great tequila."

"We sure did miss you around here," Matt understood how important the position at Delta was to Noah.

"Yeah, I can tell, everything is sitting just like I left it," Noah motioned to his IN basket and overflowing files on his desk.

Matt turned to see that someone was entering the cubicle area of the office. "C'mon Noah, the people in this office wouldn't know what to do with your assignments anyway."

"Hey, check this out Hiatt," Noah turned back to his computer and saved what he was working on. He closed out of the program occupying his desktop and clicked on a folder titled "Shoulder Cannon".

"We had 576 bugs when we initialized the software for the shoulder cannon," Noah went to take a sip of coffee.

"Before I went on vacation, the team at Delta, including you, had worked through 461 bugs that prevented optimum performance of the cannon. We are left with 115 bugs to scrub before the software phase of this project is ready for field-testing. Out of the 115 bugs remaining, about 70% of the bugs require minimal code change for improvement."

Noah went back to his coffee cup to sip more flavored caffeine. "With the remaining 35 complex bugs, I figured out two this morning that are pivotal to the best performance of *my little friend*." To the right hand side of the computer was a gun with multiple barrels mounted to a harness that contained several moving parts. The harness was mounted to a molded shoulder made out of plastic. Next to the plastic shoulder were a headset that contained a small round LCD on the left hand side and a microphone and earpiece that ran close to the cheek on the right.

Noah grabbed the headset, "Matty, put this thing on for me." Matt caught the headset as Noah tossed it over the desk. Matt stood up and put on the headset. He adjusted an LCD screen that acted similar to a photo chromatic lens. Matt had worn the headset several times during testing at the office.

"Okay Matt, when I activate the headset there will be specific commands to communicate with the weapon. The first thing you will say is 'voice recognition'. The computer will recognize your voice and you'll be the only one to give commands. The three commands I want you to test are arm, lock, and eye scan."

"I'm ready," Matt looked like a cyborg from the not so distant future.

"A few key strokes and we'll be ready for action," Noah began hacking away at the keyboard. "You are ready to initialize," Noah hit the enter key.

Matt looked at the cannon. "Voice recognition."

Matt heard the computer speak through the earpiece, "Voice recognition complete, proceed with your command." Matt was surprised by the computer's voice, a lady that was soft spoken and subtle.

"Arm." Matt watched the cannon on the shoulder come to life as the LCD screen lit up. Even though the LCD was transparent with a frame, Matt could read data scrolling in front of his left eye; he was able to see through the data and the LCD lens. The LCD quit scrolling data and "ready" with red letters was visible in the top left hand corner of the screen. With voice recognition, the LCD was capable of targeting objectives in the front or rear. The cannon was equipped with a computer eye in the front and back of the weapon's housing. Matt could lock on targets behind him by focusing on a target in the LCD screen. When the cannon was locked on a target to the rear, the LCD would only transmit a signal from behind the cannon. If multiple targets were selected in front and back, the operator would utilize voice commands to toggle back and forth between objectives in the LCD.

Noah was watching the computer, "Matt, move your eyes around the room."

The cannon followed Matt's sight around the room. Instead of responding to head movements, the cannon focused on Matt's pupil location to pick up targets in the room. The LCD screen was reading Matt's eye movements and scanning the retinal image 15,000 times per second. When the LCD captured targets from behind, the screen was able to process retinal images from the eye to secure a lock on multiple objectives from the rear.

"Matt. Find something in the room and say lock." In front of Matt was a small globe on one of the shelves in Noah's office. "Lock," The image was captured on the LCD screen and minimized to the top right hand corner. Matt was impressed that the LCD screen magnified everything in front of his left eye. Even though he was wearing a relatively small lens over his eye, items were magnified through the LCD.

Noah saw the lock Matt had chosen. "Matty, the beauty of this cannon is that you can lock onto nine targets at the same time. Even though you can do a 290-degree scan with the weapon, you'll maintain each lock in the upper right hand corner of the LCD screen. You can fire upon one target or all nine almost simultaneously. Understand, once you've locked on a target, you'll be in a position to eliminate the objective."

Matt began to lock on different items around the room, including Noah. The LCD screen would minimize each of the targets and catalog them to the upper right hand corner.

"Each target will be stored in the sequence you lock on objectives. You can clear targets and pull up any number from 1 to 9 as you scan for objectives. Once you pull up a target and say fire, the cannon will do the rest." Noah looked pleased as he pulled away from his computer and looked at Matt. Matt was still looking around the room as the gun followed in the direction of his sight. He had to close his right eye to maintain balance and not get dizzy.

Matt called out, "Eye Scan."

From the LCD screen a laser began to scan Matt's eye. The scan took 2 seconds and a subdued computer voice spoke in his right ear. "Hello Mr. Hiatt. Please initiate your next command when ready," Matt thought the function was cool.

Noah smiled at Matt and did his best high-pitched computer voice, "Matty, I belong to you and shall obey your every command," Noah began to laugh. Continuing with the computer voice, "Matty, take me off this silly plastic prosthetic and let's get to work," Noah began to laugh harder at his own impersonation.

"Why don't you utilize goggles to cover both eyes?" Matt looked like Popeye with his right eye closed.

Noah responded as if he'd explained the design of the single eyepiece before. "Nothing compares to the human eye when considering vision. The brain is able to process information much faster and eliminate errors that a computer can't recognize."

"What errors?"

"Mirrors, foreground and background, peripheral vision, and a whole host of other complex algorithms that a computer can't be taught. Vision of the human eye must be maintained toward the front for assurance that an objective is destroyed."

"What about the back?"

"You'll have to rely on information transmitted from an eye mounted on the back of the cannon. Trust me, you'll know if the cannon is picking up a target that needs to be eliminated from the back. Car chases, foot races, and other obvious scenarios are great for the cannon. You can eliminate a target to the rear in a car chase without taking your eye off the road. By the way, over 97% of objectives are targeted from the front of any weapon."

Matt smiled as he pulled the helmet off his head, "Pretty cool Noah. This will have some great uses in the field. What kind of caliber is the cannon shooting?"

Noah was quick to return an answer, " 50 caliber in each of the nine barrels." Noah continued on, "3 rounds per second in each barrel." Noah popped open the housing to the cannon. "The housing accepts 3 different loading chambers from a belt fed system. Rounds are tight and extra close to feed barrels quickly. Understand Matty, any of these barrels can be utilized to destroy one target simultaneously or nine different targets at once. The flexibility is limitless. The earpiece will preserve hearing in the operator's right or left ear. Delta can control the weapon from a computer as well. If the operator is disabled, Delta can still operate the cannon."

"Thanks for the demonstration. Keep on working on balance and mounting mechanisms so an infantryman isn't falling over trying to hold the cannon up."

Matt left Noah's office and went to his own. He had a nice view of a golf course from his window. Powering up the computer, Matt reached behind to a mini-fridge and opened the door. The fridge was stocked with sports drinks, soft drinks, and chilled coffee drinks. Matt chose a coffee drink to start the morning. The computer came to life and Matt began to check his emails. Emails had become rampant in the corporate world and Matt viewed most information as passing the buck. He hated emails. Matt's inbox showed 120 new messages. He could have deleted all of them and not missed a beat, but Matt was concerned that something of importance could be lurking in the quagmire of information.

"What a waste of time," Matt said to himself as he began to hit the "X" button on the toolbar.

"Did somebody actually think this was important enough to send along?" Matt continued to gripe to himself.

After deleting 12 messages, an Instant Message appeared in the lower right hand corner of Matt's computer.

The text said, "We should meet." The text was from Sesom.

Matt thought to himself, "I don't know anybody by the name of Sesom." He began to type.

"I don't know anyone on the payroll named Sesom. Please advise to the nature of our meeting and who you are."

A prompt reply was returned, "Too long to cover in text box, the spoken word will be more convincing than communication through a computer."

Matt was searching the directory at Delta for a first or last name of Sesom. Nothing was found.

"It doesn't appear that you work for Delta, how did you access the server?"

"I have friends who are good with computers."

Matt began to fire missiles through the text box. "Why should I trust you, you're a hack and breached Internet security monitored by the Federal government."

"If that's the worst thing I do today, this day shall be better than most." Matt detected a bit of sarcasm with the response.

"I'm busy. You might want to hack into the executives' computers and see if they're available. They may want to speak with you about an Information Technology position with Delta." Matt thought the brush off would be sufficient to quiet the hack.

"Mr. Hiatt, my persistence will not stop as your life is in danger."

Matt was becoming irritated by the Instant Messaging, "If my life is in danger, how would a complete stranger with an odd name that I've never heard of be aware of my life's risk?"

The pause grew longer with the question Matt offered Sesom.

"I have been sent to protect you and you shall protect me. Because this line is secure and I've hacked my way in, my team can only encrypt so much information before a trace is made and encryption is filtered. Please meet with me before the exposure of this operation is made known to others."

Matt thought for a second, as he knew time was working against him, "How can I trust you?"

"I'm the man on the bridge. Meet me at 10:07 at Carlita's Café," Sesom signed off and Matt closed the IM box. A hack like this meant a visit from security was looming. Matt knew that he should leave the building to prevent anyone from following him to Carlita's for his own protection...and theirs. Matt logged off his computer and went back down the hall to Noah's office. Noah was still tinkering with the cannon, headset, and keyboard. He was scrubbing the source code to eliminate bugs in the software.

"Hey Noah," Matt quipped.

"Yeah Matty," Noah turned from his computer to face him.

"Gotta step out for a moment. I'll be back at 11:00."

"See you then," Noah went back to work.

As Matt walked down the hall, he brought up the Internet connection from his Smartphone. Once again, he clicked on the Security button and accepted a live feed from his townhome.

"Leaving so soon Mr. Hiatt," One of the security guards went to retrieve Matt's .45 and KT.

"Unfortunately. Just got notice that I have a meeting I wasn't aware of," Matt put the .45 back in its harness and lifted his left leg for the KT. Matt walked to the elevator and depressed the down button. The elevator was there in seconds.

Susan was happy to see Matt again, "Quick day of work?"

"Not as quick as I'd like. Save a piece of birthday cake for me," Matt strolled by Susan's desk with his phone in hand.

Matt exited Delta and stood in the breezeway of the building. As the feed came through the phone, he saw the front door was intact and nobody was in the vicinity. He toggled to his bedroom. The image revealed two men ransacking his bedroom. Matt waited for them to turn toward the video camera. After one intruder had searched behind the flat screen TV, he tossed the TV from the wall and turned toward the camera; Matt snapped a picture with the Smartphone vis-à-vis the video camera on the wall. The other intruder was snooping around Matt's computer desk. He picked up the laptop computer and grabbed the photo of his sister's family. The intruder studied the picture for seconds and turned to face the camera. Matt snapped another picture capturing the second intruder. At that point, the intruder must have noticed the security camera moving on the wall. He rose up his handgun and shot the camera; Matt could tell the handgun had a silencer on the end of it. The feed from the camera went to noise and no signal. Matt moved to the living room. There was an intruder near the fireplace looking through shelves of books and artwork. The third intruder turned toward Matt's bedroom for a couple seconds and scanned the living room ceiling for something. Matt snapped a picture of the third intruder. The intruder smiled and shot the camera. Matt did a quick check of other rooms and logged off his Smartphone.

Matt thought to himself, "If those morons hurt Scratches, they'll pay dearly." Matt looked at his watch; the time was 7:45. He needed to kill a couple hours before his meeting.

****

10:07 didn't seem that strange to Matt. As a military planner of invasions and interrogations, Matt understood the importance of keeping events unpredictable. Whoever Sesom was, he obviously had been trained to understand unpredictability as well. Killing time wasn't a problem for Matt; he loved driving the Mustang up and down the coast. He had spent time on both coasts of North America, some of it training with the military and some of it exploring on his own time. Matt loved the water and enjoyed spray from the surf, the warmth of the sand, and scantily clad ladies. Carlita's had a nice view of the ocean from a deck or seating inside the café. Matt had been to Carlita's before, under different circumstances of course.

Matt parked on the street and plugged the meter. Much safer to leave his Mustang in a spot that can be viewed from inside the café. Matt went to the trunk and grabbed a sport coat; he needed to conceal the .45. He tossed the sport coat around his shoulder and placed his arms through the sleeves. After he worked out a few wrinkles in the coat, he took the safety off the .45. Matt grabbed a few more magazines from the trunk and put them in pockets of his sport coat. 10:05 was registered on Matt's watch and he headed into Carlita's to meet his stalker.

Matt removed his sunglasses as he entered Carlita's. The café was packed during this time of the day and a late breakfast crowd was still filtering through the front door. As Matt took a few steps forward, a woman came from the restrooms and walked by his right shoulder.

"On the deck to the left," The woman kept walking and took a seat with a man inside the café. The man glared at Matt as he walked by their table, Matt returned the stare. After Matt had woven his way through the morning crowd, he passed through a set of French doors that opened to the back deck; Matt returned the sunglasses to his head and looked to the left. The mystery man was seated at a table to the back and motioned with his right hand for Matt to come over. He was a big towering black man with a muscular physique. Sesom's head was shaved and his scalp reflected a sunny day in Los Angeles. Matt pulled the left lapel back on his sport coat to reveal his .45 to Sesom; Matt wanted Sesom to know that he was armed. Sesom smiled and his white teeth contrasted against a dark complexion.

Sesom rose from his chair and offered his right hand. Matt took Sesom's right hand and squeezed it firmly. They both sat down at the same time.

"Did anyone follow you?" The accent was West African.

"You tell me," Matt sat back in his chair.

"Not my people. Not enough to follow others," Sesom grinned again.

"So what's with the bridge this morning and my house later on?" Matt wasn't much for small talk, he got right to the point.

"I cannot believe we finally found you. The visions in my dreams produced an image of your likeness that is unmistakable. My team and I have waited for this day."

"Well let's celebrate," Matt turned as the waiter walked up to their table.

"Sir, is this the person you're waiting on?" The waiter spoke to Sesom.

"Oh yes, yes, I have been waiting too long for my friend," Sesom began to laugh and slapped Matt's forearm.

Sir, may I take your order?" The question directed at Matt.

"I'd like a white mocha, extra hot, no whip, with a sprinkle of chocolate."

"And you sir," The waiter turned his head in the direction of Sesom.

"I'd like a glass of water, filled three-quarter, topped with ice, and a twist of lemon please," Sesom did his best impression of Matt and began to laugh hysterically. Sesom's laugh was deep and booming, which was easily heard by half the patrons on the deck.

"Well if anyone followed me, they can surely find me now." Matt made reference to Sesom's loud laugh.

"What do you mean about your visions?" Matt took on a more inquisitive tone, knowing that he had experienced some dreams of his own.

"A little over two years ago, I began to dream about a man in a city surrounded by angels. There was a beach, palm trees, and sun shining bright. The dreams became more frequent and vivid. I began to dream of people following this man in the city of Angels. He was taking us on a journey, and even though I never saw our final destination, I knew that I needed to find this man."

The waiter brought back two waters with lemon twists. "Sir, your drink will be right out," Matt reached into his water and tossed the lemon twist over the rail.

Sesom continued, "At that point a stranger I had never met found me in a Moroccan plaza. I thought he was crazy, but the stranger knew about my name, where I was from, and my recurring dreams. He said that he was sent to find me."

Matt's drink had made it to the table and he took a drink, "And who is this person?"

"His name is Amen and he traveled to me from Israel."

Matt interrupted Sesom, "Amen. People actually name their kids Amen?" He took another sip of mocha.

"Is that Amen with Cleopatra in the café?"

Sesom remained serious, "Yes, that is Amen in the café. He is with a woman named Cering."

"They didn't look like locals," Matt continued to sip on the coffee; it was extra hot as ordered.

"Cering came to me from Egypt. Her ancestry can be traced all the way back to the great Pharaohs of Egypt and the oppression of Israelites." Sesom began to stroke the stubble on his face with his left hand. "She is a great warrior and comes from a wealthy family."

"To make this long story short Mr. Hiatt, there have been eleven people that have come to me and two died already, leaving our total at ten. I was the first to see visions of a man surrounded by angels and soon people began to show up telling me stories of their dreams and connections to me. These people knew intimate details of my personal life and family. As we shared stories about our visions, we began to realize that each of us had something to offer in pursuing our destiny."

Matt was focused on the beach and turned toward Sesom, "Look, I don't understand why you're laying these details on me or why my life is in danger, but I do know some thugs are turning my townhome upside-down looking for something."

"Mr. Hiatt."

Matt interrupted, "Call me Matt."

"Mr. Matt, those people in your home are looking for leverage. They cannot make an attempt on your life until they understand the knowledge you possess," Sesom raised his water and took a drink.

"What are you talking about? The knowledge of what Delta Defense is working on?" Matt began to laugh at the fact of how little he actually knew about what went on in the company.

"No Mr. Matt."

Matt interrupted again, "Matt is fine, no mister necessary."

"Okay Matt. Having recurring dreams aren't you?"

Matt seemed surprised that Sesom would know about his frequent dreams, "I've had a few dreams that recur from time to time."

Sesom looked at Matt like he was providing half-truths.

"Okay, I've had some interesting dreams that are pretty vivid over the past year."

Sesom crossed his arms and leaned back in the chair, "Please continue."

"Why should I continue with a complete stranger who's been stalking me? You haven't appeared in any of my visions."

Sesom leaned forward, "You shall come to find out that I have been sent to protect you."

"From who?"

"From the people in your townhome."

"And who are they?" The caffeine was beginning to stimulate Matt's brain.

"The same aggressors that killed two of my people and infiltrated our group."

"Why would they do that?" Matt was struggling to make the connection between Sesom's people and him.

"To find the Twelfth Disciple." Sesom leaned back again.

Matt began to process early portions of the conversation, "You stated that eleven people had found you."

"That is correct." Sesom was getting excited, as Matt appeared to show more interest in the conversation.

"If my math is correct, you should have already found the Twelfth Disciple and that person is part of your group."

"This much is true Matt, but one of the people that came to me was a phony," Sesom was still excited and beginning to show his emotion with his arms.

"He infiltrated our camp to learn about our visions and what we were planning. Then one morning, he was gone."

Matt became more focused, "Sesom, haven't you described your group as people that came to you based on their dreams and visions of the future? How is it that someone you describe as a phony can infiltrate your camp?"

"I fell into his trap. At the same time our coalition was forming to discover a purpose, there was a group coming together in opposition to our cause."

Matt repeated Sesom's words, "Our cause?"

Sesom took another drink of water and wiped his shiny head with a cloth napkin, "As we came together through dreams and visions of the future, we began to understand that our cause served a higher purpose. In the United States, I believe you call it the sum equaling the whole of its parts."

Sesom continued, "There is another group, one of bad intentions, that holds their own beliefs and visions of the future. When they learned that our coalition was forming and growing stronger through those called to follow, they set up surveillance and infiltrated our camp. They needed to know our thoughts and actions to respond to the threat of prophesy."

Matt looked confused; "You lost me at the prophecy part."

Sesom began to smile, "Didn't you go to Sunday School Matt?"

"I did, but we were more focused on Ark building, the exodus from Egypt, and Nativity scenes."

Sesom continued, "There are many words from scripture that call for a Messiah, the 2nd coming, a return of the White Horse, and other references to God's redemption. While humankind has been successful in pitting religions against each other for political and financial gain, the reality is that many teachings run together and flow from the same source...God. The group in opposition to our cause represents evil and destruction in the world. They use religion as much as anybody else."

"I'm still a little confused. What does this have to do with me?"

Sesom smiled again, "You are the 12th Disciple."

Matt smiled back at Sesom, "How is that? I haven't attended church in 11 years. I have killed people with my own hands and sent many people packing to meet God earlier than they expected."

Sesom began to laugh, "Do I look like a man that hasn't killed another man or placed people before God? That is one of the reasons we are chosen to protect the kingdom of God. Let's just say that the God of your Old Testament is alive and well. If I'm not mistaken, you have witnessed the perils of evil firsthand."

"I have."

"Then you understand your motivation to become part of the military and join Special Operations. You haven't killed anybody you liked or thought was worthy of this life. I doubt you experienced much remorse when you killed people that deserved it."

"I didn't."

"Well Matt, you shall find that our calling requires us to utilize skills to protect the prophecy of God, not a religion."

Matt began to process the 12th Disciple concept, "If I am this so-called 12th Disciple and supposed to join your coalition, why me?"

Sesom began to roar with laughter and guests from other tables took notice. "Matt, why me, I didn't sign up for this either? I have come to find out the purpose I serve is greater than myself, almost like what you do in the military."

Matt began to speak and was interrupted by Sesom, "Hold on Matt. Many of the visions I experienced brought me to you for good reason. You possess the final key in our journey as Disciples and a beginning of our calling to serve the kingdom. The dreams you've had are the gateway to our understanding and the purpose we will come to serve."

"That sounds great, but I need to get back to work at Delta," Matt began to exit his chair.

Sesom got serious, "Matt, please take your seat back. The decisions you make from this point forward are critical to the safety of Disciples, your friends, and family. If you leave now, you put each of those at great risk."

Matt stopped and looked at Sesom, "What do you mean?" Matt returned to his seat.

"You may not go back to the life you've known. If you do, they will use leverage against the Disciples and you to understand your calling and visions. Your family will be tortured, coworkers will be killed, and you will be framed as a terrorist and criminal. They will find ways to conspire against you, ruin your military career, and cause you to be tried as an enemy of your own country. If that sounds appealing, you may go back to Delta; but understand, we as Disciples were sent to protect you and will to our death. If you turn your back, you will disrupt our mission and expose us to great danger."

"How am I supposed to know this is true?"

Sesom reached into his pocket as Matt went for his weapon, "Easy Matt, I'm merely getting a radio."

Sesom pulled out what looked like a Bluetooth device and put it on his left ear.

"Dorje, stand by please…"

Sesom turned his attention back to Matt, "Down the beach at 325 meters there is a seawall made out of large boulders. Please look over my left shoulder and find the wall Matt."

"Okay, I see the wall."

"Along that wall about 25 meters before it meets the sea, there is a man peering over the rocks with binoculars. The man on the wall is watching our every move so don't appear alarmed."

Matt kept staring at Sesom, leaned back, and glanced in the direction of the seawall. There was a man on the rocks looking through optics. Sesom regained Matt's attention.

"Matt, along the side of my chair is a pair of binoculars. I'm going to retrieve them casually and set them on the table in front of you. When I say, I want you to pick them up and look directly at the man on the wall. Continue to look at him until I say so."

"Okay."

Sesom kept talking, "I'm getting the binoculars now and I'm going to set them in front of you. Don't pick them up immediately. I want you to pick them up in 5, 4, 3, 2, okay pick them up now."

Matt reached for the binoculars and put them to his eyes. He focused on a man with dark complexion that was staring right at him. The man in the binoculars couldn't believe that Matt was looking at him and raised his eyes from the optics.

Sesom spoke into his Bluetooth, "Take the target now."

At that point a spray of red liquid ejected from the rear of the man's head. The binoculars fell from the man's hands and he collapsed over the rocks. Matt didn't even hear a gunshot.

"Matt, you can quit looking now. I wasn't kidding when I said your life is in danger. More importantly, your sister's family is in more danger."

This got Matt's attention, "Why?"

"They will use your family as a means to get what they want."

Matt appeared mad, "Who are THEY?"

Sesom got serious, "We call them Samil. We must move out of the area now. Ethan and Talan, rendezvous in 2 minutes outside the café. Amen and Cering, come meet us at the table, we shall leave together."

As Sesom finished his sentence, Amen and Cering came through the doors at the back of the café. They had the look of mercenaries as they approached the table.

"Amen and Cering, meet Mr. Matt, our 12th Disciple," Sesom motioned to Amen and Cering to greet Matt.

As Amen outstretched his hand Matt spoke, "I insist that you call me Matt."

Amen complied, "Matt, I have waited for this day for many months."

Cering stepped in and offered her hand to Matt, "Sesom has said many great things about you."

Matt smiled, "Well, seeing as Sesom and I just met, I'm flattered."

Sesom was quick to delegate orders, "Amen, you will be assigned to Mr. Matt's sister and family. When we rendezvous with the vehicles out front, Mr. Matt will phone his sister and let her know of the imminent danger."

Matt was staring at Cering. She was a beautiful Egyptian woman with dark skin and long ebony hair. Cering's leather outfit was tight to her body and Matt wondered where she might be hiding a weapon, if any. Dark sunglasses concealed her eyes and their subsequent movements.

"Cering"

"Yes Sesom"

"Call ahead and let Captain Phil know we're coming and to ready for departure."

Matt looked confused, "Departure?"

Sesom maintained his serious tone, "Yes Mr. Matt, we will leave this area and plan our mission together based on information we share. Your dreams and visions will be a key to our decisions." Sesom tossed a twenty-dollar bill on the table.

Matt seemed incredulous, "Look at how I'm dressed? Do I look like a man ready for a mission."

Sesom laughed as he motioned for the group to exit through the double doors, "Mr. Matt, we have thought of these things. Don't forget that you're the 12th Disciple, not the 1st."

Matt remembered Scratches in his townhome; "I must get Scratches from the townhome and have someone look after her."

By now they were halfway through the café and Sesom was confused, "Scratches? Who is this Scratches?"

"My cat."

"You have a cat?" Sesom began to laugh and gain the attention of other diners.

Matt was beginning to get frustrated with Sesom. "Yes, I have a cat and either your Disciples or I will travel back to my townhome to get Scratches."

Sesom was still laughing, "We shall get your cat and take him to your sister's."

As the group walked through the front doors, 3 black SUVs pulled up to the café. Matt turned to Sesom, "I prefer to take my Mustang."

Sesom shook his head, "No time for the Mustang. Your car probably has a tracking device anyway."

Sesom called to Amen, "Take Mr. Matt's Mustang and stop by his townhome. There is a cat named Scratches that will need to be delivered to his sister Mary. I will advise you of the location for Mary and her family later today. The car has likely been tagged, please scan it thoroughly after retrieving the cat."

"Keys," Sesom reached out his hand to Matt.

Matt looked away for a moment and reached into his sport coat. The keys to his Mustang were equipped with a keyless entry and automatic start. With great reluctance, Matt approached Amen.

Matt gripped the keys with his right hand and made a fist.

"How can I trust you with everything that is important to me? My family, cat, and my Mustang?" Matt opened up his right hand and revealed the keys. Amen went to reach for them.

As Amen outstretched his left arm to take the keys, Matt closed his fist and did a 360 maneuver with his body and swung his fist at Amen's right cheek. Amen countered by raising his right arm and catching Matt's fist. Matt spun completely around and was face to face with Amen as their right arms were locked together and fists within inches of Amen's cheek. Amen didn't look surprised.

"It's standard and stock with 300 horse power. Not a scratch! I also expect you to guard my family with your life," Matt was ready for Amen to strike back.

"With my life Matt," Amen meant business.

Matt opened up his right fist and handed the keys to Amen.

"Across the street, lime green."

Amen smiled at Matt, "Not a scratch."

Amen took the keys and went to the back of the third SUV. He opened the rear hatch and grabbed two duffel bags from the back. He opened a pocket in one of the duffle bags and pulled out a small electronic device. The device was the size of a cell phone, but had no keys or receiver. Amen powered up the electronic device on the side. He dashed across the street to the Mustang. Matt turned his attention back to Sesom.

"Where to?"

"Middle vehicle. We'll discuss plans as we travel to the dock."

Matt had another confused look, "Dock?"

Across the street a vehicle revved up and peeled out. Matt looked up and saw his lime green Mustang as the tires began to smoke from the rear. He shook his head and went for a passenger door in the second SUV. Amen set the portable device on the dash of Matt's Mustang; the device was now scrambling any signal being transmitted by the vehicle. The Disciples were on their way.

****

Mike felt his cell phone vibrate in his pocket. He was in the kitchen of his pizzeria during a lunch rush.

"This is Mike."

"Hey Mike it's Matt, how are you?" Matt was on his way to the Port of Los Angeles.

"Up to my ears in dough, and not the green kind."

Matt could hear clamor in the kitchen. "You have a minute?"

"For you brother...absolutely," Mike went to the washbasin and began to clean his hands quickly and grab a towel. He exited the back of the building into a parking lot. Maria's Pizzeria was in New Jersey and a very popular spot for lunch hour, parties, and kids to play games.

"All right Matty, I'm all ears."

"I need you to do me a favor," Matt was holding the cell phone with his left hand and rubbing his forehead with his right. The SUV was speeding toward the Port.

"Anything brother, you name it."

"I need you and sis to take a week off and leave Jersey."

"You want us to come visit?"

"No, it's not that. I'm leaving Los Angeles right now."

Mike turned up the volume on his cell, "Where are you heading? Are you being deployed again?"

"This time the mission isn't military. It's personal. I received a tip from someone today that my life and your lives are in danger," Matt was struggling with how to explain the current situation.

"Who did the tip come from? Someone you can trust?"

"I think so. I just met with him at a café near Delta and he provided me proof enough."

Ethan was driving the SUV. Cering was in the front passenger seat and Sesom was next to Matt in the backseat. Ethan didn't seem to be concerned about local authorities or speed traps; he was more concerned about tailing the SUV in front of him.

Mike took a seat on concrete steps in the back of the building.

"Are you coming this way?"

"Not likely. We'll discuss the mission once we leave port in Los Angeles. I have a feeling I'll be heading overseas for the next several weeks, if not more. There is a man named Amen from Israel heading your way to protect your interests. Once I establish a rendezvous point from you, he should be there tomorrow. I'm leaving everything I have at the townhome, at least what's left."

"What do you mean?" Mike wanted more details about the townhome.

"A group has already ransacked my place, taken my laptop, and took the picture of you guys from Christmas last year. I saw them on an uplink from my security feed. They plan to use my family as leverage if they find you. I can't let that happen."

"Who are they?"

"The people I've spoken with refer to them as evil. They seem like a group of mercenaries sent to carry out orders for whatever reason. I'm still trying to understand why. I'm not sure if they want revenge for something I've done in Special Operations or something I plan to do. Really hard to say at this point, more intel is needed."

Reality set in for Mike, "Matty, you know how Mary feels about these kinds of things and missions in far away countries. This one isn't even military, even though the reasons behind it could trace back to some of your previous missions. I can handle Mary and the kids, but I want in."

Matt smiled, as this is what he expected from Mike, "Give me a location point for tomorrow afternoon, Amen will meet you there. After that, we will meet up as a family once I understand the nature of our mission." Matt was glad that Mike wanted to watch his back; they had never served together in combat.

"Remember that saltwater taffy place on the Boardwalk in Ocean City?"

"Frals?"

"Yeah Frals. Have him meet us outside Frals on the Boardwalk at 1600 hours. Mary and I will pack a couple bags and be prepared for travel. I hope Amen likes kids. I'll explain to Mary and let her know that we'll be meeting up with you at some point. Is the guy's name really Amen or is that cover?"

"His name is Amen and he seems well trained. I tried to deck him about fifteen minutes ago to test his skills; he passed. Amen is an Israeli; I'll tell him you'll be wearing a USMC ball cap," Matt looked at his right hand and made a fist; he was impressed with how Amen caught the punch.

"I'll be in touch. Take your phone charger and make sure Mary has her cell as well."

"Over, you take care of yourself and stay safe, out," Mike folded the cell phone to close it. He had forgotten about the lunch rush and took in a deep breath of Jersey air. Even though he had finished his service with the Marines, Mike always enjoyed the military and adrenaline high from missions and close combat. The Marines were sad to see Mike retire early from service; Mary was adamant that he pursue civil interests and stay close to family. Mike knew that Mary loved her brother deeply and their connection had been strong since the tragedy at Columbine. Mary was always concerned when Matt went abroad to protect liberty, but she deeply understood the importance of serving the US as her dad had done before Matt. Mike thought that some time off for family wouldn't be a bad thing, even if it involved his becoming engaged in combat. Mike stayed in shape and was ready for any enemy, foreign or domestic.

He opened his cell phone again and called.

"Hello."

"Hey honey, you'll never believe who I just spoke with?"

"Who?"

"Matty. Pack some clothes; I'm on my way home. We're leaving."

Mary was surprised by the urgency of departure, "Mike, this is rather abrupt."

"Yes, but I'll explain when I get home. Gotta run honey."

"Okay Mookey. See you when you get here." Mookey was a nickname Mike had picked up during his tenure with the Marines.

****

The Port of Los Angeles is a massive landscape of ships, containers, tractors, and concrete. Large cranes shot into the air to serve as arms for loading and unloading cargo. As the three SUVs approached the Port, Sesom opened his cell phone.

"Suzie, it's Sesom. We are arriving at the Port now."

"Come to the East Channel Parking Garage and meet us on the 3rd floor. We'll have a white van shuttle the group for Breakbulk departure. You can't miss the van on the 3rd floor; it's not crowded up here right now. Captain Phil is expecting you and departure is scheduled for 1:00 pm," she said.

"Well done Suzie. What's the cargo?" As if it mattered to the journey, Sesom thought.

Suzie was quick to respond, "Wheat. Destination is India and about 15 days to arrival."

"Thank you Suzie. Did Captain Phil get our supplies and gear loaded?"

"Yes sir."

Sesom was pleased, "We will see you in five minutes."

Sesom put the earpiece back in his ear and hit a button on the side, "East Channel Parking Garage, 3rd floor, rendezvous at white van. Make sure that the SUVs are combed over, we can't leave anything behind."

Sesom turned towards Matt.

"You have traveled the great oceans, no?"

"I have, not under these circumstances with complete strangers to an unknown destination," Matt chuckled.

"Mr. Matt, I am..." Matt interrupted Sesom.

"The whole Mr. Matt thing is beginning to wear on my nerves. If we're going to spend some time on the high seas together, you'll need to address me as Matt. No Mr. Matt, no Mr. Hiatt, just plain and simple Matt."

Sesom began to laugh in his recognizable boom, "Okay Matt, I will refer to you as Matt and only Matt."

"Thanks."

The SUV began to climb the ramp of the parking garage, a little shy of the anticipated 5 minutes. People arriving and departing the parking garage didn't know what to think of a motorcade that resembled the President's. The white van was out in the open as the motorcade arrived on the 3rd floor. Cering was the first to exit the SUV and greet Suzie.

"Suzie, thank you for handling our arrangements," Cering handed Suzie an envelope of American bills of high denominations.

"Cering, it's great to see you again. Please stay in touch," Suzie bowed before Cering to show her respect and approval of the payment.

"You know what to do with the SUV?" Cering was covering all bases.

"I do."

"And you don't recollect any of the events I've covered with you," Cering was pressing.

"What events?" Suzie knew the drill.

"If we need you in the next several weeks, I'll call you. Thank you again for handling this."

Suzie was a professional who understood international affairs; "This briefcase contains all of your passports, paperwork for ports, and delivery of payload documentation. Captain Phil's record and clearance with ports of any origin are impeccable. Not to forget, he and Sesom have trusted each other for years."

"Matt Hiatt's paperwork is intact as well?" Cering already knew the answer to her question.

"Mr. Hiatt's record with the military is impressive." Suzie looked in Matt's direction and gave him one of those looks of disappointment, disappointment that she wouldn't get to know him better, at least for now. She was familiar with his credentials and impressed with the package in person. Matt nodded at Suzie. He was concerned about having no clothes and going on a boat for an extended period of time. Matt was watching the other Disciples grab duffle bags, totes, and other personal effects. They were climbing inside the vehicles and checking all compartments. The group didn't want to leave the slightest trace of their presence.

Cering smiled at Suzie. "Make sure that you wash the vehicles and scrub for prints. Vacuum the interiors well and then let some dogs spend the night in the SUVs before you return them to the rental agency. That way any DNA traces will turn up some Shepherds, Retrievers, and Labradors. Just make sure they're dogs that won't tear up the interiors," Cering turned to Sesom.

"We're settled," Cering went to the back of the SUV and began to load gear on her shoulders.

"Hey Matt," Cering called out.

Matt was rubbing his left hand through his hair. He had returned the sport coat to his body to conceal the .45 tucked away in its holster.

"Yeah."

"Here. I packed you a bag; Clothes, bathing kit, hunter's knife, a few weapons, and ammunition."

Cering tossed the bag in Matt's direction.

"Thank you," Matt didn't have time to open the duffel bag, just time to load it in the back of the van.

"Let's go," Sesom's voice called out.

"Keys are on the front seat. Do you remember Captain Phil's boat's name?" Suzie wanted to make sure all bases were covered.

"Excalibur," Sesom growled as he climbed in the driver's side.

The remaining Disciples tossed their bags in the van and took a seat. Sesom started up the van. Matt couldn't believe what was unfolding. He began the morning documenting a strange dream with a recurring woman. Matt's morning jog was interrupted by a stalker who brushed off the threat of a bullet through his head. After leaving work abruptly, Matt witnessed a stranger's head turned into a canoe by sniper fire near a local café. He'd had some strange days in the past decade, but this day was beginning to shape up as a winner.

Ports are notorious for their lack of security, which was a principle reason Sesom chose to travel by boat. While the group would be isolated in a cargo ship on the sea, the thought of traveling by plane, especially when they didn't know where they were going, seemed fruitless.

The van had only one checkpoint to go through.

Sesom rolled down the window to chat with a Port Authority guard. The guard poked his head out a window in the side of a security shack.

"What's your business?"

Sesom spoke with complete strangers as if they were neighbors next door; "My crew and I are traveling on the Excalibur with Captain Phil to India. Our payload is wheat and we have been contracted by Phil to help with duties on deck," Matt was surprised by a destination of India seeing as the Disciples hadn't even discussed their mission or final destination.

"Stand by sir while I verify," The guard retrieved a clipboard with papers on it. After searching for a few seconds, the guard dialed a number on a cordless phone.

"Captain Alland, I have a group of deckhands that are requesting permission to the dock and your ship; please advise," The guard nodded his head, "okay sir, I'll send them on. Thank you."

"You are free to carry on. The Excalibur is docked at C-1 a couple miles down the East Channel. Follow the signs and have a safe trip," Sesom nodded in affirmation to the Port Officer. The Officer maintained the same facial expression and monotone voice as he spoke with Sesom, as if his demeanor would help prevent a group of terrorists from blowing up the dock or ships at sea. Matt thought the exchange between the Port Officer and Sesom was comical. From Matt's perspective, a group of people from different origins and countries sailing as deckhands on a wheat boat seemed strange. Matt still hadn't met half the people in the van; he figured introductions would come later. If the guard had pulled the nine Disciples out of the van, Matt would have been able to name only four, which would send up red flags for most any security officer. The thought of India was still weighing on Matt's mind.

"Sesom, why India?" The other Disciples took notice of Matt's question because they had no idea the trip was set for India either.

"Why not India?" Sesom began laughing again, "Matt, it's very doubtful that we will arrive in India; however, we must declare our cargo and a final destination for this vessel before sailing." Sesom was looking in the rear view mirror.

"An Egyptian company owned by Cering's family purchased the wheat on Captain Phil's ship. Because Cering's family owns several companies throughout the world that operate in international trade, we will be able to change our destination at any point on our voyage," Sesom seemed pleased with his plan.

"The idea of us climbing on a plane and traveling internationally together is dangerous for a number of reasons; our group stands out like a sore toe," Sesom missed the idiom.

"Thumb," Kimi said as she smiled and shook her head.

Sesom turned his direction toward Kimi, "What?"

"Stick out like a sore thumb, not toe." This obviously wasn't the first time Kimi had corrected Sesom's grammar. Sesom looked at Kimi confused as if he didn't know what she was alluding to by her comment.

"Airport security would take notice of our group and the thought of traveling at 900 kilometers per hour in a pipe would expose us to great risk," Sesom's statement seemed reasonable to Matt, even though traveling by cargo ship meant many days at sea.

"Captain Phil will take good care of us too," Sesom nodded in the rear view mirror as the group approached C-1. Captain Phil was already on the gangway to greet his longtime friend. The van was put in park and the Disciples immediately exited with backpacks and returned to the back to remove their duffle bags. Not much was said between the Disciples and they appeared to be all business; Matt was hoping their disposition would change over the next several days on a cargo ship.

Captain Phil was at the top of the gangway to meet the crew. Sesom went first to hug his longtime buddy and hand him a cigar.

"In the middle of the Pacific we shall enjoy this Cuban," Sesom held the cigar up to his nose and smiled at his friend. He tucked the cigar in Captain Phil's left pocket.

Phil grabbed Sesom's right hand and pulled him close for a hug, "Great to see you my brother. Has the land been treating you as well as the water?"

Sesom pulled back from Phil, "Never my good friend, you know that I love the seas. I believe that you and I have sailed them all together."

"I'd like you to meet some friends that will be traveling with us," Sesom turned toward the Disciples.

"I believe you have met Cering before and worked with her family."

Captain Phil took off his hat, "The pleasure is mine to see you again Cering and I always appreciate what your family has done for me."

Cering smiled and leaned toward Phil, "Thank you for assisting us, once again, with matters of family business." She leaned forward and kissed him on his left cheek.

Captain Phil blushed and addressed all the Disciples, "As you come on the ship enter the steel doorway, take a right and then an immediate left. Follow the hallway to the stairwell and take the stairs down a level. You will find your quarters on that level and the one below. Please help yourselves."

Cering disappeared into the doorway off the deck, Dorje stepped forward; he was built like a Sherpa. What he lacked in height he made up for in physique and fitness. He bowed to Captain Phil and spoke in very broken English.

"Thank you for letting us journey on Phil's boat. My name is Dorje from Tibet."

"Doorjay, let me know if you need anything as we travel together," Captain Phil shook hands with Dorje and he followed Cering across the deck and through the steel door.

Li stepped forward and bowed as well. Li's English was better than Dorje's.

"Captain Phil, thank you for such hospitality. Even though I'm not fond of traveling by boat and struggle with seasickness, I'm glad you're at the helm," Captain Phil put his left hand on Li's right shoulder.

"Look here Li. There are seasick patches in medicine cabinets on both levels. Put one on right now; don't wait until you begin to feel queasy. There are also some oil drops that you can put under the tongue to help with nausea. Make sure you drink plenty of fluids; they'll help with puking and dehydration. The cargo ship has stabilizers, so hopefully the trip will be decent, but the Pacific is known to be rough at times."

Li was thankful Phil understood people who were a little sensitive to the sea, "Thank you Captain Phil."

Next was Lucas from Brazil. He was huge and didn't say much. Lucas came from a very poor section of Sao Paulo and was reared in a church community. At 6'5" and bigger than Sesom, Lucas was easy to spot in a crowd. His nature was gentle and he knew that his size was intimidating for most people. He addressed the Captain in such a manner.

"My name is Lucas from Brazil. Some people call me Luke. I prefer Lucas. Thank you for letting us sail on your ship," Lucas gripped the Captain's hand and squeezed.

"Well Lucas from Brazil, welcome aboard the Excalibur. If you need anything don't hesitate to ask," Phil was glad to have his hand back.

Matt was behind Lucas on the gangway. He was still decked out in business attire and wearing a sport coat, mostly to conceal his favorite weapon still fully loaded with the safety off. Captain Phil seemed like an everyday guy. He wore jeans, a t-shirt, and a flannel shirt. His ball cap was red with a grey ship prominently displayed in the center. A sword outlined in yellow pierced the bow of the ship and the cross guard looked like a mast above the front deck, or a cross guiding the ship. In the area of the fuller on the sword "Excalibur" was stitched in blue. Matt thought the hat was cool.

"Good afternoon Captain Phil. If I would have known that I'd be sailing this afternoon, I would have dressed a little differently this morning," Matt outstretched his hand for Captain Phil.

"My name is Matt and I live in Los Angeles. I met Sesom a little over an hour ago," Matt motioned to Sesom, "and he convinced me to take a trip with this diverse group of strangers. I hope you have some shine in the cupboards." Matt thought that he could use a drink, even though he wasn't a big drinker.

Captain Phil replied in kind, "Matt, I have the real stuff in the cupboards and you can help yourself when needed. Make yourself at home as we'll be spending a few days on the sea together, I look forward to it."

"Thanks," Matt moved forward across the deck and disappeared into the steel doorway.

Kimi had trained in karate and kendo near Okinawa. She was dressed in jeans, tennis shoes, a camisole, and a red baseball cap that had her hair forming a tail through the back. Black sunglasses made Kimi look intimidating and her 5'9" frame was difficult to miss. Kimi was attractive, just like Cering, but had looks that were deceiving. The women had killed people in hand-to-hand combat and were masters with weapons. Kimi's training in kendo made her special to the group and she could defeat many enemies with a sword of any kind in a single battle. Over the past several months Kimi had been training Cering to use a wooden kendo sword. Taking a trip on a cargo ship would allow Kimi and Cering to work on balance while training with swords. Kimi removed her sunglasses as she met Captain Phil.

"Good to meet you Captain, I'm Kimi from Japan. Feel free to take us by the island and I'll be happy to treat the group for dinner at Yokohama. I have a friend that owns a restaurant in the Port."

"Thank you Kimi," Phil looked at Sesom, "I'll speak with Sesom about our schedule and see if a stop is possible. Always nice to shake away sea legs during the trip on some land."

"Regardless, the invitation is open and I'm obliged to offer dinner for your hospitality," Kimi kissed the Captain on the right cheek and crossed the deck. Phil turned a shade of red as he turned to Sesom.

"Very pretty ladies Sesom, and good natured too."

Sesom roared in laughter, "Don't even think about it Captain, you couldn't keep up. Those ladies are trained for a higher purpose than ours."

Phil began to laugh and shook his head in agreement. Ethan was in front of Phil and offered his hand.

"Captain Phil, my name is Ethan and I'm from Egypt too. Thanks for the use of your ship for our journey."

Phil took Ethan's hand, "I have a boy named Ethan living in Alaska with his own family. Great to meet you Ethan. I love visiting Egypt when I can, so much to see in that part of the world."

"My family resides in Egypt and I grew up near the Nile River. Many of my ancestors farmed from waters of the Nile for hundreds of years."

"Longest river in the world. I'll stop by Egypt by way of the Mediterranean at some point in the near future. I would like to meet Cering's family and business partners first hand. Ethan, if I can do anything for you let me know. My ship is yours."

"Thank you Captain," Ethan stepped forward across the deck and into the steel doorway.

The last of the Disciples stepped forward to meet the captain.

"Captain Phil, my pleasure is to meet you. Thank you for the use of your vessel for our trip. My name is Talan and I come from India," Talan bowed before Captain Phil.

"No need for that here Talan," Captain Phil stuck his hand out for Talan, "I've traveled the Indian Ocean many times over. You guys have some of the spiciest food in the world. I don't think I've ever been right after my last bowl of chicken and rasam," The Captain began to laugh.

"We do enjoy our food a little spicy," Talan shook the Captain's hand. "Thank you for your kindness."

Captain Phil continued, "Go along Talan and make yourself at home. My ship is yours."

Talan crossed the deck and disappeared through the doorway.

"Nice group you've got here Sesom. People from many places all over the world."

Sesom folded his arms in front of his chest, "Yes Phil, they are a diverse group and we have come together through faith and friendship, much like you and me." Sesom raised his right index finger and pointed at Phil and himself.

Phil whistled for his deckhands. They were starboard and came around on the forecastle, "You remember these guys don't you?"

Sesom smiled as he saw the two men in their late twenties

Sesom put both of his hands on a deckhand's face, "Aaron. How can I forget you my friend? I'm glad that you have stayed with Captain Phil to watch over his boat and belongings. You and I have always been connected in a very special way."

"Thanks Sesom, it's great to sail with you again," The two men hugged and Sesom put his outstretched left hand on the other deckhand and moved to him.

"John, you look stronger than the last time we met?"

John appeared to be a little embarrassed by Sesom's comment, "I took your advice Sesom. I began a routine of nothing but sit-ups, push-ups, and pull-ups. A little running here and there for the legs and some of Cap's grub pushed me up 15 pounds."

Sesom punched John in the abdomen, "You are getting stronger my friend. We shall work out together on this trip."

"That would be great Sesom."

Captain Phil was eager to set sail, "Aaron, call the tug and have them hook up. We leave in 30 minutes. Secure all ropes and get ready to pull anchor when the tug has hooked to our bow."

"Ay, Cap."

Captain Phil turned his attention toward Sesom, "Great to see you again my friend. All of your supplies have been loaded and are located in the stern on the lower level. You also have 3 vehicles for traveling once we arrive at a final destination."

"Hold onto that cigar Captain Phil. We shall smoke together once we set sail," Sesom turned in the direction of the steel doorway and went to check on his team. As he passed through the doorway, Sesom remembered how much fun he had sailing the high seas; the smell, cold nature of welded steel, storms, and great meals shared in a tight dining area adjacent to the kitchen. Sesom took a left down a long hallway. There were hall lights encased in steel mesh on each side; they provided more than adequate lighting. A heavy-duty commercial carpet lined the floors of Excalibur for traction and warmth. Sesom began to climb down the stairs to the next level.

The bottom of the stairs revealed several cabins on each side of a hallway. Disciples were already moving about the cabins and unloading gear. Sesom looked at his cell phone. There were a few bars of signal for him to make a phone call. He began to look in the cabins for Matt.

"Kimi, have you seen Matt?"

"Down a little farther on your left."

Sesom continued down the hallway and reached Matt's cabin. Matt was happy to shed his business attire for clothes that Cering packed. Sesom checked his cell phone reception and dialed a number.

"Matt. I'm dialing Amen. Please let him know the time and place he is to meet your sister."

Sesom tossed the phone to Matt. He was now dressed in a pair of jeans, a button down long sleeve black shirt, and sandals. Matt caught the phone as it was ringing.

Amen's phone began to vibrate. Because Amen had conducted surveillance throughout the week on Matt's townhome, he was familiar with the area and adjacent homes. He had studied the tendencies of neighbors and looked for anything out of the ordinary. One of Matt's neighbors across the street was out of town. Amen had elected to take refuge in the home to watch Matt's residence. Samil were definitely present in Matt's home and they were hiding out in anticipation that Matt may return. Amen went for his phone as he watched the townhome across the street.

"Hello."

"Amen, it's Matt. How are things back in the old neighborhood?"

Amen was happy to hear from the new Disciple, "Just as planned. A few of Samil are holed up in the house. Every hour or so a couple more case the place from a car."

"Any sign of Scratches?"

"No sign of a cat yet," Amen took another look through his binoculars at each of the windows. "By the way, what kind of cat is Scratches?"

"A mixed breed of some sort. She's orange with green eyes. She will respond to Scratches if you call her. Better yet, once you make it in the townhome there is canned food in the pantry. All you will have to do is open a can and she'll come running."

"Very well," Amen was keeping his eyes on the place through binoculars.

"Do you have something to write with?"

"Yes. Hold for just a second," Amen reached into his backpack near the window. Located next to Amen's backpack was a high-powered Winchester 300 Savage 110FP with a high-powered scope. There was also a modified ballistics weapon with a scope and charges on the floor.

"I've got my notepad," Amen pulled the cap off a pen with his teeth, "copy when ready."

"Rendezvous with sister Mary, brother-in-law Mike, and two children set up for 1600 Eastern Time in Ocean City, New Jersey on the Boardwalk tomorrow. Specific location is a taffy shop called Frals. There are several park benches outside the location, plan to meet at one of them. Mike will be wearing a red cap with USMC on it. Over."

"Copy. I will meet your family in Ocean City, New Jersey tomorrow at 1600 Eastern Time. I will protect them with my life Matt. Looks like the cat and I will be traveling by plane this evening. Please hand the phone back to Sesom."

"Thank you Amen," Matt tossed the phone back to Sesom, "he wants to speak with you."

Amen was providing some instructions to Sesom. "Yes, okay Amen, I can make those arrangements through Suzie. From Los Angeles to New Jersey this evening with a companion." Sesom began to laugh at his last statement, "Check your phone for an email confirmation of flight plans and further instructions. We will catch up with you at some point in the future. Good luck my friend," Sesom closed the phone and smiled at Matt.

Sesom was still in the hallway when he raised his voice, "All Disciples meet on deck in fifteen minutes to set sail. We will have a meeting following our departure." He disappeared down the hallway and found a cabin that was vacant. Matt pulled out his own cell phone; there were two new emails. He clicked read.

Sent at 11:45 am

To: Matt

From: Noah

Subject: Delta

Matty, is everything all right? You mentioned that you would be back at 11:00. Dan has been wondering where you went. I can only hold him off for so long.

Matt clicked Reply.

Reply at 12:47 pm

To: Noah

From: Matt

Subject: Delta

Thanks Noah, everything is fine. I've got some personal matters that I need to address. Sorry I didn't notify you earlier. I'll be in touch with Dan shortly.

Thanks

Original message received at 11:45 am

Matty, is everything all right? You mentioned that you would be back in an hour. Dan has been wondering where you went. I can only hold him off for so long.

Matt clicked on the second message:

Sent at 12:35 pm

To: Matt

From: Mike

Subject: Operation Amen

M, we'll be at Fral's in Ocean City tomorrow at 1600 eastern. I spoke with Mary briefly and let her know that we will be traveling. I haven't given her details yet; I will handle later this afternoon. Look forward to seeing u bro.

Once again Matt hit reply.

Reply at 12:50 pm

To: Mike

From: Matt

Subject: Operation Amen

If anything comes up, let me know by phone. Getting ready to set sail from LA. I'll be in touch.

Original message received at 12:35 pm

M, we'll be at Fral's in Ocean City tomorrow at 1600 eastern. I spoke with Mary briefly and let her know that we will be traveling. I haven't given her details yet; I will handle later this afternoon. Look forward to seeing u bro.

Matt was dreading his next move. He needed to phone Dan back at the Delta office. Dan had deadlines, directors breathing down his neck, and too many projects with too little time or money. Matt sat on the edge of his bed and looked Delta up in his contacts. The phone began to ring.

"Delta Defense this is Susan."

"Hey Susan, it's Matt. Can I speak with Dan please?"

"You bet Mr. Hiatt. Here we go," The phone was being connected with Dan's office. Once again, the phone began to ring.

"Good afternoon, this is Dan."

Matt began to rub his forehead with his right hand as he began speaking.

"Dan, it's Matt," he took a deep breath, "I've had some personal issues develop this morning that prevented me from making it back to the office."

"Hiatt. You realize that the shoulder harness project is coming up for testing and a contract may be written within the next two weeks?" Dan didn't have much patience, "You are a critical team member in field development of this weapon."

"I understand Dan..." Matt was cut off.

"Do you really understand Matt? I've got three major projects coming to fruition and one of my critical team members is out somewhere. By the way, when WILL you be coming back?"

Matt moved his hand from his forehead to the right temple, "I'm not sure Dan. Once I have an idea of when I can wrap my arms around these issues, I'll definitely be back," As Matt made his statement he was having a difficult time believing himself.

"That's not good enough Hiatt. You phone me by noon tomorrow and let me know when you're returning or else you're off the team for the shoulder harness project," Dan's ultimatum was predictable to Matt.

"I understand sir. I'll phone by noon tomorrow and let you know my status. I apologize Dan for the inconvenience," Matt felt bad for Dan, as he had witnessed the perils of management in and out of the military. Dan had already hung up the phone.

Matt pulled the .45 from the harness. The harness was in between his black button down and a tank top t-shirt. He pulled the clip to make sure it was full, removed a bullet that was chambered, and engaged the trigger to check the laser. Matt went to his sport coat and took two full clips from a pocket. The harness had leather loops near the holster to hold clips for a weapon. Matt stuffed the extra clips into the harness and put the original clip back in the .45. Matt chambered a round and kept the safety off as he returned his .45 to its holster. Matt was curious to see what weapons Cering had packed for him, but the ship was sailing and Sesom had requested the presence of all Disciples on deck. The weapons would have to wait.

Matt noticed someone in the doorway in his peripheral vision. Dorje was waiting to meet Matt. Dorje needed every opportunity to work on his English.

"Matt, my name is Dorje from Tibet. Sesom talk about you much. Very good to meet you and I look forward to know you," Dorje nodded at Matt with a grin.

Matt smiled back, "Well Dorje, I'm not sure if I've ever met anyone from Tibet, so you may be the first." Matt walked over to Dorje and shook his hand, "Let's go meet the others." Matt put his right hand on Dorje's back and motioned for him to go first.

****

Amen looked at his watch, 1:04 pm. He needed to neutralize the situation, find Scratches, purchase a pet carrier, and board a plane at Los Angles International Airport this evening at a yet to be determined time. Amen looked through the binoculars again. He could see one of the Samil goons peering out a window on the second level of Matt's townhome. He was expecting another drive by in approximately 26 minutes. Amen set the alarm on his watch for 25 minutes. He reached for the duffel bag and pulled out some ballistic charges. Each charge was shaped like a high caliber bullet, but was pliable like rubber. On the back of the bullet was a small digital display. Amen tapped the display and numbers began to appear: 5...10...15...20...25...30...5...10. Amen stopped tapping the display at 10 and turned the outer casing on the back until the 10 flashed three times. The bullet was armed and ready to be fired. Amen repeated the procedure for two more bullets. He loaded all three into a weapon with a long, large barrel. Amen looked at his watch once again, 20 minutes until the next drive by. Amen was surveying everything in the neighborhood from the second floor. He loaded three rounds into the Savage 110FP; he was certain that only two would be needed.

****

Dorje and Matt were standing on the forecastle with the other Disciples. The Excalibur had just left the dock and was being led by a towboat. Matt turned to watch Captain Phil through the window on the bridge. Captain Phil pulled the horn and the ship roared its departure from the Port. The towboat would carry the Excalibur a safe distance from the docks and set her loose.

Sesom had a couple of bottles of sparkling cider and enough glasses for the Disciples. He peeled the foil from the top of the bottles and began to shoot the corks at Captain Phil. Sesom and Lucas poured cider for each of the Disciples.

"I'd like to make a toast," Sesom held up a glass and looked around at each of the Disciples.

"To our journey together. May God's face shine upon each one of us and bring safe passage to this vessel, wherever it's headed," Sesom winked at Matt.

All of the Disciples raised their glasses and toasted Sesom. The towboat began to veer off the path of Excalibur and Captain Phil pulled the horn once again. The towboat responded with a much higher pitched horn that was equally as loud. Excalibur was leaving the Port's mouth and heading into the Pacific. The sun was directly over Matt's head and hanging high. Several gulls had followed the Excalibur from port in anticipation of scraps, cut bait, or other items to feast on from the ship. Looking up at the gulls reminded Matt of his dream and the black birds.

"You are the last to find Sesom?" Lucas's voice was deep.

"Actually, Sesom found me," Matt took a sip of cider, "I'm Matt," Matt extended his hand to Lucas for a handshake.

"Unusual for Sesom to find somebody. You are the last of the Disciples, no?" Matt was mesmerized by how softly Lucas spoke given his size.

"Let's hope so because the ship is sailing," Matt grinned at Lucas. "I'm thinking that we're going to get together and discuss our mission based on everyone's input."

"That would be good. I'm looking forward to our mission together."

Sesom's voice interrupted conversations occurring on the forecastle, "In 30 minutes we will meet in the dining area. If you don't know where the dining area is, it's next to the kitchen. If you don't know where the kitchen is, follow your nose. There is a Cajun Boil on the stove right now and you can't miss it. Lunch will be served."

Matt went to explore the cargo ship. He was curious to see about some of the toys Cering and Sesom loaded on the Excalibur.

****

Amen was looking through his binoculars. The time was 1:27 pm and he was expecting a drive-by. Samil goons would appear at the windows every few minutes, brandishing radios on occasion for communication. Amen had already picked up their channel on the radios and listened in on several conversations. The accent sounded Yemeni and their appearance corroborated his opinion. Amen knew that he would need to act quickly in order to preserve the integrity of his mission, even though his primary target could be hiding anywhere in the townhome. He wasn't fond of cats, at least not yet.

Radio chatter started up and Amen's mobile target appeared on his left at the end of the street. Amen cut the window screen in front of him. He went to the binoculars for confirmation. Two Samil in the front seat and one in the back; the vehicle was traveling at a slow rate of speed down the street. Amen focused the specs on the passenger in the front. The passenger raised the radio to his mouth and asked the men in Matt's townhome to answer. Amen held up the ballistics rifle and pointed the barrel out the window. The focus was adjusted slightly and Amen trained his right eye in the center of the crosshairs on the right front tire of the SUV. He closed his right eye for a second to check on the position of the SUV with his left eye. Amen would have to make sure the SUV was exiting the area prior to his shots; if not, the mission could be compromised. He closed his left eye and went back to his right.

The SUV passed Amen and came to a stop in front of Matt's townhome. Meaningless chatter about a soccer game ensued and Samil shared that they had seen no sign of the American. Amen was watching with his left eye and listening closely to the radio. "Xaatrak" came over the radio and Amen knew the

SUV would be leaving; he began to focus with his right eye. The crosshairs were dialed in on the top of the passenger's wheel rim. Amen was hoping for a shot between the rim and rubber to hold the ballistic charge in place. The SUV began to drive off slowly.

Amen pulled the trigger and watched through the scope, he saw a puff of dust come from the area he was targeting. Amen moved the scope to the rear of the vehicle on the passenger's side and began to count to himself, "10." He adjusted the focus on the scope while targeting the same area on the rear tire, "9." He had the target in focus and began to depress the trigger, "8." The next round soared through the air and struck the target in the desired location, "7." Amen once again focused the scope on the rear tire and dialed in his location, "6." He then changed his target to the door of the gas cap and focused the scope in the center, "5". Amen began to squeeze the trigger once again, "This one is for Trevor, 4." The round sped through the air and struck the door of the gas cap. Amen saw the break lights illuminate from the SUV; obviously the driver heard the round hit the vehicle. By this time the SUV was nearing the end of the street and a four-way stop, "3." Amen did not have a good view of the occupants in the vehicle as the windows were tinted on the sides and rear, "2." The brake lights extinguished as the SUV continued to the stop sign, "1." Amen dropped the ballistics weapon and went for his high-powered rifle, "Goodnight."

The SUV began to accelerate from the stop sign when the first charge exploded. The first explosion was followed by two more blasts that sent the SUV spiraling into the air in a ball of flames. Even though the SUV was 150 meters down the street, Amen could feel the heat from the blast through the open window, the blast also shook the ground near the SUV and would likely draw the attention of many neighbors and curiosity seekers. Amen was counting on that.

Amen's high-powered rifle was targeted on Matt's townhome. Amen dropped down to his knees and let the barrel rest on the windowsill. One Samil came to a window at the front of the townhome on the first level. Amen set the crosshairs on the Samil's forehead and fired one shot. The bullet penetrated the window and dropped the first subject. The second Samil came to another window on the second floor and peered in the direction of the SUV that was just beginning to crash to the ground in a fireball. Amen slightly adjusted the focus on his scope and set the crosshairs at the Samil's right temple. He squeezed the trigger as the SUV came crashing to the ground. The second subject had been eliminated and Amen began to disassemble the ballistics weapon. He tossed the ballistics weapon and rifle into an oversized duffle bag, closed the window, and headed for the back door. Amen exited the back door and tossed the duffel bag in the trunk of the Mustang. He walked around the house and crossed the street; people were beginning to exit their homes and filter into the street to get a better look at the vehicle.

Amen utilized Matt's keys to enter the townhome. He pulled a Glock 19 as he entered the home. Amen wasn't overly concerned about other Samil present in Matt's townhome, as he'd conducted surveillance for the past hour. He went immediately to the kitchen and looked in the pantry. Several cans of cat food were present and Amen chose two. He opened one and looked for a clean dish in the cupboards. After finding a dish with cat paws on it, Amen began to dump the contents of the can into the dish; the smell of wet cat food was unappealing to Amen. Out of the corner of his right eye came the furry four-legged friend.

"So you must be Scratches?" Scratches went for the food and Amen scratched the cat on her back.

"No time for eating right now," Amen picked up the cat and exited the townhome locking the door behind him. By now several people were in the street watching the frame of the SUV burn with intense heat. Amen heard sirens in the distance and moved swiftly across the street with Scratches. The Mustang was parked in the driveway of the house he'd used as a firing range. Amen opened the driver side door and set Scratches in the passenger side seat; he then popped the trunk and went for one of his duffle bags. Amen retrieved a small tool kit and an electronic receiver that picked up radio transmissions. The hood was unlatched and Amen disconnected the black wire on the battery. He then powered on the receiver and began to scan the vehicle for a bug. The signal grew stronger near the undercarriage. Amen knelt down and held the receiver at the front axle and moved his way back. The bug was definitely near the rear axle based on signal strength of the receiver. Amen looked around the differential and found a small GPS transmitter. Since the GPS transmitter was magnetic, Amen easily pulled the transmitter from the differential and went to the driver side door. He started up the Mustang and drove down the alley. Before he turned onto the street, Amen opened up the second can of cat food and set it on the seat for Scratches. She dug in.

"You like that stuff?" Amen began to laugh at his gesture as he held his nose.

"My name is Amen and we're traveling across the country tonight," Scratches didn't seem to care as the food was spilling over onto the leather seat of the Mustang.

"A few stops and we'll be on our way," Amen's phone began to buzz. He pulled it out of his pocket and read the screen, a message from Suzie with a subject of "Flight Itinerary". Amen put the phone down and began to look for a store to purchase a pet carrier. A trash truck was on the side of the road collecting garbage. Amen rolled down his window and tossed the magnetic GPS transmitter over the roof of the Mustang and it stuck to the side of the trash truck.

****

The dining room of the Excalibur was relatively nice considering it was framed in a steel cage. The cabinets were made of oak with a light stain. Amenities included a stove, microwave, dishwasher, coffeemaker, and plenty of counter space that made the kitchen extremely functional for sizable crews. A large dining table gave way to a dozen plus seats and Disciples were beginning to settle in for the meeting with Sesom. Even though Sesom had not defined himself as leader of the Disciples, the others had sought out Sesom after dreams provided them details and a motivation to find the African. Several in the remaining group had followed Sesom for over a year to discover meaning of their visions and lives together. The Disciples encountered Samil on several occasions, bringing their numbers to nine after the infiltration and bloodshed with pure evil. The group was solidified through their faith in each other and the whole of their parts. Coming from opposite ends of the earth made them unique, their abilities in weapons and combat made them exceptional. Matt was surprised at the absence of ego in the room.

"If you need to, get something to drink and have a seat," Sesom was pouring coffee for himself as he made the announcement. The coffee smelled good to Matt.

Matt grabbed a ceramic coffee cup hanging on the wall over the sink. The cup was large and had thick walls to endure pounding while on high seas. Sesom offered him some coffee.

"I'm sure you have many questions."

"I do."

Sesom began to pour. "There is nothing like a good cup of coffee with friends," he stopped short of the lip, "nothing."

Matt looked around the dining area. Sesom began to doctor his own coffee with cream and sugar, "You will soon know these people as friends, brothers and sisters too."

"I'm sure we'll have plenty of time for that as we cross the Pacific together."

"Yes we will," Sesom put his right hand on Matt's left shoulder and squeezed. Sesom took one of the chairs located at the end, or head, of the table. Matt went for the cream and sugar. A few sips confirmed the cup of coffee was good, and hot.

Matt took a seat next to Cering and Ethan.

Sesom was happy and opened the meeting with joy in his voice, "After more than a year, we have found the 12th Disciple."

Ethan was good at playing devil's advocate, "How can you be so sure this time Sesom?"

Matt seemed surprised, "What do you mean by this time?"

Ethan turned to Matt, "A few months ago a man approached us in Istanbul, and he claimed to know Sesom and many details of our dreams. We mistook this man for the 12th Disciple and he became part of our group. Trevor, one of our Disciples from England, never trusted the man and began to question his motives and actions. Turns out, this man who assumed the name of Seth, was a fraud and had manipulated everyone but Trevor. After a few weeks our conversations and exploration with him were leading us nowhere, and Seth seemed more interested in gathering information than sharing it. Trevor tailed Seth one day and found out his true intentions. Seth was recording all of our conversations and mailing them back to Samil. As Seth was loading memory cards into an envelope at a Turkish post office, Trevor approached him and was killed. Even though Trevor had drawn a pistol and was asking Seth what he was doing, a sniper shot Trevor in the back of the head from outside the building. More than likely Seth knew that Trevor was tailing him."

"So how did you guys find out about the memory cards and Seth's deception?"

"We have friends in high places too," Ethan looked at Sesom. "Sesom received a copy of the videotape from the post office. We all saw Seth placing the memory cards in an envelope and Trevor approaching Seth in the post office with his weapon drawn. Quite the scene. Seth has since disappeared. I look forward to seeing him again." Ethan pulled out his weapon, emptied the chamber, and handed it to Matt.

"1911. Seen many of these in the Marine Corp. Good weapon. Old-timer but very reliable," Matt handed it back to Ethan.

"That pretty much describes Trevor too. The 1911 was his gun, I'll make sure that Seth has an opportunity to see it again."

Sesom regained control, "Ethan, this isn't about personal vendettas or the fact that Trevor is gone. We must come to know our mission in order to understand our destiny."

"What about Trevor then?"

Sesom seemed incredulous when addressing Ethan's question, "He served his mission and protected us from Samil. Trevor was a perfect fit for our group and was the only one to understand the depth of Seth's deception. If it weren't for Trevor, we would have surely been in greater danger. I believe that his mission was served and he saved our lives. His visions became a reality on the day he gave his life for us. Trevor had seen the deception and understood the risks associated with Samil's infiltration."

Sesom backed off his tone a little, "Look Ethan, you and I are brothers. I trusted Seth and I'm to blame as much as anybody else. But this time we've found the missing link in our chain. He's sitting right next to you. I'm certain of that based on what he's told me already."

Matt sat back in his chair and folded his arms, "I'm still a little confused on how I've become a missing link or end-all-be-all to your journey; I didn't even know you before this morning. And, how is it that someone was able to infiltrate your group and understand everything about you?"

Cering took the liberty to answer Matt's question, "When Sesom and I met over a year ago, I sent letters to my parents in Egypt describing the encounter and how my dreams had become a reality. Amen was already following Sesom and understood the importance of his calling." That was the first time Matt heard someone reference the encounters as a calling. "I was very excited and many of the questions I had about dreams, visions, déjà vu, whatever you want to call it, began to make sense. Because Amen is a trained mercenary with the Israeli Defense Forces and responsible for the deaths of several bad men, and my parents are very wealthy and have interests in many businesses and fundraising for Egyptian leaders, my letters were intercepted by rebels. The letters ended up in the hands of Samil vis-à-vis rebels that dislike Egyptian rule and trained mercenaries from the Israeli Defense Force. The letters became a calling card for Samil to hunt us down."

Matt still wasn't following the story. He took a gulp of coffee to wake up brain cells. "Why does Samil care one way or another what you write to your parents or if you've found a calling in life. I'm not connecting the dots."

Sesom interjected, "We have come to a crossroads in the history of mankind. Samil knows this and will do everything in their power to control the outcome. Samil represents pure evil and the destruction of everything good. They realize we are in the midst of a revelation and they will do everything they can to stop us."

"Stop what?" Matt began to laugh. "Our boat from sailing the Pacific? Our arrival on the Indian coast? What is it that they are so intent on stopping?"

Sesom began to laugh too as he knew that Matt's ignorance was bliss. "Matt, through your recurring dreams, you hold the key to our destination. Once we determine and agree upon our destination, the journey will have just begun."

"Forgive me Sesom, but there you go talking like a genie that just popped out of a lamp. Let's cut to the chase and quit talking about fluff. I'm still not sure who half these people are," Matt had grown tired of the double talk by Sesom.

"You are right Matt. You met Amen and Cering at the café," Sesom motioned toward Dorje.

"Dorje is from Tibet and trained at high altitudes to guard his Holiness, the Dalai Lama. He is an expert in hand-to-hand combat, weapons, and sniper fire. I believe you met Lucas up top. He is from Brazil and ran with street gangs from a very young age. Fortunately, he was taken in by a Christian orphanage and found a higher road," Sesom took a sip of coffee. "Ethan drove us from the café to the parking garage, he is from Egypt like Cering. Li, our Disciple from China, is trained in high tech weapons and martial arts. He's not so fond of boats. Kimi is from Japan and is highly trained in karate and kendo. Cering has been training with Kimi to master kendo and they're both excellent with swords. Talan is from India and excels in Kung Foo and lathi. He has a rich understanding of Hindu culture and religious history as a whole. He handles our communication and technology needs."

Sesom paused for a moment, "These are the Disciples who are physically here. Two others that are with us in memory and spirit," Sesom paused briefly, put his head down, and laid his palms on the table. "Trevor was from England and came to us from the Special Air Service. He was a brave warrior and lost his life protecting us from Samil. When others of this group and I were naïve to infiltration from Samil, Trevor had a hunch and lost his life proving it. Liam was from Canada and had a rich history with the JTF2. He went home to visit family in Canada after finding me in Italy. His mother had fallen sick and was in the hospital with a fatal illness of some sort. Little did I know that Samil would tail Liam and ambush his family while he was visiting them in Canada. They even killed his mother in the hospital. At that time, we decided the Disciples shouldn't return home and put their families in danger; at least not until we understand the nature of our mission and minimize the risk of Samil.

Matt began to ask a litany of questions, "Why does Samil want to kill you?"

Sesom continued with his serious tone, "I'm not sure if they want to kill any of us, at least right now."

"Why would they wait?"

"We have some answers they're looking for."

Matt threaded the sentence for Sesom, "So they need to find what you're looking for before they exterminate you?"

"This is what I believe," Sesom was glad to see that Matt was beginning to understand a small part of the equation.

"My dreams are an important element to what you're looking for?"

Sesom's lips peeled back to reveal a smile, "Yes Matt. We believe that your dreams will begin our mission. Samil fears that the 12th Disciple holds critical information to our mission and its success. Like Alpha and Omega, you are the Omega that begins a certain action."

"Where do you want me to start?" Matt sat back in the chair; his arms fell to his sides as his hands rested on his thighs.

"The last dream would be nice," Kimi had a journal ready and Lucas leaned forward in his chair.

Matt paused for a moment, as he knew the Disciples seated around the table had waited, in some cases, over a year to hear what Matt would say. Matt began to realize how important his contribution would be to the team's mission. This group of Disciples sacrificed much over the past year pursuing truth, even though they had little idea of what the truth held or why Matt's story would become a beacon for their journey. Matt closed his eyes.

"My last dream occurred early this morning. I woke up and documented…" Matt paused and realized the importance of his journal as he looked at Sesom, "The details are in my journal."

"Continue Matt. We will worry about details later," Kimi began to transcribe what Matt said. She began about halfway through her journal; many of the pages had been filled already. Matt closed his eyes again.

"I had a dream that I was in a plaza of some sort. There was an enormous wall in front of me; it had very large stones that appeared to be made of sand. I remember looking up and there were several blackbirds perched on top of the wall. The black birds began to eclipse the sun and cast a shadow on the plaza," Matt went for his coffee and continued.

"Something caught my attention to the left out of the corner of my eye. There was a woman leaning against the wall with her arms outstretched, grasping the wall. She was rocking back and forth," Kimi's pen was scribbling and all the Disciples were motionless, listening intently for clues.

"The woman's head was hanging low. Almost like," Matt got up from his seat and went to a wall in the dining room, "almost like this." He stood against the wall and put his arms out lowering his head to a level below his shoulders. Matt began to rock back and forth while keeping his hands in the same place on the wall.

"The wall began to ooze blood from pores onto the woman's hands, then arms, and eventually the blood began to soak her clothing. Her clothing was light colored with a rope tied at the waistline. I remember the woman's hair was dark and straight; the length terminated around her midsection," Matt took another sip of coffee and opened his eyes, he had the undivided attention of the group.

Matt laughed a little, "I remember thinking that she looked like Pocahontas from the Disney movies." Kimi stopped writing; she didn't know who Pocahontas was.

"Who is this Pocahontas and what does she look like?"

Sesom interrupted her and said something in Japanese. Kimi returned to writing.

"It's okay Sesom," Matt nodded at Kimi, "dark skin, very smooth facial features, blue eyes that stood out like gems; she was very pretty I may add."

Kimi was drawn back into a conversation, "What was her approximate age?"

Sesom gave Kimi one of those looks and Kimi returned it. Matt closed his eyes again.

"Young, early twenties, maybe younger. She turned to face me. I remember being surprised in the dream that she noticed me, almost as if I went from spectator to participant. I thought I was merely dreaming something was happening, I didn't expect to become part of the dream." Matt's attention was captured by the smell of the Cajun Boil percolating on the stove, he was hungry.

"Sesom, how about if we enjoy some of that grub on the stove? Might help me focus a little better on the dream," Matt winked at Sesom.

"Li, would you mind doing the honors," Plates were already in the middle of the dining room table and Li began to pass them around the table. A silverware holder was fastened down to the table and held salt, pepper, utensils, Tabasco sauce, and napkins. Li went to the stove and grabbed the metal boiler that seemed to be half his size. There was already an oversized strainer in the sink and Li turned the boiler over, dumping the water for straining. There were shrimp, white fish, crab, lobster, and crawfish, onions, corn, potatoes, and half lemons that had been squeezed in a colander. Li grabbed some newspaper on the counter of the kitchen and brought it to the dining table. He began to spread the newspaper and other Disciples pitched in to help.

"Ever had a Cajun Boil?" Sesom directed the question to Matt. Matt thought the question seemed comical coming from a large man from Africa.

"I haven't," Li went back to the strainer and dumped the contents back into the boiler. He also scooped an enormous amount of butter from a tub and dumped it in the boiler. He turned the items together a few times with a large wooden spoon and brought the boiler over to the dining table. Li dumped all of the contents onto the newspaper and went back to the kitchen. A large loaf of bread was waiting in the oven and Li was careful to remove the item with oven mitts. The same hands that had beaten, maimed, and killed several men, were protected and carefully delivering bread to the table. Li took a seat at the table and pitched the mitts back in the direction of the kitchen counter.

"This will be a treat for you Matt. But before we break bread, let's honor the God that has brought us to this point in our journey," Matt wasn't a big fan of prayer. He'd heard enough of it during the Columbine tragedy. God this, God that, it wasn't that he didn't believe, it was that he didn't like people forcing God on him, in any fashion. However, out of respect,

Matt bowed his head to bless the meal. Oddly enough, he felt a little different around this group of people.

Sesom bowed his head, "Dear God of many religions and people, please bless this meal and let it nourish our souls. Please help us to be tolerant of each other and our beliefs. We ask that you bless each one of us and what our contributions are to this group. Forgive us our sins, and show us the way to salvation. Amen."

Several of the Disciples began to reach for utensils and began to stab at the boil in the middle of the table. Matt was impressed with the family style meal and everyone helping themselves. Obviously this group had spent some time together and shared several meals. Cering stole a shrimp from Dorje's fork and he began to laugh.

Sesom got back to business, "Matt, continue with your dream; Kimi, please continue transcribing."

"Where was I?" Kimi looked at her notes.

"The woman in the dream had just faced you," Kimi stabbed a potato with a fork.

"Oh yes," Matt knew he had control of the group at this point, he surveyed the mound of food and popped a chunk of potato in his mouth, "the woman turned her body toward me and her arms were soaked in blood, then she rotated her palms in my direction. She forced the faintest smile and said something like, 'please help me.'" Matt was surprised at how good the food was and complimented Li, "My compliments to the chef, very tasty Li." Li smiled and bowed his head to Matt.

"At that point I woke up and wrote the dream in my journal, a journal that is likely in the hands of your Samil friends," Matt was concerned about what was in his laptop and what was written in his journal. There were pictures of family members and other personal information that Matt was not excited about sharing with some of the most evil people on earth, at least according to Sesom.

Sesom called upon his Disciples, "I would like to know your thoughts."

Talan popped a shrimp in his mouth and kept digging through the pile as he asked a question, "Matt, you mentioned the wall was tall and made of stone. The stones were big, no?"

"Yes, they were." Matt fumbled for a napkin on his lap.

Talan addressed Sesom as he licked his fingers, "Sesom, the location sounds to be like Jerusalem, the Western Wall to be exact. The stones are large and porous. The wall runs several meters in each direction, a place of worship for many, but mostly Jews. There is a large plaza in front of the wall for many to gather. In fact, there has been fighting over the area for thousands of years, much like the land of occupation to the east."

Cering chimed in, "Yes, I have seen the wall too. Talan may be right. The wall is huge and is a place of worship for many."

"What about other similar places?"

"Obviously, The Great Wall of China," added Cering.

Ethan snickered, "Yes, but are we to search 3100 miles of wall for one woman?"

Sesom agreed, "You are right Ethan, there is a lot of wall, but I'd like us to consider everything. Matt, what ethnicity was the woman?"

"She resembled Cering. Same kind of facial features and skin tone."

"Middle Eastern. What other walls would be in the Middle East that may be of significance?" Sesom threw out the question to the group.

Lucas spoke up, "Sesom, you assume that the woman of the Middle East is not at some other place in the world?"

"I agree Lucas. But you must look for the obvious in dreams. We must not make a mole hill out of a mountain."

Kimi noticed the grammatical error, "You mean a mountain out of a mole hill." Sesom looked at her quizzically.

"Dreams are usually simple and straightforward, at least ours have been. Kimi, please read back the details," Kimi went through her notes and looked up at Matt occasionally for affirmation.

Dorje spoke up, "Matt, you speak of plaza or gathering. Were more people there?"

"No."

"The plaza made of rock as well?"

"Yes, from what I remember. The wall had huge sandstone bricks and the floor of the plaza had smaller stones that were polished," Matt's arms went from big to small as he described the sandstone.

Dorje continued in his broken English, "Do believe plaza was place for worship?"

"I'm not sure. There was obviously a connection the woman was making with the wall and she appeared to be grieving. I was a little more focused on the blood coming from the wall covering her hands and arms. The plaza was empty, except for black birds perched atop the wall."

"Any other of woman in more dreams?" Dorje looked for a pattern.

"Yes, there were several others. I had looked through the journal this morning and recounted a dream with the same woman near or in a stream. She was cupping her hands and showing me water or maybe offering me a drink, I'm not sure. She wasn't bloody or in distress, but her hair, facial features, and eyes were the same color as in other dreams," Matt shoveled more Cajun Boil in his mouth. "There was a recurring dream of me watching over this woman while she slept; nothing sexual, almost as if I was protecting her from something or somebody."

Kimi was rapidly scribbling details as Matt spoke.

Lucas spoke in a baritone, "Many of the walls in the Middle East were built as fortifications to keep enemies out. The Western Wall was an extension of a temple in Jerusalem, built shortly before the coming of Jesus Christ. The Romans did great destruction to the temple shortly after Christ's death. To Jews, the place is one of the holiest of holy. Amen may have more details on the history and importance of the wall."

Sesom was impressed with the contribution of Lucas, "Thank you Lucas. Talan, please fetch your computer and do some research on great walls in the Middle East. Gather as much information you can on the Western Wall in Jerusalem. I would like to see pictures and understand the history of this wall in particular."

"I will."

"In the meantime, let's enjoy this great meal Li has prepared for us," Sesom knew the group was hungry.

****

Amen was now the proud owner of a cat and pet carrier. His plane was leaving at 6:05 pm and he needed to check in by 4:30. It was 3:20. One more order of business before Amen could leave for New Jersey, he needed to ditch the Mustang. Amen found highway 710 and headed for Compton.

Scratches was in the front seat with Amen. She would meow occasionally and Amen did his best kitty talk to keep the cat calm. The Mustang was fun to drive and Amen tested the limits of the transmission and handling, he knew the Mustang would never make it back to Matt. Disposing of Matt's car was critical to keeping the authorities confused. If the police and military thought Matt had been kidnapped or killed, there may be fewer people on his trail. Sesom did not want Matt to be implicated in any killings or trouble with the law. Amen was unsure of when authorities would find the decomposing bodies of Samil in Matt's townhome.

Amen saw a highway sign ------- Compton 1 ½ miles. Amen had never been to Compton before. He had heard of Compton and understood the gang activity of Compton and Watts. Amen loved music and heard of a band called NWA; they sang a song about Compton. Even though Amen wasn't a huge fan of rap, he enjoyed listening to all types of music. Amen took the exit for Compton and headed west. The neighborhood was old and run down in places, but nothing to fear in Amen's eyes. He had seen worse overseas and in South Africa. The new Mustang stood out like a sore thumb, exactly what Amen wanted. He approached a rough area and pulled to the side of the road. There were gang inscriptions and busted out windows in some of the storefronts. A few citizens of Compton were admiring the Mustang and pointing to the custom rims Matt had purchased. Amen went for his phone and searched the Internet for a cab company in

Compton. A local taxi company and phone number flashed on Amen's screen; he touched the phone number on the screen, the phone began to ring.

"Red's Cab Company."

"Who is this?"

"Red."

"I need a cab in Compton at the intersection of East Compton and South Butler."

"You lost or something."

"No. I just need a cab to the airport. How long?"

"How you payin'?"

"Cash"

"I'll be there in 10 minutes."

"Thank you. I'll be on the corner in a blue blazer, blue button down, and jeans. I have dark hair and I'm wearing sunglasses."

"I'm on my way," The phone hung up.

Amen exited the vehicle and went around to the passenger door for Scratches. He grabbed the pet carrier and went to the trunk of the Mustang. Amen had a travel bag, his high-powered rifle, and ballistics weapon in the back; he removed all three. By this time, some curiosity seekers had taken notice of the car, Amen, and the cat. Amen was very much aware of their presence and anticipated their arrival. One of the younger teenagers wasn't afraid to approach Amen.

"Say man, nice wheels."

"Thanks, how old are you?" Amen was lining up his items on the corner.

"15. I'll be 16 in two months. I've already started driving with my pops and a permit."

"Congratulations. You a pretty good driver?"

"I think so."

"You ever driven one of these?" Amen finished unpacking his items from the back and closed the trunk.

"Oh, no sir. My dad has a 1983 Ford pick-up with 294,000 miles and I'm learning on that; it's a stick."

A crowd was beginning to form around Amen and the young teenager near the Mustang. Some of the older boys were looking through the windows to get a closer look at the interior.

Amen played dumb, "So, is red your favorite color or something?"

"You don't come around here much, do you Holmes?"

"No. This is my first time to Compton. I heard a song about Compton a few years back. Not quite like Sinatra's New York, New York." The crowd around him began to laugh and cover their mouths with their fists.

Amen was ready to bargain, "Anybody have some water for my cat. I just bought this carrier and it came with a bowl. She's kinda thirsty."

An older teenager stepped in front of the younger one, "It'll cost you."

"I'm ready to pay cash for the water."

"It'll cost you a dime."

"That's it. That seems reasonable." Amen fumbled around his right pocket for some change. He pulled out a few quarters, a nickel, and a couple pennies, "Will you take a quarter?"

"No, you don't understand. A dime is a ten dollar bill in Compton."

"No problem," Amen pulled out his money clip and fetched a ten-dollar bill. There were hundreds, fifties, twenties, tens, and fives in the money clip. The group pulled in for a closer look and huddled around Amen. Amen handed the $10 bill to the older teenager.

The younger teenager commented on the money clip, "Yo man, that's more than my pops makes in a month."

"Really, well I'm willing to give a nice tip if you can have the water here in five minutes or less."

"You're on," The older teenager pulled out his cell phone and called a nearby friend.

"Hey Sneakers. Get a bottle of water and come to the corner of East Compton and Butler fast. No time for questions, get here now," The teenager closed his cell phone and looked Amen over.

"Man. You in the wrong kinda clothes, with way too much money, in a place that ain't necessarily Mr. Roger's neighborhood. Most of the people in this group are packing, cops rarely come through this area, and when they do, they just run all the lights 'cause they scared. You scared?"

"No."

The older teenager eyed Amen with a perplexed look and laughed, "And why not?"

"Because I drove to Compton on my own will. There's nothing wrong with the vehicle and it's got a full tank of gas. I know that you guys mean business and I'm here to conduct business. I need some water for my cat, Red's taxi will pick me up shortly and I'll be on my way. You don't know if there are friends of mine nearby with high-powered rifles and scopes with cross hairs focused on your heads or," Amen looked down at the man's genital region, "that area." Amen got the attention of the older teenager.

"Alright man, but you better pay up because the water will be here in seconds."

"I've never made a promise I didn't keep," Amen thought about the Mustang and how he wasn't returning the vehicle to Matt. Matt would be disappointed because the car was a prized possession and Amen indicated he would take care of the vehicle. A car came whizzing around a corner and parked in an abandoned liquor store parking lot close to the group of boys and Amen. Sneakers jumped out and ran to the older teenager.

"Here man, what the hell is going on?"

"You'll see. Give the man the bottle."

"Yo man, this dude is decked out in blue. Are you kidding me?"

"No. I'm not kidding you. This dude and I have a deal. Give the man some water!"

Sneakers handed the water to Amen, "Thank you." Sneakers just backed up and watched Amen. Amen went to the pet carrier and poured some water for Scratches.

"Scratches, meet Sneakers," Amen took the money clip out of his pocket and pulled out a $100 bill.

"Nice doing business with you," He handed the bill over to the older teenager, "the water is even cold."

"Yo man, my pleasure," A red taxi drove up and an older man pulled up next to the Mustang.

Red had to roll down the window manually on the passenger's side, "Did you make the call?"

"I did," Red put the car in park and got out. The older teenager spoke up, "Yo Red, good to see you."

"You too Michael. You hustling my friend here?"

"Absolutely," Red smiled at Michael and began to load the bags in the back of the taxi; he put the pet carrier in the backseat. Red's taxi was clean and waxed twice a month, he was proud of his business and provided a great service to Compton and surrounding areas.

"When you're ready sir," Red went back to the driver's side and entered the taxi; he pushed the meter handle down.

Amen looked at the group. "Thanks for your help," He turned toward the young teenager and asked him a question.

"So you turn 16 in a couple months?" The young teenager stepped in front of the older one.

"I do."

"Would you like to do some business?"

"Yes sir, if I can?" The teenager was eager; he turned his red ball cap bill to the back.

"See this Mustang? Well here are the keys," The other boys began to gasp, giggle, and slap each other with high fives and fist bumps. The teenager knew the deal wasn't' done.

"What's my end of the bargain?"

"Two things. Stay in school for one and wear many colors in your lifetime. Secondly, there is a good chance that the police may look for this vehicle in the near future. The owner will not report it stolen, but you may need to visit a chop shop and do a little work on it," The teenager was surprised Amen knew what a chop shop was. "If your pops asks you where you got the wheels, have him call Red," Amen pointed in the direction of Red and made sure that he heard what was said. Everyone knew Red in Compton.

Amen continued, "I have a brother named Lucas that used to run with some of the toughest gangs in Brazil a few years back. He got out and found his calling in life to protect others."

"He a cop?"

"No. He's a Christian."

Amen checked around the area to ensure that all of his gear was loaded. He opened the front passenger side door and sat next to Red, the window was still down.

"If you find any personal information in that vehicle, I ask that you please destroy it, for your safety. If you go looking for trouble, you'll find it."

The young teenager was still in shock from the gift Amen gave him; he nodded his head and waved at Amen. Amen turned to Red, "To LAX," The current time was 4:08 pm.

****

"Li, that was a great meal, thank you," Sesom was picking his teeth with a toothpick.

"Fantastic Li, I haven't had a home cooked meal like that in years. The bread was especially good," Li acknowledged Matt with a nod and began to clear plates from the table.

"Sesom, why so much faith in me? I've had a few dreams, what's the big deal?" Sesom went from picking to chewing the toothpick.

"I've had visions and dreams about you for the past two years. Some of those dreams and dreams of Disciples led us to you in the City of Angels. While many of the Disciples found me, your situation was a little different. I had to find you," Li brought coffee over and began to warm up mugs.

"Once we discovered your townhome and position with Delta Defense, we began to do our homework."

"What kind of homework?" Matt brought the ceramic mug to his lips.

"Your name has great significance in Christianity. Matt is short for Matthew and Matthew was the 8th Disciple called to follow Jesus. Your last name is Hiatt. If you take the short form of your first name, Matt, and put Hiatt on the end, MattHiatt is formed and closely resembles the 13th Disciple of Christ, Matthias."

Matt was learning a lot, "I didn't know that a 13th Disciple existed."

Sesom continued, "Matthias never received much attention because he replaced Judas after the betrayal. Matthias became relevant only after Christ died. On the other hand, Matthew was a very educated man with considerable wealth. He was a tax collector and left a very lucrative lifestyle to follow Christ and his teachings."

"Do you know how many Matthews are in the United States alone?"

Sesom continued, "Tens of thousands. Do you know how many people in the United States are named Matthew Hiatt? 153, at least that's all we could find. There was only one listed in the City of Angels."

Matt was surprised to hear that more people weren't named Matthew Hiatt. He knew that Hiatt wasn't a popular name, but Matt didn't know how scarce it was in his country.

Ethan translated Hiatt for Matt, "The name Hiatt means *at the high gate*. Your ancestry came from England to escape British rule. Your father had a very successful career with the Air Force and contributed greatly to the Missile Defense program of the United States. The fact that your family experienced the tragedy at Columbine High School and loss through the terrorist attacks of 9/11 makes you, how should I say it, unique."

"Isn't everyone unique in their own right?" Matt inherited the gift of modesty from his father.

Ethan countered, "Of course Matt, but how many families and individuals excel in a time of turbulence and trials during life? Many people bury their heads in the sand and become consumed with their own self-pity. You finished high school with honors and immediately entered the Marine Corp upon graduation. They witnessed your physical abilities and knew that your mind was strong in the midst of adversity. I'm sure that your promotion into Special Operations was rapid and you saw much of the world by the time you were 23."

Matt began to clap his hands together. "Wow, you've done some homework. I'd seen much of the world by the time I was 22 though," Matt winked at Ethan; Ethan smiled in return.

"I don't understand something though?" Ethan sat back in his chair.

"What's that?" Matt raised his coffee mug and took a sip, almost time for a refill.

"The United States had a few opportunities to take out Osama Bin Laden in Afghanistan and along the Pakistan border; yet, they let him go. I don't understand," Ethan was genuinely concerned about the US's intentions in the Middle East based on previous actions, or inactions.

Matt knew where Ethan was going, "I'm confused about some of the direction as well. My company in Special Operations is made up of a dozen Marines; the Commandant of the Marine Corps handpicked us personally. We've seen some pretty nasty stuff during the past 3 years, and the opportunity to wipe out Osama Bin Laden with his entourage. We called in our position and asked for advisement from command. We had everything in our arsenal aimed at Bin Laden's caravan and our command told us to stand down."

"Why?" Ethan didn't understand.

"No idea," Matt shook his head. "Imagine looking at the man responsible for your parents' deaths and not being able to pull the trigger. At that point, I really didn't know what our mission was and why we were canvassing the mountains of Afghanistan. They called us the dirty dozen back then, one of our group quit the company after the incident with Osama Bin Laden and asked to be reassigned."

****

"What's your name?" Red had a white beard and a baseball cap with his company's name on the front.

"You don't want to know?" Amen enjoyed the breeze from his window being rolled down.

"Everybody's got a name," Red was being persistent with the wrong person.

"Everybody but me. Not to be rude Red, but there is a possibility that people interested in my name and flight plans might find you and become interested in what you know. It's best if you know nothing."

"I understand, just trying to make some conversation," Red glanced in the direction of Amen and smiled. "What you did for Robert back there was generous."

"Who's Robert?"

"The young teenager that took interest in your Mustang?"

"Oh yes, he seemed like a good young man. I hope that he doesn't get too involved with gangs and find himself in prison for life."

Red shook his head in affirmation, "I know his father and I doubt he'll let that happen."

"That's good. What about the boy's mother?"

"She passed away five years ago after a short battle with cancer. Lu was a great woman and an even better mother."

"So why does the boy wear colors to denote gang affiliation?"

"Out here, it's better to be affiliated with a gang than not be affiliated," Red was happy to have his passenger talking.

"They seem like nice kids though."

Red was quick to reply, "Most of these kids are good and have the best intentions. They just want to be loved and that's what the gang provides in many cases. Unfortunately, they're born into a life that's tough from the start. They're surrounded by crime, drugs, and peer pressure to belong."

"How do you get away with having a cab company called Red's?"

"The kids know me as Red. I've always been Red to them. I've taxied their parents, relatives, friends, and enemies over the past several decades. I can name most of the residents in Compton because I've lived here all my life. There are several people making an honest living in Compton setting the right example for these kids; we just need more of those people. Once again, what you did for that boy was special."

"Just make sure his dad doesn't take a strap to his back for something I gave him."

"I will."

"I have a couple items in the trunk that are for you too."

Red looked at Amen with surprise, "And what kind of items do you have in the trunk for me?"

"The first is a sniper rifle with a high powered scope. The second is a ballistics weapon that shoots charges at objectives. You can set the charges for up to 30 seconds. When they reach their objective, the timer will begin to count down until detonation. I sighted both of them in for you this morning at 75 meters," Amen smiled to himself as he looked straight ahead.

"What would I need those for?"

"I'm not saying you need them at all, but they are worth a considerable amount of money. I want you to have them."

"Should they be taken to a chop shop as well?" Red gave Amen one of those looks.

"Let's just say that the weapons are very accurate and lethal if necessary."

"What kind of business are you in?"

Amen thought about the past year with Sesom, "Let's just say that I'm in the business of protecting assets and other people's interests."

"Me too," Red didn't go any further with the question.

"You got family?"

"Ten brothers and sisters; two of my brothers passed away."

"Big family."

"All I got is family and this cat. I wasn't a big fan of cats until I met this one."

"LAX is coming up, what airline?" Amen went for his cell phone and brought up the message from Suzie.

"Just drop me off anywhere in the departure area. I'll make do from there."

"You got it."

The airport was busy, but Red was able to squeeze in an open spot in the unloading zone for departures. Amen and Red exited the cab and went to the trunk.

"Please keep these two bags as a token of my appreciation," Amen pointed to the duffle bags that contained a high-powered rifle and ballistics weapon. He then pulled out a bayonet military style knife and put it in his travel bag. Next was the Glock 19, Amen pulled the gun from the holster and released the magazine in the bag. He pulled back on the slide and a bullet popped out of the chamber; Red caught it and handed it to Amen. Amen placed the bullet in the travel bag and zipped it up. Scratches was beginning to let out a few meows and Amen walked around to the passenger side door to unload her.

"You ready to travel across the country," Amen looked at his watch, 4:23 pm. Scratches was quiet as all she wanted was attention. Amen pulled out his money clip and peeled back two $100 bills.

"Thanks for showing up quickly and getting me to the airport," Amen stretched out his right hand and offered up the money.

"But your cab fair is only $28.00."

"Well, then your tip shall be $172.00. I insist that you take the money, please don't disrespect me by not taking the money. I would hate to have to reload the Glock now that it's packed and secure," Amen smiled at Red.

"Thank you sir, and thanks what you did for those kids back there."

"Now remember Red, if anyone asks questions about my cab ride, I provided you no information."

"Absolutely, and that's the truth too," Red wanted Amen to know that he was all business.

Amen grabbed the bag from the back and picked up the pet carrier, "Thank you again Red." Amen walked through the double doors and disappeared into a mass of people. A quick glance at the departure screen showed United Airlines flight 316 **on time** for New Jersey leaving shortly after 6:00 pm. Amen looked up and down the massive hallway to find a sign for United Airlines.

"How may I help you?"

"Two traveling to New Jersey," Amen pulled a license from his wallet and handed it to the attendant. The attendant began to punch away on the keyboard in front of her.

"May I have the ID of the other passenger?"

Amen set the pet carrier on the scale in front of the attendant, "You will find some identification around her neck."

The attendant leaned over the counter and whispered, "Oh."

"Very well Mr. Jordan, you may board with the cat at gate B8. Are you checking any bags today?"

"Just one."

Amen removed the pet carrier and set his travel bag on the scale. The attendant printed a tag and wrapped it around the handles of the bag. She handed Amen two boarding passes for first class and his ID for the flight to New Jersey. Amen felt better knowing that his flight was on schedule and he was checked through to New Jersey for a non-stop flight. There was only one thing Amen had forgotten throughout the day, to eat and nourish his body; he was hungry.

****

The Disciples finished their late lunch and everyone was helping clean up. Matt, Sesom, and Cering returned to the dining table.

"Matt, I just received a text from Amen."

"Where is he?"

"LAX. He will be leaving for New Jersey shortly and landing at Newark. Good news, he has your cat."

"That's probably a sight to see," Matt and Sesom began laughing.

"He also eliminated Samil invaders at your townhome and others watching your place," Matt waited for Sesom to share other information he was reading. "He says not to contact your place of work, the military, friends, or family right now. Depending on when authorities find Samil intruders in your townhome, many questions will develop. Best if you're listed as a missing person or a person of interest," Sesom looked up at Matt.

"Dan at Delta is expecting a phone call from me tomorrow."

"You must not phone him," Sesom shook his head and was adamant about Amen's instructions.

"I'll be fired and stripped of my security clearance. They will also notify my commander with the Marines at Pendleton tomorrow. The Marines will be looking for me as an absent without leave case. The military isn't fond of Special Operations' combatants who turn up missing, for any reason," Matt knew that his disappearance would be alarming to several people and the Marines. A person picked by the Commandant for Special Operations that goes missing would become a high priority for the Marines.

"We will deal with issues as they're dealt to us," Sesom was firm in his statement, but sympathized with Matt's life changing news.

"Maybe Cering's family will provide me a job after we're done with our mission?" Sesom and Matt began to laugh again, Cering joined in the laughter too.

****

Amen's footsteps resonated on the wood planks of the Boardwalk in Ocean City. He took in the sandy beaches and raging force of the Atlantic; the spray was cool on his face. He was glad to have packed a pair of jeans, t-shirt, and running shoes. Even though he seemed out of place with a pet carrier in his right hand, he strolled down the Boardwalk as if he owned it. A family was snapping a picture nearby and Amen offered his assistance.

"Would you like me to take your picture?"

The father looked down at the pet carrier and said, "Sure," with some hesitation in his voice.

Amen took three pictures of the family and offered the camera back to the patriarch.

"Sir, do you know where Fral's is along the Boardwalk?"

"Of course. Continue down the Boardwalk for another 300 yards or so and Fral's will be on your left."

"Thank you sir," Amen picked up Scratches and continued down the Boardwalk. The smell of sand and surf was wafting through the breeze coming from the ocean. The Boardwalk was busy with families, couples, and individuals taking in the ocean or enjoying a book along the rail. Amen hadn't seen a market like this before, one with multiple shops and amusements for children of all ages. Having the ocean nearby made the area a spectacle for visitors.

In the distance Amen saw a storefront sign for Fral's and began to look around for park benches to rendezvous with Matt's family; he could see a man with a red baseball cap on.

As Amen drew closer to the man, he noticed that his appearance was similar to Matt's in some respects. The man was a little bigger in physique, but carried himself very well. Amen and the man made eye contact and the stranger began to walk toward him. As they grew closer to one another, Amen noticed the hat was stitched with USMC on the front in yellow thread.

"You must be Amen."

"And you Mike."

Amen set down the pet carrier and extended his hand to greet Mike. Mike's hand engulfed Amen's.

"Matt had you bring his cat?"

"I'm afraid so. There is really nothing left in his townhome, so he insisted I retrieve his cat."

"What about the Mustang?"

"You don't want to know."

Mike began to laugh, "Matt's going to throw a fit about that. He saved up in Special Ops for years to buy that baby."

"Best if we just didn't bring it up when we see him again."

"I agree."

"Where is the rest of your family?"

"Mary has the kids in Fral's and they're picking up some taffy."

"What is this taffy?"

Mike gave Amen a look of surprise, "You've never had salt water taffy? Oh boy, are you in for an American treat." At that time Mary, John, and Rebecca came out of the store. Mary was a very attractive woman with brunette hair that was pulled back into a ponytail that draped down to the small of her back. Mary was wearing a black camisole, jeans, and sandals. She carried Rebecca and John was walking beside her with a bag of salt-water taffy. Mary's sunglasses were resting on the top of her head. John saw his dad and began to run over to him.

"Daddy, daddy, look what we got you," Mike scooped John from the Boardwalk and held him up to his chest.

"Alright buddy, my favorite. I want you to meet a friend of mine, his name is Amen. Can you give him a piece of taffy please?" John reached in the bag and pulled out a piece of taffy wrapped in wax paper.

"Here."

Amen took the piece, "Thank you." He unwrapped the taffy and put it in his mouth. After chewing the taffy a few times he looked at Mike and smiled. Mary and Rebecca walked up to Amen. Amen noticed that Mary appeared a little older than he imagined.

Mike did the introductions, "Mary, this is Amen, the man Matt called us about yesterday."

"Is my brother okay?"

"Yes. He is with several of my people."

"And just who are your people?"

"We have been sent to protect your family and Matt with our lives. Your lives are in danger, including the little ones."

Mary knelt down and rested Rebecca on her thigh. "You are traveling with Scratches?"

"A long story, but yes, at Matt's request."

John pointed at the cage and wanted to get a closer look, "Kitty." Mike set John down in front of the pet carrier.

"When will we meet up with Matt and the others?"

"We will meet up with them in Japan. They set sail for India yesterday and we should be meeting them at Yokohama in nine days."

"Nine days? What about my pizzeria?"

"The condition of your pizzeria is far less important than the safety of your family."

"Agreed," Mike stated with some hesitation. He wanted to hear more.

"We will travel from here to Washington DC and catch a flight to Tokyo tomorrow. We must not travel by way of New Jersey or New York, as the enemy will have intelligence operators at both airports looking for us."

"You realize we have two small children," Mary was concerned about traveling with her son and daughter.

"I do, and we have a cat too," Amen smiled at Mary. "Please understand that whatever you need I have been instructed to provide. We will travel by first class and purchase a seat for Scratches. More importantly, your safe passage to Yokohama is my priority. Did you bring IDs for travel?"

"Yes, but we didn't bring our passports and the children don't have any," Mike was concerned about how they would travel internationally.

"I'll have them prior to our departure tomorrow."

"Why you?" Mike continued the questioning?

"Why me what?" Amen knew the question was coming.

"Why should I trust you with my family?" Mike stonewalled.

"For the same reason I am entrusting my life with your family." Amen began to quote from Psalm, "And the Lord shall help them, and deliver them: he shall deliver them from the wicked, and save them, because they trust in him. My job is to deliver you back to your brother." Amen gave Mary a glance as he spoke directly to Mike.

****

The equipment in the lower section of the Excalibur amazed Matt. The belly was divided in two; the first half, in the bow, was loaded with exercise equipment, weights, and a boxing ring, the second half, in the stern, was loaded with military equipment and three vehicles. There were handguns, rifles, machine guns, grenades, grenade launchers, rocket launchers, and some larger weaponry stored in crates. The three vehicles were modified SUVs with bullet proof glass, reinforced solid steel undercarriages, and roll cages throughout the cabs. All three vehicles were black and reminded Matt of his ride from the café to the Port of Los Angeles. Just above them was wheat stored in multiple compartments on two separate levels.

Matt would usually start with weights and move to cardiovascular machines. The treadmills, ellipticals, and rowing machines were mounted below TVs hanging from the ceiling. The weight training area had several machines, benches, free weights and dumbbells racked out against the wall and near benches. All the cardiovascular and weight training equipment was placed on industrial rubber mats to protect the hull. Matt was most impressed with the boxing ring set up for mixed martial arts, kendo, and karate training. Matt sparred with Sesom and trained with Talan in karate the day before and was looking forward to kendo training with Kimi and a mixed martial arts match against Ethan today. The Disciples were always training to learn different techniques and attack sequences. Because the Disciples came from all over the world, there were plenty of fighting techniques and strategies they could share with each other.

When Matt entered the gym, Cering and Kimi were sparring in kendo and Dorje was working on the tumbling mats. The women dressed as if they were going to play a game of

Lacrosse. Cering had improved her kendo skills over the past several weeks and was beginning to land offensive strikes against Kimi. The women were deceptively tough and strong. Matt went to a neutral corner and watched the two women spar.

Cering swung her training sword high and Kimi ducked and rolled to her right. Kimi countered with a swing shin high at Cering. Cering jumped and jabbed her sword into the ground blocking Kimi's attack. Kimi retracted her sword and began to twirl it in front of her like a plane's propeller.

"Remember, when you are attacking from the ground, make sure you pull back and reset before attacking an enemy again," Kimi continued, "you don't want to be in a ground attack for too long as the position reduces your ability to attack from multiple angles," Cering nodded at Kimi.

Kimi twirled her training sword faster and moved the weapon around her body. Her first strike was high and straight down toward Cering's head. Cering raised her sword and blocked the strike by gripping the sword on opposite ends and raising it above her head. Cering went for the counter by spinning counter-clockwise and aiming for the left side of Kimi's abdomen. Kimi dropped her sword tight to her side and blocked Cering's shot. Cering was exposed and Kimi raised her right leg and kicked Cering in the chest sending her to the ropes. Kimi paused for a moment.

"Remember, your sword must act as protection first, even in an offensive strike. Keep the kendo stick in front of you when possible to prevent an offensive strike from someone's legs or arms. If you can't, you must utilize your karate skills to protect your body from an enemy's sword." Cering shook her head again in affirmation, "I understand."

The women continued to fight and Kimi would stop on occasion to provide instruction. Matt went to the weights and began to work his triceps and biceps; he would run through ten sets of twelve reps before he was finished. Sesom, Ethan, and Talan came into the gym with a stack of papers.

Sesom held the papers up for Matt to see, "Matt, I believe we have all the paperwork we need to make a decision about a destination for the Excalibur." Matt kept on pumping iron as the three men took seats on benches near him.

"We have searched the internet for walls of the Middle East that hold great significance," Sesom reported with enthusiasm.

"Jericho has some of the oldest walls in the world, and while the Apostles documented travels through Jericho and a few miracles were performed by Jesus there; other than being ancient, the walls have little significance." Sesom shuffled the papers and focused in on another territory, "Turkey has several walls, but as Lucas mentioned, many of them are fortress walls built years ago to keep enemies out." Sesom continued to flip through pages, "Ancient Egypt may have had walls to contain the Israelites during the 12th Dynasty of their rule; however, much of the information surrounding the walls is mythical and based on assumption."

"Where could other historical walls be?"

"Babylon, just south of Bagdad, was fortified with walls around the entire city several thousand years ago. Once again, these were fortress walls to keep enemies out; really not built for religious worship or significance," Sesom set the papers down as Matt continued his workout.

"Talan and I pulled up as much information on the Western Wall as possible. There is much history and an equal amount of mystery surrounding the wall and I believe the wall and plaza match the descriptions of your dreams. The first temple built in the area supposedly contained the Ark of the Covenant, until it was destroyed by the Babylonians five hundred years prior to the coming of Christ," Sesom grabbed the stack of papers again and showed Matt a picture of the Western Wall and plaza. Matt stopped his reverse curls.

"I'll be…" Matt reached his hand out for the picture.

"What do you think?" Talan wanted confirmation they had found the right place.

"That's amazing. That's the place of my dream," Matt continued to study the picture and placed his finger over the wall.

"Very much history there Matt. The Jews and Muslims have fought over the Western Wall territory for years, thousands of years," Talan pointed to the wall as well. "The area through here and where you see the mosque are considered to be the holiest of places for Jewish worship. The wall and plaza are considered to be an extension of the first temple built in the area."

"Wow, but how…" An alarm sounded on the ship and Sesom went for a phone on the wall. An alarm seemed strange to Matt, as the seas were calm and the skies clear. Matt continued to study the picture.

"Yes Captain," Sesom was serious as alarms on the Excalibur were rarely sounded.

"You have to come up here Sesom. You'll never belicve what I'm looking at!" Captain Phil was shocked by what he saw.

"I'll be right there."

Sesom turned to the group, "Everyone topside now. Cering, Ethan, Kimi, and Talan, grab some weapons, including grenade and rocket launchers," Matt's weapons were in his room.

"What about me?"

"You follow me to the Captain's Bridge," Sesom and Matt began to climb stairs to the deck. After four flights, Sesom exited a door from the stairwell to the deck and immediately went for the Bridge at the bow of the ship. One more set of stairs and they entered the Bridge. Phil was looking through binoculars out to sea. Aaron was steering the ship and John was watching controls.

"What's going on?"

Matt came bursting through the door to the Bridge.

"Like I said Sesom, you're going to have to see this to believe it," Captain Phil offered the binoculars to Sesom.

"Where am I looking?"

"Starboard at about 2 o'clock," Sesom began to focus the binoculars.

"I see two small vessels with three to four men apiece heading right for us," Sesom pulled his eyes from the binoculars and looked out over the sea, he then went back to the binoculars, "they are maybe 1000 meters from us."

Matt took interest in the conversation, "Are they Samil?"

Sesom continued to look through the binoculars and answered Matt, "Samil is stupid, but they're not this stupid."

Captain Phil looked at Matt, "They're pirates. Rare for the Pacific in these parts, but pirates nonetheless."

Sesom dropped the binoculars, "Aaron and John, down below, we'll handle this with Captain Phil. These guys are armed and likely mean business."

"Ay Sesom," The young men left their posts and Captain Phil took over.

Lucas, Li, and Dorje had shown up and were on deck. Sesom opened a window and called out for them, "Who's armed amongst you?"

All three of the men smiled and seemed eager for some action. Sesom gave instruction, "Cering, Kimi, Ethan, and Talan are on their way up with more artillery. Keep your weapons hidden until the time is right."

Matt wanted to get his firearm, "Should I get..."

"No. No time. Stay put," Sesom brought the binoculars back up to his eyes, "eight hundred meters maybe."

Captain Phil offered some insight, "One group will likely board while the other stays tight to the ship. They usually load hostages in the boat running alongside the ship."

"Hostages?" Matt was surprised that pirates would take hostages, "Don't these guys usually look for maps and buried treasure?"

"Not these guys," Captain Phil had a serious tone. Phil loved his ship and pirates had never boarded the Excalibur while he was Captain.

Cering, Kimi, Ethan, and Talan arrived at the Captain's Bridge. Sesom was quick to provide leadership.

"We will steer the ship so pirates board from the starboard side. Go to Captain Phil's quarters. From his office, you will be able to see everything on the starboard side of the Excalibur. One of the boats will likely flee when the time is right. Make sure that you don't launch missiles or grenades until the boat is clear from the starboard side."

Cering had the grenade launcher strapped around her shoulder and an artillery box with more grenades in her right hand. Kimi was carrying an AT-4 single shot rocket launcher. Ethan and Talan carried LWRC M6A2 automatic weapons. Cering was curious, "Will there be a signal?"

"Yes, when one boat is running away from us with their engine at full speed, that will be your signal," Cering smiled at Sesom and disappeared with Kimi, Ethan, and Talan.

Sesom called out the window again, "500 meters, do not fire a weapon until the first boat has boarded; you will know when the time is right." Sesom turned to Captain Phil, "You just camp here. Go ahead and kill the engines."

Captain Phil brought the throttle down on the Excalibur. Sesom turned to Matt, "Let's join the guys on the deck."

Matt and Sesom went down the flight of stairs and met up with Lucas, Li, and Dorje on the forecastle. The pirates' boats were now in clear view and rushing toward the Excalibur.

"We will let the first group board, then we will take care of business," Sesom removed his shoulder strap and weapon. He tossed the strap through the window of the Captain's Bridge and tucked his handgun near the small of his back; Sesom pushed the gun down a little farther than normal as he knew the pirates would search across his waistline, if they had the chance.

Both pirate boats came alongside the Excalibur and they shot rope guns to the bow of the ship. They called for the Disciples to tie off the rope lines as they were going to board. The pirates also warned the Disciples that funny business would be met with gunfire and magnetic mines would be placed on the side of the Excalibur. Sesom looked down on the pirates.

"Okay, as you please. Please don't damage our ship," Sesom noticed that the pirates were equipped with long-range radios. Disciples were attaching ropes to tie-offs so pirates could climb aboard the ship. Five pirates began to climb ropes; they were equipped with machine guns and knives. The first pirate to board the Excalibur appeared to be the leader. He wore a red beret; all of the pirates were Caucasian with Slavic facial features. The first pirate aboard the Excalibur was also first to speak.

"Who's in charge?" Matt recognized the accent as Russian.

"I am," Sesom stepped forward. Disciples had tied off ropes and were filing in behind Sesom. The other four pirates boarded the vessel; this wasn't their first rodeo but they had no idea they were in the presence of mercenaries, snipers, martial artists, and Disciples trained to kill with their bare hands.

The leader gave commands in Russian to his counterparts boarding the ship. Two of the pirates went to search the ship while the other two began to spread the Disciples apart.

The leader was dressed in cargo pants and a black muscle shirt. He stood a little over six feet and was physically fit, even though he looked small compared to Sesom.

"What's your cargo?"

"Wheat. We're on our way to India."

"Who's steering the ship?" The leader motioned to the wheelhouse above.

"My second mate. When we saw you were boarding he took over navigation."

Another command in Russian came from the red beret. The pirates began to line up the Disciples and Matt was the first to be pulled from the group toward their leader.

"Why only one white man? You appear to have a very diverse group. Are you sure he isn't in charge?" The remark was meant to be inflammatory toward Sesom. Matt was beginning to get angry with the pirate pushing him around and shoving the barrel of his AK-47 in his face.

"Him?" Sesom began to laugh loudly and some of the Disciples cracked a smile. "He's my newest deckhand. He doesn't know his bow from his stern," Sesom began to laugh even harder.

Matt spoke to the overanxious pirate in front of him, "Get the gun out of my face."

The pirate was edgy and didn't like Matt addressing him.

"What did you say?"

"Get the gun out of my face."

The pirate went to lunge the gun even further into Matt's face; before he could, Matt grabbed the barrel, emptied the chamber, and released the clip in less than one second. He kneed the pirate in the stomach, pulled the AK-47 from him, and popped him in the chin. The pirate dropped to his knees and lost consciousness face down on the deck.

Matt now had a gun, "Next time take the safety off." Matt put the clip back in and chambered a round.

The leader raised his AK-47 in Matt's direction and was met with a Glock 29 at his right temple.

"Don't even think about it. Your safety is on too, but mine isn't. Lay your weapon down at your feet," The leader did as told and went to his knees. Sesom heard a thud behind him and to the left. Li had dropped the other pirate and was holding an AK-47 over him.

"Lucas and Dorje, go find the other two pirates and bring them back to the bow," Sesom picked up the AK-47 and pulled a cigar out of his pocket. He strapped the AK-47 to his right shoulder and removed a lighter from his pocket. Biting off the end, he put the cigar in his mouth and lit up a Corona.

"You guys should have picked a different boat," Sesom began to puff on the cigar and Matt came over to him.

"What are we going to do with these guys?" The leader seemed interested in the answer too.

"Send them on their way," Sesom winked, "I'm sure they know not to bother us in the future." Sesom turned his attention to the leader.

"Where is the main ship? There's no way you're out here on your own."

"I don't know."

"I find that hard to believe," Sesom stood silent until the other prisoners arrived on deck.

Lucas and Dorje came from the hull and two prisoners walked in front of them; hands on their heads, one was bloody around the left eye. Sesom turned his attention back to the leader.

"Call your other men up. Let them know it's clear," Sesom continued to puff on the Corona and maintained complete control of the situation. The leader stood up and looked over the starboard parapet wall. He yelled something in Russian and the boat waiting below peeled off the Excalibur and made a run for it. Sesom took another puff of his cigar.

"Why is it that you do not listen? I specifically told you to have the rest of your crew board our ship. Their blood will be on your hands," Sesom pulled the cigar from his mouth and looked at the remaining bud.

"What do you mean?" The leader didn't understand Sesom.

"Look to your right," Sesom pointed in the direction of Captain Phil's quarters and a window opened up on the starboard side of the ship. Kimi put the barrel of the AT-4 out the window and waited until the fleeing boat was a safe distance from Excalibur. A flash came from the window and a rocket intercepted the boat within a second. The detonation from the rocket sent debris from the boat a hundred feet in every direction, all five pirates aboard the boat perished instantly.

"That blood is on your hands," Sesom put the cigar back in his mouth.

"Line them up," The pirate Matt had rendered unconscious was beginning to come to. "Pat them down. I want all their radios, weapons, cell phones, and GPS devices. Leave them with nothing but their clothes on," Sesom kept a close eye on the Russian leader as he already made one dumb decision for the pirates. Lucas kept watch with one of the seized AK-47s. A pile of radios, tracking devices, cell phones, knives, and a few pistols were taken from the pirates.

"You may go now," The leader didn't hesitate as he provided Russian commands to the remaining pirates. They began to climb back down the ropes to their boat. Once all of the men successfully boarded their boat, the Russians fired up the engine and left the starboard side of the Excalibur. They didn't look back.

"Matt. Have you ever used an AK-47?" Sesom pulled the cigar from his mouth again. He looked up to Captain Phil in the Captain's Bridge and gave him a signal to resume speed.

"Yes. The gun is available throughout Afghanistan. Many Russian troops left 47s behind during their war with the Afghani people."

"Two rounds to the engine of that boat. Seeing as you've fired the weapon before, you will understand the distance before the boat is out of range."

Matt utilized the parapet wall of the starboard side of the bow to rest the barrel of the machine gun. Even though the Excalibur was listing side-to-side 3 degrees, Matt had a clear shot of the engine as the pirates pulled away.

"200 meters." Sesom puffed his cigar. Matt was studying the distance and timing the rise and fall of the list.

"250 meters."

Matt fired one round that went through the engine of the boat. The boat began to sputter as the engine died. The pirates began to curse the Disciples of the Excalibur in Russian and waved their fists at them.

"275 meters."

Matt fired off another round that struck the boat's engine again. A puff of smoke billowed from the top of the engine and it caught fire. The Russians scrambled to put the fire out with ocean water and a fire extinguisher on board.

"Are you sure you don't want 5 or 6 rounds in the hull of that dingy?" Matt was still angered by the pirate shoving a gun in his face.

"No. They are in God's hands now. If they are lucky, their ship will find them floating about. If they are luckier, another boat will come by and pick them up. They are unarmed and unable to hurt anyone," Sesom burned the cherry of his cigar. "Most likely they will die of thirst and be forever lost at sea."

"Tragic," Matt stood up and watched the pirates put out the fire and curse the Excalibur.

Matt turned to Sesom, "Do you believe in curses?" Matt caught a whiff of Sesom's cigar and noted the smoke was aromatic, unlike the inexpensive cigars his Special Operation's buddies smoked on occasion.

"Only those who act against the wishes and will of God shall be cursed. A few pirates angry that their mission failed and now stranded may curse all they want; curses won't change our outcome or theirs," Sesom pointed at Matt with the two fingers holding the cigar and spoke softly. "But those who test Abraham's promise, deny the flight of Egypt, or refute the Commandments handed down from Moses to all people of God shall be cursed for an eternity."

"Alright big guy, no need to get preachy on me," Matt responded as Sesom smiled and began to laugh.

The Russian boat was becoming a speck on the sea as the Excalibur charged toward the Orient.

****

Amen journeyed safely to Tokyo with Mike, Mary, Rebecca, John, and Scratches. Traveling with small kids was a challenge, but Amen was surprised at the good nature of the children and how John was just happy to spend time with Mike. Mike had poured unlimited hours in his pizzeria and endured some very tough years post 9/11 to keep the business afloat. Mary was supportive of Mike and assumed the love and care for John and Rebecca that her mother demonstrated to her all through her life. Tokyo had parks, shrines, temples, and even a Disneyland. Rebecca was too young to enjoy the rides and attractions of Disneyland; however, she enjoyed watching Mickey Mouse, Donald Duck, Pluto, and a plethora of other characters that seemed ubiquitous within the park.

Amen had put Matt's family up in the finest hotels in Tokyo and waited on them hand and foot since arriving five days prior. Amen mostly hung out in the background to let Matt's family enjoy their time halfway across the world; he knew their lives would never be the same. So far, Amen hadn't spent much time with Mike or Mary since arriving in Tokyo and now found himself on a park bench with Mary and Rebecca at Disneyland. Mike had taken John to run around the park and take in a ride or two. Rebecca was fast asleep in Mary's arms.

"Thank you for watching over our needs," Mary was wearing sunglasses and taking in the sun, carefully protecting the exposed parts of Rebecca's skin.

"It is not only my pleasure, but my duty. Your brother gave me specific instructions prior to meeting up with you in Ocean City," Amen was a cool character always observing his surroundings.

"How long have you known Matt?" Mary was thinking that they might have met during Matt's time in Special Operations.

"About five minutes," Amen was matter of fact about the relationship.

"Five minutes and you've come half way across the world with us?" While Mary was surprised, she understood the dedication and commitment of those who served in the military and those who served others as a way of life; they rarely considered their own needs.

"We met briefly in a café and we didn't have much time for small talk or getting to know one another. I've spent more time with Matt's cat and his family than with him," They both began to laugh.

Amen continued, "Matt was very specific about Scratches and that she come along, I'm afraid she's the only remaining part of his townhome left in tact."

"What do you mean?" Mary continued to rock Rebecca and keep her close. She carried herself with much more poise and calm than that of a typical 29-year-old woman.

"When I arrived at Matt's townhome, a group of very bad people had already invaded and seized or destroyed many of his possessions," Amen shifted his body on the park bench to watch some visitors run past in the direction of Mickey Mouse.

"Who are these people?" Mary had experienced evil already and not much surprised her.

"We call them Samil. The origin of the word comes from Hebrew and means Angel of Death."

"What do they want with my brother?"

"We are not sure if it's your brother or a person closely connected to him. They were getting very close to Matt and monitoring his location and movements."

"How do you know?"

"I found a positioning device on his Mustang."

"His new Mustang?" Mary took interest in the car because she knew how proud Matt was of the vehicle.

"His new Mustang."

"I'm surprised Matt didn't have you bring that too."

"I think he wanted me to," Amen was speaking as if hiding something.

"What happened to the Mustang?"

"You don't want to know."

"Do to."

"I dropped his Mustang off in Compton, and right now it's either in a thousand pieces being sold as parts or modified beyond recognition with a new V.I.N. and title. Regardless, we will never find it, and neither will anybody else."

Mary began to laugh a little at first and then she began to roar hysterically. Amen began to laugh with her until they both had tears in their eyes.

"He'll want to kill you," Mary was trying to get her composure back.

"I know, why do you think we're staying at the best hotels and seeing some of the popular spots in Tokyo. You're my only hope," Amen continued to laugh and Mary started up again. Mike and John came back to the park bench.

"What's so funny?" Mike wanted in on the laugh.

Mary was waving her hand in front of her face while she continued to laugh. "You know the Mustang Matt purchased a few months back?"

"Yeah. Amen didn't want to share the grim details of the Mustang's fate with me earlier."

Amen and Mary began to laugh harder. Mary was speechless with laughter; Rebecca began to fidget and wake in her arms.

"What happened to Matt's car?" Mike was beginning to sense that Matt wasn't going to be happy with the undisclosed secret based on Mary and Amen's giggling.

Mary slowly gained her composure in order to keep Rebecca asleep and to speak with her husband, "Well, it appears that Amen had to ditch the Mustang before he met up with us," Mary looked in the direction of Amen.

"Well where did he ditch it?" Amen began to shuffle on the park bench.

"Compton."

"Compton?" Mike cracked a smile at Amen, "Why Compton?"

"The authorities are likely looking for Matt as we speak. I had to make sure there were no traces of his vehicle to confuse those looking for him," Amen seemed satisfied with his answer.

"What would the authorities want with his Mustang?"

"When I went back to Matt's townhome, there were two men waiting for Matt to arrive. I showed up instead, across the street with a high-powered rifle. The two men waiting for Matt are no longer waiting," Amen knew that his revelation would invoke curiosity in Mike.

"What did you do with the men?"

"Left them in the townhome, as they lay. The scene was pretty messy. Three men were casing Matt's home in an SUV too; authorities are probably still picking up pieces from that SUV exploding into thousands of pieces at the end of Matt's street," Amen glanced toward Mary. "The men I told you about, Samil, they are well connected and have people infiltrating police, fire, government, the military, you name it. Regardless of what happened at Matt's townhome a few days ago, Samil will do their best to paint Matt as a bad person and blame him for the deaths."

"Oh my gosh," Mary was establishing how tangled the story was becoming.

"Who's Samil?" Mike felt left out.

Amen provided Mike an abbreviated version of what brought them to this point in Tokyo. Amen was an excellent communicator and had served the Israeli military very well. While he was still very involved with the Israeli military, they had allowed him to take leave. The Israeli military understood the importance of fighting holy wars and maintaining a strong presence in Jerusalem. They weren't about to lose control in a Holy Land again or permit evil an opportunity to subjugate the Jewish nation of Israel.

"How are you funded and how many people are supporting you?" Mike knew that money was important in the matters of military affairs and protection.

"Unlimited," Amen was quick to put Mike's fears at ease. "We are funded through a family in Egypt. The family is connected to one of the Disciples traveling with Matt right now. There are 40 people involved with our operations; including specific people that we trust with travel, money, intelligence, and communications."

"I'm still a little unsure of what Matt's role is in this?"

"Matt has experienced dreams and visions over the past several months that will lead us on our mission," Amen folded his hands and rested his elbows on his knees. "Our journey will begin once Matt discovers the nature of his visions. All the other Disciples found Sesom; Matt is unique in the sense that Sesom found him."

"Unique in what way?"

"Unique in the sense that Sesom is the Alpha and Matt the Omega of our group."

"What is your group by the way?" Mike didn't know if the group was religious, military, mercenary, or some other faction.

"We are made up from people all over the world. Muslim, Buddhist, Hindu, Christian, Jewish, Existential, and agnostic are represented by the Disciples. Two have already died to protect the essence of our journey," Amen took a more serious tone as he leaned back against the bench. "All of us are specially trained in combat, martial arts, or both. Many of our beliefs dovetail into a Supreme Being, while a few in our group are undecided and don't know what to believe yet."

"Why are your beliefs important to this mission?"

"Dreams and visions have brought us together. Our orders have not come through a chain of command, but through what we've experienced personally. Our calling transcends the physical."

"Heavy stuff," Mike was done with trying to understand the whats and whys that brought his family to Tokyo. He was excited about spending time with family, seeing his brother-in-law, and possible action against an unrecognizable enemy. "How about some hot dogs and French fries?"

"Yeaaaaaaahhhh, let's go Dad," John was tired of the adult conversation too.

****

Matt took a shot to the small of his back and fell to his knees. He leaned forward and allowed his fists to hold up the weight of his upper torso. A kendo training sword held in Matt's hands reminded him of a simple closet rod; Kimi had trained Matt hard the past several days.

"Is this the part when I get to tap out?" Matt was dripping sweat into the facemask of his helmet.

"No mercy for those in training," Cering began to laugh as she was spinning a real kendo sword around her body outside the sparring ring. Cering's skills in kendo were improving at an accelerated pace.

Matt felt the beat of his heart in his back where the kendo sword landed. He rose to his feet and began to twirl the stick in front of his body. Kimi tucked her sword underneath her right arm and took a defensive posture. Matt went on the attack and came from the top left side of Kimi's shoulder. Kimi responded with a twirl and one-handed brace of the sword over her head. She immediately kicked Matt in the chest, which backed him up a few feet.

"Don't leave yourself exposed when on the offensive," Kimi returned to her defensive stance. "Kendo experts will utilize martial arts when necessary to submit an enemy. If you attack from above, you must be prepared to use your legs to protect against an attack from below."

"Let's take five," Matt removed his helmet and went for a water bottle nearby.

"Are you excited to see your sister tomorrow?" Cering was eager at the chance to dock in Tokyo and stand on firm ground.

"My sister, brother, niece and nephew. I haven't seen them since I returned from Afghanistan," Matt exited the boxing ring and took a seat on a nearby weight bench.

"Afghanistan is no vacation," Cering was familiar with history of the Middle East and the struggles Russians and Americans had encountered in that desolate area.

"Yeah, I doubt I'll be going back anytime soon. I'm sure the Marines and Delta Defense aren't pleased with my sudden absence and any situations surrounding my disappearance."

"Are you ready?" Kimi was eager to continue training and invited Cering into the ring.

Cering was becoming an expert with a kendo sword. She twirled the sword over her head, down around her chest, from side-to-side, and backed up into a defensive stance, "Are you?"

Kimi laughed, "You are becoming a warrior, I'm not sure how much longer I can hold you off."

Matt learned a lot by watching Kimi and Cering fight with kendo swords. He would watch their moves and imitate them outside the ring. Matt wasn't a warrior yet, but he'd trained four to five hours each day to learn kendo since they left the Port of Los Angeles. With time to lift weights, cycle, train in martial arts and kendo, Matt was improving his strength and combat skills. While the idea of traveling by way of a massive cargo boat didn't appeal to Matt initially, he'd come to understand the importance of taking this time to train and recharge his batteries. Matt spent time with each of the Disciples learning their combat techniques and something about them personally. Li was one of the most interesting Disciples because of his speed and agility. During training, Li would attack quickly and employ all of his limbs to submit an enemy. Once Li was successful at overcoming an opponent, he would become completely peaceful and begin a breathing technique through his nose to slow his heartbeat and adrenaline flow. While they were training, Matt asked him about the meditation exercise.

"Mr. Matt," obviously Li hadn't received the lecture from Matt about his name, "Your mind is best defense in battle. Eyes, ears, skin, must be able to know surrounding. Control and use of your mind important to staying alive."

"What do you mean by skin?"

"Skin can alert you to changing air, temperature, and the look of an enemy. Just as people can only see a few colors of the sun, skin has more uses than touch," Li's broken English was making sense to Matt.

"The whole when you can take a pebble from my hand thing," Matt remembered an old TV show when he was much younger.

"What is this pebble you speak of?"

"Never mind," Matt forgot his audience and knew that any attempt to explain the pebble from his hand TV show would fall way short of understanding.

Sesom came up to Matt and laid his hand on Matt's shoulder.

"Tomorrow we will arrive in Yokohama, the largest port in Japan. Your sister's family will meet us for dinner," Matt turned to face Sesom. "Your sister's family can continue on by plane to Jerusalem, or we can be one big happy family on the Hiatt cruise line of Excalibur."

"Is there room on the boat?"

"We make room."

"Let's bring them on the boat then. I'm a little worried about how two young children will handle traveling on a large cargo ship though."

"No worries. Kimi and Cering are excited about meeting your sister and helping with her small children. As you say in the United States, women's intention."

"You mean **intuition**."

"Yes, just like I said, intention," Sesom believed in his English as much as he did a mission.

Kimi and Cering were in a fierce training battle. Cering was beginning to match Kimi's skills and landing blows that would be fatal to an enemy. Sesom and Matt watched the two ladies fight in the ring and were captivated by the speed with which the swords were maneuvered and struck each other.

"Very tough women," Sesom looked to his side at Matt.

"Indeed they are," Matt raised the water bottle to his mouth and squeezed, soaking his face and hair.

"Sesom, what do you believe we will find in Jerusalem?" Both men took a seat on a nearby weight bench.

"Answers, many answers," Sesom was vague as usual.

"Answers to what?"

"To our visions and dreams. To our questions about faith and spirituality. To the essence of our mission."

"Are you afraid?" Matt was projecting his own feelings.

"Yes. I'm afraid we are being called to become involved in something bigger than we comprehend. We must maintain openness to our findings and not rush to judgment in that which we don't understand. Evil in our world and the strength of Samil are cause for concern. At no other time in man's history have we seen evil become so powerful and prevalent in our world," The words rolled off Sesom's tongue with little effort or emotion; he had obviously pondered his calling over the past year.

"The woman of my dreams doesn't appear evil, but someone who is trying to share a message. The stream, wall, and other encounters with her have been peaceful and troubling at the same time," Matt was doing his best to philosophize with Sesom.

"The woman needs us and we need her to understand our objective."

"Hey Sesom," Cering was pointing in his direction and calling him out, "how about some time in the ring to brush up on your kendo skills?"

"Only if Matt and I spar with Kimi and you," Sesom nodded his head at Matt.

"Deal. Get your gear on and get ready. The ring isn't big enough for all of us, we'll move our fight to the mats," Cering pointed in the direction of some tumbling mats nearby.

****

Captain Phil was sounding the horn. Disciples began to line the forecastle of the Excalibur as the islands of Japan were in clear view. The day was beautiful and seas were dark blue with a few white caps. Dolphins were swimming alongside the Excalibur as she continued to blow her horn.

Sesom entered the bridge, "Beautiful sight isn't she?"

"You bet. There are so many ports and great fisheries in Japan. I can't wait to grub on some fresh catch."

"You've contacted the authority and gained access at Yokohama?"

"You bet. Suzie copied Amen on details of our arrival; they may be waiting for us at the Port. I ordered up some fuel, more food, and fresh water. Anything else you need Sesom?"

"No Captain, I think we'll be fine with what you've ordered."

"We'll overnight in Yokohama and begin our trip for the Arabian Sea tomorrow morning," Captain Phil had a map behind him to plot their course. "Cering has made arrangements for us to offload our wheat at the Port of Ashdod, bringing us close to Jerusalem," Phil pointed at Jerusalem. "We'll be forty miles from the city once we dock at Ashdod."

"We will come up through the Arabian Sea?" Sesom looked at the territory on the map.

"You bet. We'll come up through the Arabian to the Red Sea, from there we will navigate the Suez Canal to the Mediterranean. Once we make the Mediterranean, we will dock at Ashdod," Captain Phil grew a big smile on his face, "This is my first trip up the Red Sea."

"I hear that it can be a tight trip," Sesom looked at the Captain.

"It is, especially around the Suez where they have to dredge to keep the depths safe.

"How many days from Japan?"

"Give or take ten, depending on how much I push the engines."

"Great," Sesom was looking at a calendar on the wall.

"What, boss?" Phil evoked general concern.

"We will be in Israel at the time of Rosh Hashanah."

"Roshawhoskie?" Captain Phil was unaware of the Jewish holiday.

"Rosh Hashanah, the Jewish New Year."

"Is that a problem Sesom?"

"We'll have to see when we arrive. I'm sure that many Jews will make the pilgrimage back to Jerusalem for the holiday. May make our job a little more difficult," Sesom was now tapping his finger on the calendar to mark the beginning of the Jewish New Year, "Amen will be happy though."

Sesom yelled out the bridge to the Disciples, "Dorje and Ethan, prepare the lines for tie offs. We will be docking on the port side of our ship," Dorje looked at Sesom in a strange manner.

"This side Dorje," Sesom utilized an outstretched left arm to indicate the left side of the ship.

****

"So what's the plan Amen?"

"The Excalibur should be docking any minute. Based on my discussions with Sesom, we will be traveling to the Arabian Sea and heading north to the Red Sea. The Red Sea will take us through the Suez Canal and we will dock at Ashdod in the Mediterranean."

"Where is Ashdod?"

"Israel. I'm very familiar with the area," Amen gave a nod to Mike.

"I thought we were traveling to India," Mike appeared confused.

"Change in plans. The Disciples have changed our destination to Israel."

"So much for me getting back to Maria's anytime soon," Mike looked out over the Bay.

"How is the restaurant performing in your absence?"

"Fine. Which angers me even more," Mike put his hands on his hips. "I have a great crew that has stuck with me since we opened. The Assistant Manager is military as well. He was injured in Pakistan while on a tour with the Marines. When he came back to the States after being medically discharged, he showed up at the door of Maria's and wanted work."

"Did you know of him prior to the arrival at your pizzeria?"

"No. But some of my Marine buddies tipped him off and encouraged him to come see me once he was discharged. There are countless injured in the armed services that seem to get lost in the shuffle after their return from duty. Seems like DV on a license plate is the only marker for those wounded in war, their stories seem to be buried forever," Mike was done discussing his thoughts on the military and war. "Why Ashdod?"

"Very close to Jerusalem and the Holy Land. Forty miles separates the Port from the city of Jerusalem."

"Any reason we're heading into Jerusalem?"

"Not sure, other than the fact that the Disciples have likely discussed the decision. I'm sure we'll find out more once your brother arrives."

John was hanging with Amen and his dad. Mary was walking with Rebecca on Osanbashi Pier. The sun was shining and the water was dark blue. On the horizon in Tokyo Bay there was a ship sounding its horn. Amen recognized the sound as he'd traveled by boat with Captain Phil on the Excalibur.

"Here they come," Amen held his left hand over his eyes to block the sun and gather a glimpse of the Excalibur. Mike and John did the same.

"Cool dad. Is that our boat?"

"That's the boat carrying your uncle and his friends. I think we'll be traveling on it for the next several days."

"Alright," John began to dance around while pointing a finger in the air; he spun around until he fell down dizzy. Mary came over with Rebecca, "Is that them?"

"It is," Amen knew that Mary would be excited.

Mary looked out over Tokyo Bay in her sunglasses and oversized straw hat. She was wearing a sundress and sandals; Rebecca was dressed in a similar fashion to Mary, minus the hat. Mary picked up Rebecca and pointed to the ship on the horizon. She was excited to see her brother. The Port Authority of Japan came over to the family and told them to remain a safe distance from the ship as it docked on the pier. They moved up a walkway and kept an eye on the Excalibur, as it appeared to be growing larger and larger on the horizon.

"Wow, what a ship," Mary was surprised at the enormity of the ship.

"Wait until you see the inside," Amen cracked a grin, as he knew the family would love the ship.

"Are we staying on the ship tonight?" Mike wanted to continue on with their travels.

"No. We will stay at the Pan Pacific tonight," Amen turned and pointed in the direction of the hotel just behind them. "I'm sure that Captain Phil and the others are ready to rest their sea legs tonight. The Excalibur will remain at the pier as its refueled and loaded with fresh supplies."

Mike looked at the hotel and nodded, "Very convenient."

"Convenience is important when traveling on a boat. The Excalibur has been outfitted with several modern amenities that keep it comfortable and safe at the same time."

The Excalibur was now sidled up to the pier, and Dorje and Ethan were chunking ropes from the bow, port, and aft. Other Disciples were securing areas of the ship and preparing for fresh supplies to be loaded. "Excalibur" was written prominently on the side of the ship with the same logo Captain Phil wore on his hat.

"Excalibur, how fitting," Mary was waving at the crew and caught sight of her brother. Matt gave her a wave back. John and Rebecca were waving at the massive steel structure in front of them. Employees of the Port Authority at Yokohama were tying off ropes and wheeling up a gangway for the crew of the Excalibur. Seagulls were calling each other and sailing over the Excalibur, almost as if they were watching over her. The birds were hoping that the Excalibur would toss some cut bait or unwanted fish overboard for a snack.

Matt came down the gangway first once the half-door on the parapet wall was opened. He was carrying a small overnight bag and a light jacket over his shoulder. Mary was the first to greet him.

"You need to shave," Mary went to hug her younger brother.

Matt dropped the bag and jacket to the ground while looking over his sister, "You don't like my rugged, been-at-sea-for-10-days look?"

"Not really, but you're still handsome."

"Now that's better," Matt embraced his sister with a long hug and closed his eyes. He could remember his mother hugging him in a similar manner. John was tugging at Matt's leg.

"Hey John John," Matt picked him up and gave him a hug, "you're going to like some of the people we're traveling with."

"I like Amen," John pointed at Amen in his slacks, nice shirt, and shades. Amen gave Matt a little wave like a kid and smiled. Matt put John down and took a few steps toward Mike.

"Who you holdin' Mookie?"

Mike smiled and tickled Rebecca's chin, "We just found her at Disneyland. Pretty cute isn't she?"

"Oh yeah. Must get that from her mother," Matt took Rebecca from Mike's arms and hugged her. Matt stretched out his arm for Mike and shook his hand. Mike pulled him close and gave him a hug.

"You look pretty rough man. Almost like you've been spending some time in Hindu Kush."

"Not quite. I've done some time in those mountains and the Pacific is much more forgiving and gracious," Matt gave his brother-in-law a wink and handed Rebecca back to her father.

"Thank you Amen," Matt shook Amen's hand and patted him on the shoulder.

"You have a great family," Amen enjoyed the past week with Mary, Mike, John, and Rebecca.

To honor Matt's privacy, the Disciples remained on the gangway while he met with his family. Matt turned to them and waved them down.

"I'd like you guys to meet some friends," Matt put his hand on Dorje's shoulder, "This is Dorje and he's from Tibet," Dorje dropped his bag and shook hands with Mike and Mary while bowing.

"Cering is from Egypt. Her family is well connected throughout the world and is funding this operation. We have her to thank for the digs and travel arrangements," Matt evoked some sarcasm.

"Thank you Cering, we appreciate the time we've spent together as a family in Tokyo. Amen has been great," Mary was genuinely thankful.

"This is Sesom. He was the first to make contact with me in Los Angeles. He is from West Africa."

"What a pleasure. Mary and Mike, I've heard so much about you," Sesom had a large grin on his face.

"We've heard about you too, Sesom," Mike outstretched his hand to welcome Sesom to terra firma.

"This is Li. He's from China and happy to be off the Excalibur," Li shook hands with Mary and Mike and lay down on the pier. Li's equilibrium was off and he was still rocking back and forth, even though he was on solid ground.

"Next we have Lucas," Mike was amazed by the size the Brazilian. Matt continued, "He is from Brazil, a town outside of Sao Paulo."

John was amazed by the size of Lucas too, "Big man daddy."

"Yes he is," Mary and Mike shook hands with the Brazilian.

"Ethan is also from Egypt. He and Cering graduated from the same high school."

Mike was surprised, "Really."

"No." Matt started laughing.

Ethan stuck out his hand for Mike and Mary, "See what I've had to put up with for the past several days."

Mary was quick, "I can't imagine."

Kimi was excited to see John, "How are you?" She stretched out her hand.

"Good."

"I've heard some great things about you?"

"Really?" John began to hide behind Mike's leg.

"Really." Kimi shook the hands of Mike and Mary.

"Kimi has been teaching me kendo and other mixed martial arts; she is from Japan."

"Welcome home," Mary gave Kimi a smile.

"Thank you. I believe we're dining with some of my friends this evening in Yokohama. It's great to be back home."

"My name is Talan and I'm from India. I've heard many stories about Matt's family. Nice to finally meet you."

"And you too Talan," Mary and Mike welcomed Talan with a handshake.

Captain Phil was next in line. He had a model of the Excalibur that he handed to John.

"I'm Captain Phil. It's a pleasure to meet some of Matt's family," he put an arm around Matt and looked at Mary, "Matt shared the story of your parents with me and I'm sorry for your loss."

"Thank you. They were special."

"I'm sure that Matt has you to thank for turning out okay," Phil gave Mary a grin.

"Maybe a little."

Matt butted in, "Yeah right. If it wasn't for you and Mike, I might be dead by now."

Phil looked at John and removed his hat; "You ready to travel on this boat tomorrow?"

"Yes," John was preoccupied with his new model toy.

"I have two guys that will overnight on the Excalibur. Their names are John and Aaron. You have a suite next to the Captain's quarters on the main deck; it'll be large enough for you and the kids. We made some slight modifications to ensure that your comfort is topnotch."

"Thank you. We look forward to traveling on your ship to the Middle East. Been a few years since I've been to Israel," Mike felt confident in Captain Phil's care.

"Me too," Phil was excited about his trip up the Red Sea.

"What's the plan Amen?" Sesom was ready for a hotel and hot shower.

"The Pan Pacific Hotel is within walking distance," Amen pointed to three buildings on the Bay. "I've got a shuttle for bags and anyone that needs a ride; car seats too," Amen was beginning to understand the duties of being a father while caring for John and Rebecca.

"I'm going to hang with John and Aaron until we receive our fuel and other supplies. I'll meet up with you for dinner," Phil motioned in the direction of Mike and Mary, "pleasure to meet you folks, I'll see you tonight."

"Thanks Captain Phil," Mary gave him a hug, "we'll see you at dinner."

The Disciples were tossing their bags in the back of the shuttle. Everyone had agreed to walk, including Mike and Mary, to the Pan Pacific Hotel. Li was still lying on the pier and asked Ethan to load his overnight bag in the van.

"I'll be there shortly," Li was waiting for the pier to stop rocking before he walked to the hotel; he rolled over on his side.

"We'll check you in and leave a key with the concierge," Ethan was beginning to laugh, "let me know if we need to bring some dinner back to the pier for you." Li rolled back over on his back and closed his eyes.

Mary, Mike, **Matt**, John, Rebecca, **Sesom, Lucas, Kimi, Cering, Ethan, Dorje** and **Talan** began their walk to the hotel. *Li* continued to lie on the pier next to the Excalibur. **Amen** closed the door to the shuttle and drove to the hotel. Supplies began to show up for the Excalibur and a fueling boat was pulling up to the starboard side. Captain Phil wanted to ensure that access to the boat was limited and that all supplies were loaded by crane to the main deck. John and Aaron would be armed overnight to protect themselves and the cargo.

****

Matt was happy to see Scratches and was carrying her around the hotel room. She was purring and glad to be in Matt's arms. He let her down and tossed a fuzzy mouse on the floor.

"Great meal Matty and it's sure good to see you," Mike was tucking the kids under silk sheets of an oversized bed in a beautiful suite. Rebecca had fallen asleep during dinner and was fast asleep; John wasn't far behind.

"Really great to see you guys too," Matt settled into a chair near a desk.

"What is this all about Matt? Amen filled us in with some interesting details, but I'm not sure if we comprehend what's really happening," Mary sat down on a couch near Matt; Mike sat on the armrest of the couch.

"I'm not sure if I understand either," Matt looked out the window, "I'm pretty sure that the course of events that brought us here has nothing to do with my military career or Delta Defense."

"Then what is it?" Mary tucked her feet close to her body on the couch.

"I began to have vivid dreams about 7 months ago, shortly after returning from Afghanistan. I thought that I may have a little PTSD or something similar, so I didn't think anything of the dreams," Matt stood up and moved to the window of the suite.

"Then I began to document the dreams and I found that a woman was recurring in several of them, maybe ten or so.

Some of them were quite alarming while others were very peaceful and lucid, almost as if I expected the dream or knew I was in it."

"Do you know this woman? Have you seen her before?" Mike moved next to his wife on the couch.

"No. She appears to be of Middle Eastern descent, but I don't remember encountering the woman on any previous tours," Matt was still holding back the curtains and peering out the window.

"Do you trust these Disciples that you're traveling with?" Mike was straightforward.

"I do. I don't have any reason not to. They obviously reached me before the members of Samil did," Matt turned and faced his sister and brother-in-law. "When I was at the café and Sesom was telling me about Samil and how they would pursue me and my family, I had a sense of déjà-vu, like I'd already been there with him having the same conversation."

Matt continued, "Then Sesom handed me a pair of binoculars and told me to look down the beach to a seawall. When I did, there was a guy surveying us at the café. When he realized that I was looking right at him, he raised his eyes above the glasses and Sesom ordered his execution. I didn't even hear a shot. I saw a bloody spray and the guy collapsed over the rocks. The Disciples knew they were being tailed and likely knew that Samil was getting too close to me."

"How do you know that wasn't an assassination of one of their own?" Mike wanted to play devil's advocate before completely believing.

"I gave that a fleeting thought, but the Disciples went into action immediately. Amen took my vehicle and went back to my townhome and the rest of us immediately departed for the Port of Los Angeles. A lady met us at a parking garage with passports, paperwork, and everything else we needed to travel abroad on a ship. They knew exactly what they were doing," Matt sat back down on the chair and Scratches jumped into his lap.

"Amen was good to you, wasn't he?" Matt wanted validation from his sister and brother-in-law.

"A complete gentleman. He's taken care of the kids too. The time has been good for me and Mike," Mary placed her hand on Mike's.

"What about Maria's?" Matt knew that Mike had poured his hard work and money into the pizzeria over the past several years.

"Pat has the place under control," Mike seemed satisfied that nothing had happened out of the ordinary. "He's watching our house too. I told him to be careful and set the alarm."

"That's good. Let's hope it stays that way," Matt was rubbing the top of Scratches' head; her purr was audible to everyone.

"Are you okay Matt?" Mary loved her brother, she was concerned.

"I'm good. I enjoyed being at sea. Who knows, after this I may disappear and go work on one of those crabbing boats."

"Me too," Mike loved anything that was risky or deadly.

Mary gave Mike a look, "I don't think so," Matt and Mike began to laugh quietly.

"All I know," Matt got serious, "Is that in about ten days this will all make more sense."

"I don't know how I feel about going back into Israel," Mike was serious too, "A real hotbed over there right now. With the threat of Iran and constant skirmishes between the Palestinians and Israelis, we may be going to one of the most dangerous places on the planet right now."

"We just need to make sure the children stay safe," Mary looked in the direction of John and Rebecca.

"And you too," Matt winked at his sister.

Matt went for the door and was ready to turn in for the evening, "I'm going to send an email and call it a night...goodnight."

Mike and Mary said goodnight at the same time and Matt went to his hotel room. He pulled up an Internet connection and logged into his personal email account. He sent Noah an email with regard to the shoulder harness they had worked on. He knew that Delta would be monitoring incoming emails from their database, so he sent the request to Noah's personal email account.

To: Noah

From: Matt

RE: Shoulder Harness

Noah,

I know this is an odd request and I've been unreachable for several days. I can't explain right now, but things prevented me from making it back to the office or my home. I'm sure that Delta is pestering you concerning my whereabouts because of our friendship, and for that, I apologize.

I have one request that you may be able to help me with. I could use a shoulder harness on my travels in Israel. I know that Delta is probably field testing the item right now and I'd like you to divert one to me. If they ask you about the weapon, just tell them I took it. Please send the item to The Olive Branch, in c/o Cering, at 740 Olive Street, Jerusalem 91999. The address is a warehouse belonging to a person I'm traveling with currently.

Your friend,

Matt

As Matt clicked send on the email, he didn't know how Noah would feel about the request. Matt knew that Noah could pull off the shipment and cover up the paper trail, but there was a great amount of risk Noah would take to fulfill the request. The government and many defense contractors couldn't account for several billions of dollars earmarked for wartime operations, so a small shoulder harness gone missing had pretty good odds of going unnoticed.

****

The trip to Ashdod was largely uneventful. The Excalibur's stabilizers did a great job of enduring rough seas. Mike trained with Kimi in kendo while Matt and Cering became good sparring partners. Cering and Kimi enjoyed hanging with the children and Sesom was happy to have all of the Disciples in the same place. Everyday, the Disciples would sit down with Matt, Mike, and Mary, if she was willing, to discuss Jerusalem and map out the Western Wall.

Most of the Disciples were confident the woman of Matt's dreams would be in the plaza during Rosh Hashanah. They were equally concerned that the Western Wall would be packed with worshipers and Jews making the pilgrimage to bring in their new year. All of the Disciples would be needed for surveillance and protection. In order to cover the plaza, they needed to call on Phil to cover Matt, Mike, and Sesom while they looked for the mystery woman.

Cering and Kimi shopped in Yokohama before leaving port. They purchased several kids' toys, books, and stuffed animals for John and Rebecca. They even purchased game consoles and several controllers so the Disciples could play war games, sports, and physically interactive games for entertainment. Dorje was a true competitor and loved the interactive games; he wanted to play over and over until he won.

Rebecca and John did well on the voyage. John said the ocean was "neat" and thought it ran on forever. They experienced some amazing sunsets traveling west to Israel and Mary always wanted to be on deck when the sun was dipping into the ocean to end another day.

"Reminds me of mom and dad," Mary said to Matt.

"How?" Matt was curious.

"How bright the sun is, how the sun changes reflection over the waves and glistens on open waters. The sun seems so big as the ocean swallows her up in the evening," Mary paused for a moment, "and then she's gone and it's completely dark, but you can still hear waves crashing along the hull."

Mary faced Matt, "When mom and dad died on 9/11 and I came to Columbine to tell you at school, my life changed forever. I not only felt like your sister, but became a father and mother figure as well. I remember walking up to you on the football field, then us walking around Clement Park together; you were still in full pads. We both cried so hard at our tremendous loss that day."

"I remember the Air Force commanders showing up from Buckley, Schriever, Peterson, and Lowry to watch over our needs. Even though Lowry shut down in 1996, there was still plenty of missile defense research and deployment taking place at the Base." Matt looked out over the rail of the Excalibur.

"Seems ironic that mom and dad died in a plane that crashed into the Pentagon."

"Very ironic; Dad was performing some top secret Defense Department research and tests at Lowry after the Base closed," Matt paused, "Columbine was a tragedy that affected millions of people in Colorado, 9/11 was a tragedy that shook the foundation of an entire world. I almost felt like people could finally understand the horror of Columbine once 9/11 occurred. We'd lost our entire family and several friends by the end of 2001 like so many other Americans," Matt turned to his sister.

"Do you think that has anything to do with your calling?" Mary had given Matt's visions considerable thought while on the boat.

"I don't know, but I sense that things will heat up as they play out over the next couple of weeks. I don't have a very good feeling about what we're going to find."

"Me neither," Mary took Matt's hand and they began to walk the deck of the Excalibur. She was happy to be with her brother.

The trip up the Red Sea and Suez Canal was everything Captain Phil thought it would be. The large Excalibur seemed out of place with sailboats and small fishing boats running along side her. Occasionally they would encounter another cargo ship carrying containers or petroleum, but they were few and far between. Captain Phil enjoyed the Suez Canal because he actually had to steer the ship. The Suez Canal had been an area of substantial commerce for a hundred years, and there were beautiful plantations with lush green foliage and many trees in some spots. At times the Excalibur felt like a cruise liner; the meals were great, there were plenty of things to do on the ship, and the exercise facilities were first-class. There was a lap pool that John took interest in and the whirlpool tubs were a favorite with everyone aboard the ship.

****

Ashdod was a beautiful port and the Disciples were pleased to be in such an important place in the world. Mike summed his feelings up well when he arrived in port.

"I've only been to Israel twice, and each time I'm here, I feel like God could reach down out of the sky at anytime and put man in his place."

There was something about the Holy Lands of Israel, especially Jerusalem. Such significance with regard to history, Judaism, Islam, and Christianity contained in a country no bigger than the size of New Jersey. The day was beautiful as the Excalibur tied off in port. A nice warm breeze was coming off the ocean and the waters were amazingly clear. There was much to do at this Port, compared to Yokohama, as vehicles would need to be offloaded and armaments would be carried to the hotel, and then on to Jerusalem. Captain Phil was working with Port Authorities to offload wheat onto tractor-trailers.

"Cering and Amen, you will go forward with Matt's family and check into the Grand Beach Hotel in Tel Aviv. Take one of the SUVs, they are filled with gas," Even though Sesom didn't fully understand his power, he was a natural born leader. Cering and Amen went to prepare their cargo, the SUVs were held on platforms tied off to chains that would be offloaded with a crane.

Mike, Mary, John, and Rebecca waited on the pier as John, Aaron, and the Disciples brought bags from the Excalibur to them. Down below in the hull, Sesom, Matt, Talan, and Lucas began to unload crates with automatic weapons, grenade launchers, sniper rifles, automatic pistols, grenades, knives and flak jackets. Communication equipment was being unloaded by Talan and placed in individual bags. Each of the Disciples and Mike would have a bag of their own with military gear, pistols, grenades, and military bayonets. The sniper rifles, automatic machine guns, and grenade launchers were placed in bags of their own with special nicknames. For instance, a sniper rifle may be contained in a bag named "Lucy". A grenade launcher may be stored in "Willie". An automatic weapon may be stowed away in "Echo" or "Hugo"; Sesom stated those were dogs' names, but Matt argued that Snoopy and Clifford were more appropriate. Everything had a purpose and Sesom was very particular about his wishes; the other Disciples were accustomed to how Sesom wanted things done and why.

Sesom barked at Matt, "Take these chains and attach them to the eight hooks on the SUV's platform. "Make sure they go over the top of the safety cage and come together at a point on top of the vehicle. Please make sure that you put a heavy blanket over the top of the SUV.

The first vehicle to be offloaded would be driven by Amen with Cering as his copilot. Amen knew Israel like the back of his hand. Having relatives there and growing up near Jerusalem, Amen would provide most of the intelligence with regard to customs, security, and other logistics. Amen was also well connected to the Israeli military. While the Port of Ashdod had much more stringent standards for imports and exports than many other ports of the world, the Israeli military had tipped off the Port Authority on the travels of the Excalibur and asked that they provide lenience and passage for unloading. There was no argument from the Port of Ashdod as the Israeli military controlled many covert operations in the territory, and it was best not to ask, unless unwanted attention from the government and military were desired.

Matt hooked up the chains at eight points and brought them together on a hoist that was set up at the end of a vertical plate clamp. Above the Excalibur he could see a spotter for the crane operator. Matt gave the thumbs up and the spotter began to provide hand signals to the crane operator. Certain hand gestures and movements meant different things to the crane operator, and being precise came with the job. The hoist was raised from the top of the SUV and the platform lifted into the air. Matt was surprised how smooth the platform began to climb from the hull of the ship. The other Disciples were still loading items in bags and Matt went to assist them; once finished, they tossed all of the bags in the back of the other two SUVs. The other SUVs were on platforms and Sesom ordered Lucas to retrieve the portable tracks to move them into position for hoisting. Matt prepared the chains for the second platform. The crane was dropping more chains into the hole for Matt to retrieve. The Disciples repeated the process until the SUVs were safely on the pier. The remaining weapons' cache was locked up and stowed. Securing the ship was extremely important to the Disciples and Captain Phil. Armed guards would be necessary to watch over the Excalibur in the Port of Ashdod. Samil likely knew the Excalibur was a preferred method of transportation for the Disciples. Docking on a pier in the middle of a hotbed was risky.

Matt, Sesom, and Talan were prepping the SUVs with travel bags and other supplies on the pier when a Port Authority Officer approached them.

"Are you the Captain?" Sesom seemed like a reasonable choice based on his stature and presence.

"No, let me get him," Sesom put his fingers up to both sides of his mouth and whistled.

"Phil, you're parked illegally," Sesom winked at the officer.

"What? What do you mean?" Phil took Sesom seriously for a moment.

"Just kidding my friend. Someone needs to speak with you."

Parts of the Excalibur were draining into the harbor. A fueling ship was replenishing the supply of gas for the Excalibur; another ship was pumping potable water into the tanks for drinking, washing, and showering. Aaron and John were tying down areas of the ship with tarps and securing portholes and doors. Phil came down the gangway and met the officer.

"I'm Captain Phil and this is the Excalibur," Phil had a rag and wiped his hand before shaking with the Officer. Phil had been checking petroleum and hydraulic fluids and lines before the Port Authority arrived.

"My name is Michael and it's a pleasure to have your ship at Ashdod," the men shook hands.

"How can I help you?" Captain Phil respected any port that he visited.

"Nothing in particular. Just wanted to let you know that the Excalibur made a name for herself traveling the Pacific a little over a week ago."

"What do you mean?"

"The Israeli Defense Department received a memo that Russian pirates were looking for a ship called the Excalibur. Apparently, your ship came into contact with a group of pirates and they went missing at sea. The only remnants of their counterparts were found strewn across several hundred meters of ocean in an area that you traveled."

Sesom interjected, "You see Phil, you're famous."

The Officer went further, "More than that, Captain Phil, they have put a bounty on your boat of $10 million rubles."

Sesom was incredulous, "That's it. Only $10 million rubles," Sesom shook his head and continued to load the SUVs.

"According to our intel, relatives of other pirates went missing in their exchange with your ship. They are calling for all pirates to be on the look out for your vessel."

Captain Phil removed his hat and scratched his head, "Thank you for the tip. I'm not surprised by their brazenness and stupidity."

"Yes sir," the officer continued down the pier. He was armed with an automatic weapon on his shoulder.

"I think it's time to order more trinkets; countermeasures for torpedoes, short-range missiles, and other toys," Sesom patted Phil on the shoulder.

"Sooner or later this is going to become a full-fledged battleship," Captain Phil put his hat back on and returned to the Excalibur.

"You guys about ready?" Sesom was eager for another hotel stay, hot shower, and supper with the Disciples. They would discuss tactical operations of their trip to the Western Wall.

"Yes," Talan and Matt had loaded and double-checked everything in the SUVs.

"I'll go get the others and we'll leave in five minutes. As we enter the city, make sure that you're armed and loaded," Sesom gave them a serious look and jogged up the gangway.

****

The trip into Tel Aviv was short and uneventful. All of the Disciples, Mary, Mike, John, and Rebecca checked into the Grand Beach Hotel on the coast of Tel Aviv. Tel Aviv was going to serve as base for the Disciples as they traveled in and out of Jerusalem. Sesom wanted Mary, John, and Rebecca to feel and be safe while the Disciples conducted business in Israel. Amen worked with Cering to hire bodyguards that also served in the Israeli Defense Force. Several rooms had been reserved on the main floor to ensure the protection of the Disciples and Matt's family. Captain Phil, Aaron, and John were also staying at the Grand Beach Hotel on a separate floor. Bodyguards would be stationed on both floors and monitor all access to stairwells and elevators. Nobody but hotel personnel would be allowed access to the areas near the Disciples and Matt's family.

Sesom called a logistics meeting for 8:00 pm following dinner. All of the Disciples and Mike would be required to attend the meeting. Sesom requested the presence of Captain Phil in order to be briefed on the journey to the Western Wall the following morning at sunrise. Cering had requested the use of a conference room with a projector for Sesom's meeting. Much intel had been gathered on the Western Wall, and Suzie put together a great video presentation of the plaza and its surrounding areas.

After the Disciples gathered with Captain Phil and Mike in the conference room, Sesom called upon Amen to handle the presentation of information on the Western Wall.

The lights were dimmed at the front of the room where the projector screen was located.

"Here you will see a satellite image of the Western Wall in the Jewish Quarter," Amen changed the slide with a handheld remote.

"You will notice to the northeast, the Islamic Quarter is close by and a mosque sits atop the Temple Mount; this mosque is referred to as al-Aqsa. The Dome of the Rock is located to the north and has a splendid gold roof; Dome of the Rock is one of the oldest Islamic buildings in the world. Rosh Hashanah started yesterday and the plaza adjacent to the Western Wall will be crawling with Israeli Police, Israeli Army, and Israeli Defense Forces. Many Jewish pilgrims and residents of Israel will travel and worship at the Wall beginning very early in the morning," Amen changed slides.

"We will travel to this street, HaOmer, and set up our rendezvous point and a depot for our weapons. We will maintain some weapons and artillery in two of the SUVs." The next slide was displayed.

"People, predominately Jewish, will be gathered 24/7 at the Western Wall throughout the New Year celebration. Based on Matt's assessments and physical characteristics of the woman in his dreams, she will have a better chance of finding us than we will her. Therefore, a meeting is more likely during the day than at night." Amen pointed a laser at a large group of worshippers during the previous year's Rosh Hashanah.

"There are some large trees located over the wall to the east and one large tree to the south. Dorje and Li will take lookout positions from these areas," Amen pointed the laser at the locations for both men. "You two will need sniper rifles, binoculars, MREs, and plenty of water. You will go up before the sun and come down during the night."

"Anybody we look for in particular?" Li had seen the face of Samil, but he wanted specifics about this mission.

"Good question, Li. Cering, can you toggle to the pictures Matt uploaded for us?" Cering opened up a media program that contained pictures of the Samil invaders that visited Matt's townhome.

"Matt was able to capture these images with a security feed prior to the ransacking of his townhome," Cering toggled between three high-definition pictures as Amen spoke. Mike looked at Matt, and Matt shrugged his shoulders as if he didn't know the men.

Amen continued, "I saw two of the men at Matt's townhome from across the street while conducting surveillance. The third man likely took sensitive information from Matt's residence."

"How sensitive?" Mike knew this affected his family too.

"Email accounts, financial information, pictures, websites; basically anything Matt had on the computer. Luckily, Delta Defense has a strict policy about security clearance and information sharing. There was nothing on Matt's computer that tied him back to Delta Defense, other than emails he may have sent to coworkers. They will eventually find out about his place of work and possibly target Delta," Amen brought attention back to the projector screen.

"This man and this man are deceased. They were speaking Arabic when I intercepted their communication. Samil has been focused on recruiting and training in Yemen, Somalia, the United States, Lebanon, and small sections of Afghanistan and Syria. While the logical decision appears to have Syria and Lebanon cover the territory of Israel, we could encounter a man or woman from any country in the world on a mission for Samil to Jerusalem." Amen brought up a slide of the Western Wall.

"The plaza is segregated, so men and women will be worshipping at different locations. This may make finding a woman a little more difficult, but we will be scanning worshippers with a camera that has already been set in place by Israeli Defense Forces. Here is a live feed from the camera put in place," Amen pointed to Talan. Talan had a very small handheld controller that was similar to a game controller.

Talan began to speak, "This controller communicates with our computer. The computer contains software that downloads a link to satellites orbiting the earth. The signal is encrypted to our video camera, so hacks will not be able to intercept our feed and what we're viewing. The satellite will send digital information from the camera back to our computer. In turn, we can control movements of the camera with this controller and zoom to 40 times magnification. We will be able to see an eyelash up close if we need to. This will prevent Matt, Mike, and Sesom from having to enter the plaza without knowing our subject is there."

"Subject?" Matt laughed at the formality.

"Sorry Matt. Wonder woman," Talan didn't know what to call her.

"As you can see, I'm controlling the feed right now and the plaza is very busy. We can zoom into this worshipper and read parts of their Torah if you'd like to," Talan selected a man in robes rocking back and forth in front of the wall with a book.

"Amazing!" Sesom was even awed by the clear picture coming through the computer being displayed by the projector.

"Where is camera mounted?" Dorje was tilting his head to try and figure out the location of the feed.

"North end of the plaza on a rooftop adjacent to the wall."

Sesom interrupted, "So we will have the north, south, and east sides of the wall covered. Are we concerned about the west, which faces the wall?"

Amen anticipated the question, "Yes, as this will be a place of many people coming and going from the plaza. Unlike the trees to the south and east, and our camera mounted to the north on a rooftop, we will cover the west by foot. Ethan will handle duties on the ground to the west of the plaza."

Amen continued, "Don't forget that the plaza will be crawling with undercover and uniformed Israeli Defense Forces. They have received numerous threats of terrorism, which is fairly common for any Jewish holiday."

The meeting continued and questions were posed and answered. As with most military meetings and gatherings of Disciples, contingencies were developed and escape routes planned. Ethan would cover the west, Dorje would climb a tree to the east, and Li would nest in a tree to the south. Sesom, Matt, Mike, Talan, and Amen would operate from one of the SUVs parked along HaOmer. They would be controlling all communications and surveillance from the camera. Lucas would be located on the grounds of the plaza near the southern entrance of the Western Wall Tunnel. Cering and Kimi would be dressed the part and worshipping from the segregated area at the right of the wall. Wearing long garments and hats to conceal their identities and weapons were ideal for their cover. Captain Phil would drive the SUV reserved for Cering, Kimi, and Ethan. Ideally, the Disciples would leave without incident after finding the woman in the plaza. Realistically, Samil had sent several operatives to the Western Wall to conduct surveillance and identify Matt and several Disciples.

By invading Matt's townhome, Samil had plenty of intelligence to determine a source of the Disciples' interest. One of the principle reasons Matt, Sesom, Amen, and Talan remained in the SUV was to prevent Samil from identifying them sooner rather than later. Samil had a picture of Mike and his family, forcing a decision to keep Mike with Matt, Sesom, Amen, and Talan in the SUV. Undercover Israeli Defense Forces would guard the SUVs and the street would be closed at the end of HaOmer. The Disciples would leave at 5:30 sharp and each of them had been instructed to wear their Type IV ballistic vests. They would arrive in Jerusalem just before sunrise to gain positions in the plaza, trees, and key locations for surveillance.

"For those of you entering the plaza, you will carry this card to indicate your passage without search. The Israeli Defense Force has signed off on the use of these cards and understands our mission. Security at the plaza and wall will be briefed to let us pass as long as we have these cards on our person. As you enter a security checkpoint, which you will, flash the card without bringing attention to yourself. You will be granted passage into the plaza and tunnel," Amen had been in close communication with his friends serving the Israeli military.

Amen was ready to wrap the meeting, "Any more questions before we set out tomorrow morning?"

The room remained quiet, as the Disciples were ready to load their gear and prepare clothing for tomorrow's journey. Amen didn't hesitate, "We're dismissed and we'll meet at the entrance of the hotel at 5:25 am Please be ready to leave."

Sesom motioned for Mike and Matt to stay after the meeting.

"Mary will remain here while we travel to Jerusalem. Armed guards will continue to provide security for Mary and the two children. Aaron and John will also remain here as well, to offer Mary assistance with the children and whatever she needs."

"Do we have communication set up with the guards, John and Aaron?" Mike knew the dangers of leaving his wife and two children.

"We do."

"Very well, Let's get some rest," Mike went back to the hotel room. Mary and the children were peacefully asleep with the TV on. Mike turned the TV off, changed into shorts, and joined his wife in bed. Armed guards were stationed at the elevator and stairwell on the main floor and floor above. There was some risk in having armed guards at the Grand Beach Hotel, but there was more danger in not having guards available to protect the Disciples as they met, slept, and ate. One suicide bomber could end their mission.

****

The Disciples met at 5:25 am as planned at the front of the Grand Beach Hotel. Each of them had duffel bags and comfortable clothing that concealed weapons and ballistic vests. Dorje and Li wore gear that would allow them to scale trees and remain comfortable for several hours perched high above the plaza. Kimi and Cering were traveling with kendo swords that were smaller and easily holstered at their sides.

The trip to Jerusalem took 35 minutes. Not much was said during the trip, as Disciples knew the importance of their responsibilities and preparation for the Western Wall. As they entered the Old City of Jerusalem, Matt was in awe of the Dome of the Rock structure and the brilliant gold roof displaying a tribute to the people of Islam. The Disciples traveled down HaOmer and were met by a roadblock at the end of the street. Amen was driving the first SUV in the caravan and spoke briefly with two armed soldiers at the barricade; the other Disciples could hear the conversation through their earpieces. After a few seconds, one of the men went to the barricade and opened it up for passage. Amen traveled through and the other SUVs were waved through the roadblock. They traveled to the end of HaOmer and parked the SUVs off road under some trees. The Disciples were quick to grab gear and get into position, with sunrise twenty-five minutes away. Sesom, Amen, Talan, Matt, and Mike remained in an SUV that contained the communications' equipment.

Talan loaded a wireless card into the computer and clicked on the link for the camera mounted on a nearby rooftop. The computer received a signal from the camera and Talan was now looking at the plaza that was lit up with hundreds of worshippers in attendance. Talan took a network cable and connected the computer to an audio/video port in the SUV.

Once connected, Talan was able to feed the signal through the SUV to the TV screens located above the front seats. Areas to the east and south of the wall were relatively dark, but an orange light began to appear on the eastern horizon promising the beginning of another day in Jerusalem. People were beginning to fill the plaza and Israeli Army soldiers were in several positions with automatic weapons. A service was scheduled for sunrise and a rabbi was preparing readings for a blessing.

"Needle in a haystack," Matt was watching from the back.

Amen turned around from the driver's seat, "Like I said earlier, this woman has a better chance of finding us."

"We will wait for sunrise before we begin our search," Talan was still hacking away on the computer. He began to call out to the other Disciples in the area of the Western Wall.

"Dorje, communications check," Talan was going through each of the transmitters to ensure that all of the devices were working at their peak.

"Here, beginning climb."

"Li, communications check," Talan was looking at the receiver's signal.

"Climbing, much better than boats," The signal was picking up branches and rustling of the tree.

"Lucas, communications check."

"Here at the Western Wall Tunnel, security tight as predicted."

"Cering."

"Working our way through the crowd to the Wall."

"Kimi, communications check."

"With Cering, the plaza is crowded already."

"Ethan, communications check."

"West side of plaza, I can hear you fine."

"Phil, communications check."

"I see you and hear you."

"Amen, check."

"Good."

"Sesom, check."

"Loud and clear."

"Matt, communications check."

"Gotcha."

"Mike, check."

"Clear."

Talan had strong signals from all the Disciples, Mike, and Phil. "The units appear to be working fine. We can communicate with each other as you please, over."

Sesom came over the radio, "Please hold positions until you hear otherwise."

The sun was beginning to shine to the east of the plaza. With very few clouds in the sky, Dome of the Rock began to illuminate over the Western Wall. Over a loudspeaker from the east came an announcement in Arabic calling for members of Islam to start the day with prayer. The rabbi along the Wall was working with other worshippers to set up a power amp and speakers for his service. Many Jewish residents, pilgrims, and leaders were piling into the plaza to join in prayer and celebration of a New Year.

Talan began to scan the crowd of worshippers in the plaza. Mike, Matt, Amen, and Sesom watched the TV screens in the SUV.

"Impressive," Matt was referring to the number of people on the screen.

Talan spoke in his earpiece, "Kimi and Cering, I have your location on the right hand side of the wall."

"Thousands of years of history along that wall," Sesom was impressed as well.

Talan began a scan of women in the plaza, there were close to a thousand already. "Matt, continue to watch the TV screen to see if you recognize your dream girl," Talan turned to him and smiled.

Many of the worshippers had their heads down in prayer. As daylight showered the plaza, for every woman that Talan zoomed to view two more would enter.

"Be patient, Matt." Sesom knew that Matt would prefer to be in the plaza looking for the woman.

Disciples continued to scan the plaza until the prayer vigil was ready to begin. The time was 7:55 am and several worshippers were seated or standing to hear the Rabbi speak of God and the importance of the Western Wall in Jewish history. All of the Disciples were in place and ready. A Jewish man began to sing a Yiddish song about the flight of Jews from Egypt, and Israel as a chosen place for Jews to reside. Amen interpreted the song for Mike and Matt as they listened to the singing. Without warning, the camera shook violently and a large explosion came from the plaza.

Matt turned to see the plaza area from the SUV and a very large ball of fire rose high into the sky over the Wall. Talan was quick to establish contact with Disciples in the plaza area.

"Ethan, come in."

"I'm here, large explosion to the northeast side of plaza, closer to Lucas' location," Ethan was running toward the area of the explosion as hundreds of Jews began to flee from the Western Wall. Amen brought his hands up to his face and slammed the steering wheel.

"Lucas, copy." Talan had his camera feed back and was surveying the damage, located just below the camera.

"I'm here, just inside the Western Wall Tunnel," Lucas was rising to his feet as he dived into the entrance as the explosion went off, "stand-by."

There was much commotion in Lucas' earpiece. People were running, screaming, and lying dead or injured on the plaza floor,

"Talan."

"Yes, Lucas."

"Come now. Bring all first aid supplies from the three SUVs."

"Copy, Lucas," Talan turned in the direction of Sesom.

"Li and Dorje, maintain your positions, everyone else to the Wall to assist the wounded. Cering and Kimi, are you okay?"

Cering answered, "Yes, much help needed for those injured, maybe one hundred or so. I see possibly thirty dead."

Amen's phone rang; an Israeli agent was on the other end, "Yes, I'm alright." Amen continued to listen to the man on the other line.

"I understand, we're moving right now." Amen was obviously disturbed by the news.

"Let's go," Sesom exited the SUV and grabbed a duffle bag with first aid supplies in the back. Talan went to the 2nd SUV and did the same. Captain Phil had already retrieved the duffle bag and was heading up to the west entrance.

"Everyone ensure your safety is off and ready to fire. Be advised, many of the police and military located in the plaza will not know us from terrorists. Weapons advised only if necessary," Sesom's first priority was the Disciples. Disciples clamored up the hill to the west entrance as people were fleeing the scene. The plaza was smoky and smelled of burning flesh and sulfur. Cering, Kimi, and Lucas were tending to the wounded while Ethan stood watch. The possibility of another bomb or bombers was real, and Ethan wanted to protect everyone left in the plaza. Li had his sniper rifle resting on a branch just below his stomach. Dorje had a good view of the plaza and people scrambling to safety, he saw the other Disciples enter the area of the blast. He was armed with a sniper rifle resting on a branch chest high.

Matt and Mike had seen carnage before in Iraq and Afghanistan; they were also trained to administer CPR and basic medical procedures required in the field. Matt knew the drill.

"We need to separate those critically wounded that can't be moved from those with minor injuries. Evacuate all minor injuries now," Matt was yelling commands. Several civilian Jews remained to render aid or help evacuate those injured. Captain Phil emptied the contents of all first aid duffle bags. The bags contained oxygen, supplies for IVs, antibiotics, bandages, splints, and tourniquets. There were children crying looking for their parents and parents wailing for their children. Sirens could be heard in the distance.

From the southwest a man entered the plaza in a sprint. He had a heavy coat on for a warm fall morning. Ethan saw him first, "Li, you got him?"

"Yes," Li had the sight at the base of the man's neck.

"Take him," A shot rung out in the plaza and everyone but the Disciples ducked for cover. The man fell forward and slid on the stone floor.

"Everyone stay down," Ethan knew the guy was strapped with bombs. Before Ethan finished yelling "down", the man exploded into another ball of flames. The Disciples felt heat from the blast.

"Ethan," Dorje saw something through his scope.

"Yes, Dorje," Ethan held the earpiece closer to his ear canal.

"3 o'clock about 75 yards, Seth is at the edge of the plaza. I don't have a shot, other people around him."

Ethan made a quarter turn and locked eyes with Seth. Seth took off in a sprint and three other Samil goons followed him. Ethan didn't think twice and took off after Seth and his companions, Kimi followed Ethan in the chase.

Matt was assisting a teenage boy who had been hit by shrapnel. Mike was close by tending to the boy's mother who had life threatening injuries.

"Phil, toss me an intubation kit. I've got a blocked airway," Mike motioned for Phil to throw the bag. Captain Phil was expediting first aid supplies to all responders.

"Remember teeth and lips, no trauma," Matt was nearby reminding Mike to be careful with insertion of the metal apparatus.

"Gotcha," Mike carefully opened a passage into the trachea and inserted a small tube into the woman's windpipe. "Come here," Mike motioned to a Jewish man offering assistance.

"You are going to breath for this woman. Let me attach the bag and I'll show you how," Mike attached a clear bag that forced oxygen into the windpipe when depressed. He would let the bag inflate and begin the process again about every three seconds.

"Every three seconds you will depress this bag and let it refill. Watch the woman's diaphragm and chest during inflation; this will let you know that she is inhaling and exhaling with your help. I'm going to run an IV while you're breathing for her." The man just looked at Mike and shook his head in affirmation. Nothing was said.

"What's your name?" Matt noticed the young boy was becoming conscious.

"Caleb," the confused boy looked at Matt.

"We had an explosion in the plaza, just stay down for me." Matt had administered first aid in much worse circumstances.

"Okay. My mom…" Matt interrupted the boy.

"She's about ten feet from us, my brother is tending to her injuries," Matt gave the thumbs up to Mike to see if the boy's mother was improving. Mike gave thumbs up back.

"Looks like she's improving Caleb," Matt looked him right in the eyes.

"What happened?"

"We're not sure yet, but we know that the explosion caused much damage. You just sit tight for me and we're going to get you out of here," Matt looked up again as smoke began to lift in the plaza. He looked toward Mike to check his status. Mike handed an IV bag to a woman nearby and instructed her on how to administer 250 mg of antibiotic through a line. Something caught Matt's attention over his brother's shoulder.

Very close to the northeast section of the Western Wall was a familiar face. At first Matt thought the woman was Cering or Kimi, but Kimi gave chase with Ethan and Cering was close by assisting the critically injured. The woman had long black hair and a smooth complexion. Her hair was tied back in a ponytail bow and she was giving aid to a man with body lacerations and facial contusions. Matt noticed the blood on her hands.

The woman was wearing a dress that terminated at the knees and her skin was caramel in color. She worked hard to stop bleeding from the man caused by the blast. She stood up abruptly, turned her head in each direction, and called out, "Please help me." Matt was lost in the moment. His vision in the dream had become a reality and his senses became acute. Even though he couldn't hear the woman, he could read her lips. Her eyes were blue and familiar, although a lighter shade than what Matt recalled from his dream. Sesom noticed Matt in a trance above the boy he was assisting and called out to him.

"Matt, what is it?" Sesom was wrapping a bandage around a policeman's head.

"It's her, the woman I told you about."

"Where?"

"I'll be right back," Matt grabbed a few supplies and headed in the woman's direction. As Matt ran to the woman, Sesom called over the radio that a rendezvous had been made with their subject in the plaza and to keep a close watch.

"Dorje and Li, maintain your positions and cover our movements," Sesom wanted eyes in the sky to catch the obvious.

The woman saw a man coming in her direction and she froze, almost as if she was seeing a ghost. She had seen the man in several dreams over the past months. Left standing with her jaw open and clothing heavily soiled in blood, she dropped to her knees. Matt knelt down beside her to assess the man's injuries.

"I can't believe it's you," the woman couldn't take her eyes away from Matt. He was relieved she spoke English.

"I can't believe we found you," Matt began to cut the pant off the man's right leg. The clothing was soaked in blood. The Jewish man had been hit with shrapnel below the waist and was losing blood at an incredible rate; he was already white and his eyes and mouth began to darken to a deathly gray. The woman offered assistance.

"What can I do?" she asked, in almost a whisper.

"Cut off all of his clothes with this knife. We need to check his entire body for injuries," Matt had stripped off the pant of the man's right leg and was pressing hard on the area just below his common femoral artery. The major injury was low enough for Matt to administer a tourniquet to the leg.

"Amen, do you copy?" Matt needed help.

"Go ahead," Amen could see Matt working hard on an injured man.

"I need you to have the paramedics bring a test kit and blood for this man; one liter of each. Very little time, maybe five minutes or less before we lose him."

"Copy," Amen went to the paramedics and grabbed the gear himself and came to assist Matt.

"Phil," Matt was tightening the tourniquet.

"Yeah Matt."

"Can you bring me two bags of saline, two IV kits, and some Cefa or whatever antibiotic you've got?"

"On my way." The contents of the first aid duffle bags brought to the plaza were diminishing rapidly.

"What's your name?" Matt looked up at the woman.

"Elisabeth."

Amen was able to draw blood from an open wound. The blood was put on a swatch and inserted into a meter reader. The digital display flashed "**WAIT**" as Matt finished the tourniquet and began the process of looking for a vein in the man's right arm. Phil dropped off IV bags and kits.

"Elisabeth is a nice name. Can you help me with something?"

"Yes," she was eager to help.

"Attach this line to the bottom of the bag; just twist it on," Elisabeth was quick to respond.

"Push the red handle down and release the fluid into the line," Matt found a vein, inserted the needle, and taped it down; he grabbed the IV line. Matt checked the line for any air bubbles and quickly attached the saline solution to a catheter. Amen was working the other arm of the injured man inserting a needle. The meter reader came back with a response, "Type O".

"Perfect. We have plenty of type O in the ambulance," Amen attached the saline bag to an IV line and released fluid into the tube. He took another line and attached one end to a bag of type O blood and the other to an inlet on the saline tube. Amen needed the woman's help.

"Excuse me," Amen addressed the woman assisting Matt. Matt interrupted,

"Amen, this is Elisabeth. Elisabeth meet Amen. I forgot to introduce myself, I'm Matt," Matt looked up to the woman and nodded his head. Matt continued, "This is the woman I was telling you about," Matt gave Amen a look out of the corner of his eye.

"My honor Elisabeth. Can you please hold this bag for me?"

"Of course, anything you need," Elisabeth appeared to be the age of a woman attending a university.

"Was this how your vision played out in the dreams?" Amen looked up in Matt's direction as blood began to flow from the bag into the man's arm. Amen reached up to slow the amount of saline flowing from the bag and he handed the woman the bag of blood too.

"Not at all. I'm sure about Elisabeth though," Matt pulled 500 mg of antibiotic into a syringe and looked up at Elisabeth, who was blood stained and holding three bags of fluids. Matt administered the antibiotic through the IV and shifted from his knees to his rear to support his body. Matt pulled a pair of latex gloves off his hands. He put his hands behind his back to support his body.

Helicopters, both military and news media, began to arrive at the Western Wall. Police and military set up a barrier to the west and blocked the entrance to the Western Wall Tunnel. Matt looked up at the helicopters and closed his eyes, allowing his face to bask in the warm sun. Amen alerted the Disciples of other troubles in Israel.

"Four bombs exploded simultaneously in Israel at 8:00 this morning, one in Jerusalem, one in Sderot, and two in Tel Aviv. Iran has claimed responsibility for all of the bombings and called a jihad against Israel and all Jews."

The Disciples were quiet, as they understood the importance of maintaining the integrity of culture and country. Who were they to tell Israel how to run their affairs or manage military operations? All of the Disciples had seen the face of war and understood its complexity; rarely were wars fought for the reasons publicized. Matt looked at the top of the Western Wall; there were no black birds perching atop the structure. He then realized the symbolism of the black birds as he looked around the plaza: death. He turned his attention back to Elisabeth; she was still holding three bags of fluids over the injured Jewish man.

"Let me help you with those," Matt rose to his feet and grabbed all three bags. "Do you know this man?"

"No," Elisabeth was wringing her hands to get blood flowing.

"Are you here with someone?"

"No, I'm by myself."

Two emergency responders came over with a gurney and IV pole. One of them addressed Matt, "What's his status?"

"He's lost a considerable amount of blood. There is a fatal wound to the common femoral artery on his right leg. His blood is type O and I've given him an antibiotic. Breathing appears fine and unobstructed. Pulse at 87 and blood pressure is 80 over 55," Matt noticed the man's color was returning to his face in small blotches.

The responders checked the man for spinal injuries and carefully loaded him on a gurney. One of the technicians took the bags from Matt, gave him a smile and a "thank you", and hung the IV equipment from the pole. An ambulance was waiting nearby to rush two victims to the hospital.

****

Ethan was catching up with three Samil who were fleeing the Jewish Quarter, Kimi wasn't too far behind. The men split up at the intersection of Shonei Halachot and Misgav Ladach. Seth went one way and his accomplices went another. Ethan followed Seth and Kimi pursued the others. There were many residents and tourists on the streets and sidewalks of the Jewish Quarter, many of them curious about the blasts being reported on the news.

The two men running from Kimi were heading for the Islamic Quarter. One of the men stopped to pull his gun and fire a round at her. She ducked into a doorway and pulled her Glock 19 and returned fire, just missing a Samil as he rounded the corner. People who were left in the streets began to scramble and duck for cover. Kimi kept her weapon drawn and pursued the men again. A shot was fired at her as she rounded the corner; she rolled on the street and fired back, hitting one of the men in the chest. The other man raised his .45 to fire at Kimi and she put a round in his shoulder. The man dropped his weapon and ran. Kimi put away the Glock and pulled out her kendo sword. She easily caught the man. Kimi dropped him to his knees with a crushing blow from the kendo sword on his shoulder. He grimaced in pain as he received another blow to his back. The man rolled on his back and Kimi was directly over him. She put her right foot on the man's chest.

"Don't move," Kimi had the man's attention.

"Don't worry," The man was in no shape to argue with Kimi's request.

"Sesom."

"Yes Kimi," Sesom was relieved to hear from her.

"Send someone to pick me up. One Samil is dead and I have another in custody with a flesh wound," Kimi jabbed the kendo sword into the man's entry wound to remind him who was in charge.

"Copy. Talan, go get Kimi and use the tracking device to find her location. Captain Phil, please drive Talan to her location," Sesom pointed at them in the plaza as he spoke through his earpiece. The two men left their positions and went to the SUV with communications' equipment.

Ethan was closing on Seth and Seth knew it. Seth radioed for a Samil driver to pick him up on a roundabout on Sultan Suleiman near a high school, just past Damascus Gate. The two men were moving quickly through the smaller streets of the Islamic Quarter and under Herod's Gate. Seth would dump carts, trash, and whatever else he could to prevent Ethan from gaining ground on his position. Seth's efforts weren't enough as Ethan was quick and out for revenge against one of Samil's lower leaders. Trevor and Ethan became close brothers as Disciples, and Ethan vowed to avenge Trevor's death when the time was right.

Ethan pulled a slim-frame Glock 38 and was 30 meters behind Seth. Ethan could have taken a shot and killed Seth from behind, but Ethan wanted to meet Trevor's killer and former Disciple face-to-face. Sultan Suleiman was a hundred yards away and the roundabout was in plain view. As the men approached the roundabout, an older model European car pulled up and the passenger-side door opened. Ethan unloaded three shots. The first shot hit the driver in the head as he opened the door for Seth; the next two shots blew out tires on the passenger side. By the time Seth turned to see Ethan's location, Ethan was on top of him.

Ethan greeted Seth with a jump kick to the chest that slammed him into the rear door of the car. Seth gained his composure and returned a right kick aimed at Ethan's left temple. Ethan ducked and swept Seth's left leg. Ethan was on top of Seth and gave him a right jab to the jaw. Seth wedged his right knee under Ethan and sent him flying into the open passenger door. Seth returned to his feet and did a roundhouse kick that missed Ethan and broke the window of the car door. Ethan gave an uppercut to Seth that left him dazed, followed by a back kick to the forehead. The kick from Ethan backed Seth up a few feet.

"You're done," Ethan picked up the Glock nearby and put the gun back in its holster.

Seth was bleeding from his nose and lip; he had a shaved head and wiry build. Seth's eyes were hazel and hollow, as if he lacked a soul beneath the surface.

"I wouldn't be so sure," Seth was slowly moving his arms back and forth as he crouched in a defensive position.

"Infiltrating our group is one thing, killing a Disciple brings a most certain death sentence," Ethan stood tall with his arms at his side.

"If that was the case, you would have killed me with your weapon," Seth was debating a moot point.

"I will respect you enough to kill you with my bare hands," Ethan opened up his palms to reveal he had no weapons.

Seth charged Ethan and threw a roundhouse right punch. Seth's punch missed and Ethan countered with a right kick to Seth's stomach. Before Seth knew what hit him, Ethan did a one armed stand and wrapped his knees around Seth's neck and throat; he twisted his legs and hips to form a scissor lock. Ethan dropped Seth to the ground and looked him in the eyes.

"I will make sure that you die slowly, so I can see your eyes as you enter the gates of hell," Seth was struggling to release the grip of Ethan's leg lock while trying to regain his breath from the earlier strike to his stomach. He could only gasp for air and struggle. Ethan's knee on Seth's neck prevented him from saying anything. Ethan continued to make his leg lock tighter and tighter as Seth struggled to break free. Ethan continued to look Seth in the eyes as he faded into darkness. Seth's eyes began to gloss over and his ability to struggle greatly diminished; Seth's last sight would be Ethan choking him to death. As Seth's vision faded and his body grew limp, Ethan watched his eyes for a sign. With Seth's last breath and final exhale, Ethan watched Seth's eyes grow wide and pupils dilate as a look of fear fell across his face. Seth was dead.

****

Mike's phone began to vibrate; he was finishing up with the woman in critical condition and checking her vitals. Mike went for the phone and saw Mary was calling,

"Hey," Mike was brief.

"Is everything alright? The Israeli Defense Force just let me know about the blasts. One was pretty close to the hotel at the Marina."

"Are you okay?" Mike knew the danger of being in a Holy Land with bombs going off.

"We're fine. The kids and I are on the beach near our hotel. Security has tightened up everywhere around us. The hotel has issued an advisory against anyone leaving. John and Aaron are on the beach with us. I think we're pretty safe," Mary was watching John build a sandcastle with Aaron and John.

"A blast went off at 8:00 in the plaza of the Western Wall. Some Disciples were in the plaza, but away from the explosion. Several people were killed and many injured. I'm not sure how Israel will respond, but Iran is claiming responsibility and calling for a jihad against Israel and all Jews." Mike was motioning to an arriving ambulance.

"Where's Matt?"

"He's nearby. I need to assist the paramedics with an injured woman. Keep your phone close by; I will call in a few minutes."

"I love you," Mary was looking out over the beach to check on John.

"I love you too," Mike hung up and began to work with the paramedics to transport the lady. Caleb was fully conscious and by his mother's side. They weren't the only family members hanging on to life or dead in the plaza. There were several responders in the plaza and hundreds of military personnel being positioned in and around the Western Wall. Bomb sniffing dogs were moving up and down the plaza and Western Wall Tunnel. The Disciples were soiled in blood and sweat.

Mary looked at Rebecca, who was sound asleep under an umbrella on the beach. John, John, and Aaron were fighting back the tide to prevent the melting of their sandcastle. Mary left her beach towel to approach the three guys.

"Aaron," Mary turned to check on Rebecca who was yards away.

"Yes ma'am," Aaron squinted as he looked up in Mary's direction.

"Can you watch Rebecca for a few minutes? I'm going to stop by the restroom and grab some drinks from the snack bar."

"You bet," Aaron jumped up and headed to the beach towel Mary had spread out next to an oversized umbrella.

"Momma, look." Little John was very proud of the sandcastle the three men had built.

"Wow, you've got shells, seaweed, and big walls to protect the people from the ocean," Mary gave John a smile as she pointed at the items.

"Yeaaaahhhh," John got back to work as the tide was coming in.

Mary was wearing a one-piece bathing suit with a cover up on below her waist. Even though Mary maintained her shape and could easily flaunt a bikini, her conservative style was more elegant and classy. As she walked up the beach to the hotel, she noticed more security in and around the hotel. Unlike the United States, people carrying automatic weapons in public were fairly common in this part of the world. She feared the United States would come to know the presence of military and armed security in their streets within a few years.

Double doors opened and Mary headed for the changing rooms. The changing rooms were quite nice, equipped with towels, lotions, steam showers, and whirlpool tubs. An adjoining spa provided guests with massages, facials, and manicures for a nominal fee with their stay. Mary came out of the restroom and walked to the sink. She primped her hair and turned on the water to wash her face. The water was warming as she put her hair in a bun. Mary cupped her hands and began to splash her face with water. The water felt refreshing on her face and eyes. A hand towel was to the left of the sink, and Mary dried her hands and covered her face. As Mary drew down the towel and looked into the mirror, there were two women in hotel uniforms with covered faces on both sides of her. Before Mary had time to react, a towel was placed over her mouth and she instantly noticed a pungent smell. The towel over her mouth and nose was soaked in chloroform, and Mary began to sense darkness taking over. Her last thought before passing out was of John and Rebecca.

****

Sesom approached Matt and Elisabeth, "We must exit the plaza and regroup with the other Disciples." Sesom activated his earpiece, "Ethan, come in."

"Yes Sesom," Ethan was walking back to the Western Wall.

"Location?" Sesom maintained his general concern for the well being of the others.

"On my way back to the plaza, just north of your location. Seth is dead."

Sesom wasn't surprised, "Meet at the SUVs outside the plaza."

"Copy, Over."

"Kimi, come in," Sesom began his roll call.

"Here with Talan and Phil, be back in a few minutes, one detained." Talan and Phil were bandaging the Samil's shoulder injury.

"Dorje."

"Can see you Sesom," Dorje was still perched in the tree.

"Li."

"Clear." Li was watching activity through the scope of his sniper rifle.

"I have Cering, Lucas, Amen, Matt, and Mike in the plaza with me," Sesom was looking around to account for Disciples and Matt's brother.

Sesom looked at Matt and Mike, "Something is not right. I can sense it. Have you been in touch with Mary?"

Mike answered, "I just got off the phone with her a few minutes ago. She's at the beach with John, Aaron, and the kids. She mentioned security was tight."

Sesom activated his earpiece again, "Phil?"

"Yeah, Sesom." Phil was driving the SUV back to the Western Wall.

"Phone Aaron right now and have him stay close to Mary. He should stay at her side with Israeli Defense Forces at all times," Sesom still had a sense that something was very wrong. "Take our prisoner back to the hotel in Tel Aviv, we will rendezvous with you later."

"Ay, Sesom," Phil located his cell phone and dialed Aaron. Aaron's cell phone was vibrating, as he was busy tending to Rebecca. He missed the first two calls from Captain Phil. Captain Phil mashed the accelerator to the floorboard and sped toward the Grand Beach Hotel.

Elisabeth took a bottle from a responder distributing water. She began to rinse her hands and arms of the bloodstains left by those seriously injured from the explosion. Sesom looked at Matt,

"Are you sure?"

"I am," Matt stood up and wiped his hands on his pants. Matt took bottled water from Sesom and began to clean the blood from his hands. They both looked at Elisabeth.

She returned the glance, "What?"

Matt did introductions, "Sesom, this is Elisabeth."

Sesom stepped over to Elisabeth and stretched out his hand, "The pleasure is mine. Do you know why we are here?"

"No."

"Have you experienced recurring visions and dreams?"

"Why?" Elisabeth was stalling.

"Because we believe your life is in danger," Sesom could read Elisabeth's body language and sensed her defensiveness.

"Because I live in one of the most dangerous parts of the world?"

Sesom's size and voice were intimidating, "No, because some of the most dangerous people in the world are trying to find you."

"Why should I trust you?" Elisabeth had the demeanor of a young, rebellious college student.

"If you don't, you won't live past today. Much like I told Matt," Sesom pointed in his direction, "You will put family members and people you love in great danger if you do not follow us," Sesom raised his eyebrows.

Elisabeth didn't want to believe Sesom, but she had seen visions that were alarming. She had also experienced life-changing events over the past year and knew something was imminent. Little did she know that people would travel from all over the world to converge on the Western Wall to find her. The Disciples didn't know that Elisabeth had been worshipping at the Western Wall for several months, every day. Elisabeth's heart had been heavy for the past year and her mind filled with sad thoughts. The Disciples would come to know a very complex woman.

Sesom pushed his earpiece, "Amen, where can we go and meet with Elisabeth?"

"Hess is a good place. I know the manager and I'll call him now."

"Dorje and Li, make your way down to the SUVs. All Disciples meet at the vehicles." Something was still perplexing Sesom, something wasn't right.

Dorje and Li were careful about climbing down the trees. Amen spoke with one of the Israeli Defense Force Commanders to let him know that two Disciples were positioned in trees to the east and south. The Commander radioed military personnel in and around the plaza to let them know about Dorje and Li's positions. Amen, Cering, Lucas, Matt, Mike, Sesom and Elisabeth began to leave the plaza to meet up with Ethan at the SUVs. The Western Wall area was eerily still as many killed and wounded were being escorted from the plaza.

Sesom turned to speak with Matt, "We will meet with Elisabeth," Sesom's sentence was cut short by the sound of three F-15's and one F-35 Stealth bomber flying overhead.

Sesom redirected his attention to Amen, "What kind of a response?"

Amen knew exactly what was happening, "Active personnel and reservists have been called up to fight against the jihad and hostile countries in the territory. Turkey and Russia have pledged support in spirit, although they will avoid the campaign. China has not commented on the matter, they will likely wait until the United States takes a position before they respond." Israeli troops were already moving north to the Lebanon border and east to the Syrian border.

The United States was responding with Tomahawk missiles being launched from two submarines in the Arabian Sea targeting the country of Iran. The deployed Tomahawk missiles were programmed to destroy key positions in Tehran thought to be equipping nuclear weapons with enriched uranium. Although military commanders knew the Chinese wouldn't respond favorably to the US sticking their nose in another Arab campaign, the risk was worth the reward for the US and Israel.

"Why the Stealth?" Matt knew exactly what he was looking at overhead.

"Tactical strikes against positions in Iran," Amen's answer seemed rhetorical.

"What payload is on that stealth?"

"Tactical nukes with small warheads," Amen knew this answer would draw the attention of all Disciples.

"Nukes up the ante of any campaign in this part of the world," Mike shared his opinion on the matter.

The planes moved quickly across the city of Jerusalem to the east. As Disciples made their way to the SUVs, reporters from various news outlets approached them. A slew of questions bombarded the group as they made their way to the SUVs. One of the reporters was persistent with Matt, not only because he was American, but because his clothing was particularly bloody.

"What happened in there?" The reporter was young and aggressive.

"No comment," Matt kept walking from the western portion of the plaza to vehicles parked to the southwest.

A microphone was shoved in Matt's face, "Is the United States working with Israel on an offensive strike?"

"Get the mic out of my face," Matt looked straight ahead and kept walking. The man kept up his persistence and a TV station began to record Matt as he walked along.

Another question, "What were those planes flying overhead and where were they heading?" Matt had enough. He grabbed the microphone from the reporter and chunked it; the reporter looked astonished. Matt snatched the TV camera and smashed it on the ground as he continued to walk toward the SUVs. The cameraman became angry and took a swing at Matt.

Matt caught his punch and wisely told him, "You don't want to see me angry. Leave it alone."

"You're going to pay for that!" The cameraman still wanted to play tough guy as the reporter went chasing after his microphone. By now, several news media outlets were covering the Western Wall bombing and taking note of the scuffle between Matt and a news crew.

Sesom came over to Matt, "Enough, we have no business with these people." Sesom escorted Matt to the SUVs and the Disciples loaded their gear.

"Who is Seth?" Mike directed his question at Ethan, who had just returned to the vehicles.

"A bad man that killed one of our Disciples and infiltrated our group," Ethan loaded a duffle bag into one of the SUVs.

"I believe that Matt told me about him," Mike looked in Matt's direction and Matt nodded in the affirmative.

Sesom took charge, "Ethan, this is Elisabeth."

"Nice to meet you. Sorry about the circumstances," Ethan shook Elisabeth's hand.

"You just killed a man?"

"Yes. He was a bad man though," Ethan was surprised that Elisabeth even cared based on the past twenty minutes of chaos at the wall.

"No time for this," Sesom wanted to get to Hess and understand Elisabeth's perspective.

Dorje and Li came to the rendezvous point together.

"Nice shot," Ethan complimented Li. Li nodded and bowed his head.

"No more Seth is good." Li smiled at the group.

Elisabeth, Matt, Mike, Sesom, and Amen loaded into one of the SUVs. Lucas, Li, Dorje, and Cering loaded into the other. Captain Phil, Kimi, and Talan were on their way back to the Grand Beach Hotel in Tel Aviv. The manager at Hess was expecting Amen and his companions. Even though the streets were flooded with police and military vehicles, many people were staying inside glued to news reports and announcements from the government.

****

The trip to Hess was a short one, and many people in the restaurant were watching televisions and enjoying some of Jerusalem's finest sausage. The Disciples pulled around back and met with Gittel, the restaurant's manager. Gittel pointed to two parking spaces reserved for employees of Hess. Amen jumped out of the first SUV.

"My friend." He hugged Gittel and kissed him on the cheek.

"Good to see you Amen." Gittel squeezed him hard, "Follow me this way." The other Disciples, Mike, and Elisabeth trailed Gittel and Amen into the restaurant.

"I have a private room in the back," Gittel was working his way through the kitchen. After years of knowing Amen, Gittel knew not to ask what Amen's business was or whom his companions were when he dined at Hess. Gittel and Amen had grown up together in Jerusalem. Exiting the kitchen, the Disciples received more than a few stares from patrons in the dining room. After all, many of them had bloody, disheveled clothing. All of the patrons went back to their business of eating, discussing, and watching the news. The Disciples began to unload gear as they found seats around a very large rectangular olive wood table.

"What would you like?"

"Let's start with tea, hot and iced. Some baygeleh with cream cheese and honey would be nice too." Amen did the ordering.

"Sure thing," Gittel was happy to be serving one of his best friends.

Sesom sat next to Elisabeth. By now, shock was setting in for Elisabeth; her appearance was pale and she remained silent. Matt was sitting across from Elisabeth and felt bad for her. He began to wonder if his dreams might have brought bad fortune Elisabeth's way.

Servers began to bring in pitchers of iced tea, kettles of hot tea, and bread for the table. Many Disciples were still cleaning up in the restrooms when refreshments arrived.

"Elisabeth."

"Yes."

"Tell me why we're here?" Sesom was speaking in a very soft tone.

"I'm not sure."

"I'm trying to understand you, but given the circumstances of today and the fact that we found you based on dreams and visions, I'm struggling to believe you." Sesom wasn't being forceful with his approach.

"I know," Elisabeth wiped her eyes and nose.

"Where are your parents?"

"I haven't seen them in over a year," Elisabeth grabbed a glass and poured some iced tea for herself. Many Disciples returned to the table and took interest in Elisabeth's conversation.

"Why not?" Sesom continued with a very soft and understanding tone.

Elisabeth took several gulps from the glass, "We had a falling out, a major disagreement."

"Over what?" Matt asked the question from across the table as he put butter and honey on baygeleh.

"I'd rather not get into it," Elisabeth took a napkin and wiped her eyes, "Excuse me, I'm going to wash up." Elisabeth left the table and went in the direction of the restroom. Sesom gave Cering a nod to follow her, for Elisabeth's protection and to ensure she didn't run.

"What are you thinking?" Matt tore a sizable piece of bread with his teeth from what he'd prepared and began to chew.

Sesom poured hot tea and added sugar, "Obviously she's hiding something with regard to her parents. I'm not sure if the falling out with her parents has anything to do with us, or why we're here."

Ethan crossed his legs and shuffled his weight in a wooden chair, "How do you intend on getting her to talk?"

"We must work with her. She will talk. Elisabeth has not seen her parents for over a year and she probably craves the companionship of family, which is what we'll be for her."

Cering followed Elisabeth into the bathroom. Elisabeth wasn't surprised she was being followed; Cering's company made her feel safe. As Elisabeth began to clean her face, Cering spoke,

"We are here to protect you, our intentions are good."

"I know. Based on what you did in the plaza, I know that you're a good group," Elisabeth had a paper towel and was cleaning her face.

"We have come a long way to meet you. Though your life may be in danger, there are aspects of your life that we seek to understand."

"That's what I'm afraid of," Elisabeth looked at Cering in the mirror.

"You can trust Sesom, he is a good man with great compassion," Cering smiled back through the mirror.

Elisabeth continued to wash her arms and face, "I don't deserve compassion."

"You'd be surprised, just talk to Sesom."

Gittel came back to the private room and checked on his guests, "Amen, would you like food?"

Amen looked around the room as several Disciples shook their heads. The Disciples had an amazing appetite, and seeing as many of them had been through battles and bloodshed, eating wasn't a problem.

"Yes. Bring plenty of sausage and corned beef hash with cabbage. Vegetables to go around the table would be nice."

"Coming right up," Gittel went to the kitchen and wrote up the order. Cering and Elisabeth returned to the oversized table.

Elisabeth started up a conversation with Sesom again, "I don't know where my parents are, but I believe they are still living in the West Bank. My father is very wealthy, partly inherited, partly self-made. My mother stayed at home to raise my two brothers and me. My brothers are older."

Elisabeth took another gulp of iced-tea, as Sesom and the Disciples remained quiet. "My oldest brother rebelled against western influence and left the West Bank to serve Al Qaeda. I haven't seen him in five years. My middle brother is very intelligent and earned a degree from Cairo University. He works with OPEC on oil exploration and refining. He and I stayed in touch until I was banned from seeing the family a year ago."

Sesom leaned forward, "Why were you thrown out of your own home?"

"I wasn't necessarily thrown out because I was attending Hebrew University at the time and staying in the dorms. My parents cut me off and banned me from returning to their home."

"Why?" Elisabeth had Mike's curiosity.

"Very complicated…"

Matt laughed, "Look at this group of people, it doesn't get much more complicated than this!" Then he became serious, "When I saw you in my dreams, you were always alone. There were times when you seemed happy and others when you appeared sad. The last vivid dream I had was about two weeks ago. You were at the Western Wall with your arms stretched out against the stones. There was blood oozing from the wall and running down your arms, covering your clothing. You were crying. You then turned in my direction and said, 'Please help me.' Then these guys showed up," Matt motioned his arm in the direction of fellow Disciples, "and so did the bad guys. My home has been destroyed and I have nowhere else to go. My brother's life was in danger too, so his family came with us to Israel."

"There was blood oozing from the Wall onto my arms?" A few tears fell down Elisabeth's face.

"Yes." Matt was sad to see Elisabeth's tears.

"What is it, Elisabeth? Something terrible has happened to you," Sesom redirected attention back to her story.

"Both terrible and beautiful," Elisabeth wiped her eyes with a cloth napkin.

Sesom said, "Start with the beautiful."

"You won't believe me," Elisabeth wasn't trying to be difficult, she genuinely didn't think the group in front of her would believe her story.

"You might be surprised what I believe in," Sesom's faith was deep.

"I'd been attending Hebrew University for a couple years and found a boyfriend. My parents didn't approve of him because he was Jewish. Even though we'd only been dating four months, something very strange happened." Elisabeth looked around the table; all eyes were focused on her.

"I had an inexplicable dream. A woman came to me one evening and she asked me to walk with her. When I said, 'okay', we instantly traveled to a beach setting. As we walked along the beach, we talked about my family and studies at the University. She was a beautiful woman. Her face was glowing and she smiled incessantly. She spoke softly and put her hand on my shoulder occasionally, as if to give support physically and emotionally. Then she said the most bizarre statement." Elisabeth pulled a piece of bread from a loaf.

"She stated that I had been chosen and would become pregnant. Then she said my daughter would pave the way for His coming."

"Who's coming?" Sesom was amazed.

"I don't know. When she said that I would become pregnant, I was a little surprised. After all, it was a dream."

"So what happened?"

"I became pregnant. I found out about two months after the dream. I became sick in the mornings and felt terrible. When the doctor said I might be pregnant, I couldn't believe the news," Elisabeth was shaking her head.

"Why?" Sesom remembered the comment about Elisabeth's Jewish boyfriend.

"Because...because I'm still a virgin." Elisabeth's body slumped, as if she was releasing weight from her shoulders.

"What?" Matt was confused.

"I am a virgin," Elisabeth felt a little uncomfortable revealing such details. Sesom wasn't surprised.

"How can you become pregnant if you're a virgin?" Matt's questions began to annoy Sesom.

Sesom gained control of the conversation, "Where is the child, your daughter?"

Tears began to roll down Elisabeth's cheeks. She didn't know how to answer the question. Men and women had traveled across the world to protect Elisabeth's interests, and their arrival may have been too late. Elisabeth stalled.

"Elisabeth, where is your child?" Sesom was thinking the child would be about six months old.

"I don't know how to tell you this?" Elisabeth was frightened by the idea of sharing such personal details.

Sesom countered, "You can share anything with us, we are here to protect you."

Elisabeth began to spill the story, "My parents didn't approve. My boyfriend, Eli, was Jewish and they couldn't believe I would associate with a Jewish man. After about three months of my pregnancy, my mother could see that I was carrying a child and became furious when I confirmed her thoughts. My father threatened to have Eli killed. I am his only daughter, and I was pregnant with a Jewish man's seed." Elisabeth went for more iced-tea. Sesom had a bad feeling. If the child had been given up for adoption, the Disciples would have a difficult time finding the girl.

"Please continue."

"My parents wouldn't allow me to keep the child," Sesom dropped his head, "and they called a family doctor."

Li had just taken a bite of bread and his mouth froze.

Sesom kept his head down, "Continue."

"They called a family doctor and I was taken to a clinic to have an abortion." Tears continued to flow down Elisabeth's face, "After that, I was banned from my own home and from speaking to my brothers. My parents cut me off and I haven't spoken with them since."

Matt chimed in again, "How can?" and was quickly silenced by Sesom.

"Enough Matt. No more questions," Sesom gave him a look from across the table.

The Disciples were speechless. For over a year the Disciples had found each other, lost Liam and Trevor, and felt the excitement of knowing their mission after finding Matt in Los Angeles. All of them had been chosen, and some of them felt as if they'd failed their mission. Sesom grabbed Elisabeth's hand and she leaned her head on his shoulder.

"I'm sorry you went through that. We're here to help guide and protect you from now on. You have been chosen." As Sesom completed his sentence, Gittel arrived with plates of sausage and corned beef hash. Many of the Disciples failed to notice food had arrived, and Gittel felt a sense of despair in the room.

"Is everything okay Amen?" Gittel whispered to his friend.

"Yes Gittel. Thank you for the food and service. You may place food around the table," Amen took a plate and smiled at his friend.

Sesom's phone began to vibrate. He pulled the cell phone from a pocket and saw Phil's name on the screen.

"Yes."

"Sesom, Mary's missing. The children are with John and Aaron, but Mary didn't return from a trip to the bathroom," Phil was short of breath.

"When?"

"Maybe thirty minutes ago. John, Aaron, Israeli Defense, and hotel security have checked the grounds. She's gone," Phil was standing in front of the hotel.

Sesom looked at Mike and Mike instantly knew that something was wrong; the ringing of his cell phone interrupted Mike. The caller ID was blocked. Sesom nodded at Mike to answer the phone and hung up on Phil.

"I think it's time for a trade," the accent on the other end of Mike's call was thick and Middle Eastern.

"What do you mean 'trade'?" Mike was confused.

"Your wife for the girl."

"What are you talking about?" Mike still didn't understand what was going on.

"Mike," Mary was on the other line, "don't give them anything." Mary screamed as the cell phone was pulled from her. Her screams echoed and faded, as if she was in an abandoned warehouse. A door slammed in the distance.

"Like I said, the girl for your wife." Mike became angry as the man spoke.

"If you think," the unidentified caller with a thick accent cut him off.

"You are in no position to deviate. Be at Bayt Lahiya with girl at 8 pm. As you enter Bayt Lahiya from Hevel Aza, there will be a man with a sign that says, 'Israel is Satan', ask him where to go." The phone hung up. Mike didn't know what to do or say.

∀*∦∦*∆

Gittel worked hard to host a tasty lunch for the Disciples, Mike, and Elisabeth. The sausage, corned beef hash and cabbage, bread, soups, and drinks were exceptional. Matt and Mike took five minutes to clear their heads and walked the streets of Jerusalem. Disciples were rarely shaken by tragic news, as they had experienced so much of it during their lives. Missions were regularly compromised and improvised in the military and covert operations; the current situation of the Disciples was no different from what they'd seen in the past. Matt and Mike returned to the table.

"Cering."

"Yes Matt."

"The warehouse address you gave me in Jerusalem tied to your Egyptian businesses?"

"What about it?"

"I had something shipped there a few days ago. The weapon will help us get Mary back."

Sesom was curious, "What kind of weapon?"

"I was scheduled to field test a shoulder harness before you guys showed up. If it works, Samil won't know what hit them."

Amen commented, "What do you mean by if it works?"

"The morning I met you at the café, I had just left Delta and spoken with the project manager for a shoulder harness cannon. He was very close to debugging the software and sending the weapon out for field-testing. I was supposed to handle field testing of the weapon and ready it for production."

"How do you know the weapon was sent?"

"I won't, at least until we stop by the warehouse tied to Cering's business."

"How are you doing Mike?" Sesom's strongest trait was compassion.

"I need to stay positive for the kids, you guys, and Mary. If anyone can bring her back, it's Matty."

Elisabeth was beginning to wonder if she would be handed over to Samil in Gaza. Even though she was Palestinian and would be welcomed in Gaza or the West Bank, she hadn't heard of Samil and didn't know if the Disciples would betray her.

Sesom began to map out the reconnaissance mission into Bayt Lahiya over the next couple of hours. Amen was very familiar with the area and knew the dangers involved with crossing into Gaza.

"You and Elisabeth will be on your own," Sesom didn't want to compromise the mission with other Disciples. "You will carry small GPS devices so we know your position at all times. If you deviate from the path in and out of Bayt Lahiya, Israeli Black Hawk helicopters will be standing by for us to retrieve you and Elisabeth." Elisabeth was pleased to hear that the Disciples wouldn't leave her behind. Sesom continued, "Matt will have a panic button stitched inside the tongue of his boot. If Samil discovers you are bugged with GPS tracking, you will only need to press the device in the tongue of your boot. You must press the button hard to activate the transponder. The transponder will give us your position at all times."

Amen took over for Sesom, "Once you successfully rendezvous with Mary, you will radio us and travel quickly toward the border station at Hevel Aza. Many Samil and PLO allies will surely make your escape difficult. We will come in with the Black Hawk helicopters and destroy the border station. We will also provide cover for your escape. If they follow you beyond the Gaza-Israeli border at Hevel Aza, they won't make it 100 yards into Israel before they are destroyed."

Sesom turned toward Mike, "You can take the night off and stay with your kids."

"I don't think so. Matt is my brother and I'm going to see him through this mission."

Sesom wasn't going to argue, "Very well. Elisabeth, have you ever fired a weapon?"

"No."

"You may need to tonight. You must be ready to cover Matt and Mary as you escape Bayt Lahiya. Cering will show you the basics of handling a weapon when we return to the hotel. Has Mary fired weapons before?"

"You bet. She's good with side arms and machine guns." Mike proudly said the statement.

"How will we get past the gate?" Matt was curious.

"Both sides will let you through. If Palestinians give you any problems, we will have Israeli Defense snipers help see you through the gate." Amen was well connected in Israel and parts of PLO occupied territories.

"Won't this draw attention to us?"

"Possibly. But don't forget that we're in the middle of a war right now. Minor border scuffles and a few Black Hawks aren't going to draw much attention. Most of our Israeli Defense Forces and Armies are heading toward the Lebanon and Syrian borders. Any conflict in Gaza or the West Bank will seem like an internal affair for Israel."

****

The time was 2:49 pm and Gittel was clearing plates. Many Disciples were chatting about family members back home and the beauty of Jerusalem. Elisabeth and Cering discussed who the Disciples were and what purpose they served. Elisabeth had no idea the Disciples had been in a game of cat and mouse over the past year. The fact that two Disciples died already made the situation even more desperate for Elisabeth.

Sesom spoke loudly, "Mike, Matt, Amen, Elisabeth, Cering, and I will stop by the warehouse and check out the mystery package. Dorje, Li, and Lucas will head back to Tel Aviv. We will meet in the lobby of the hotel at 6:00 pm for dinner." Sesom turned to Gittel, "The meal was fantastic and service even better. We appreciate Hess letting us take up room and having privacy."

"You're always welcome Sesom," Gittel gave Sesom a hug as he stood up from the table. The size difference between the two men was laughable. Amen gave Gittel a hug and thanked him for the meal. All of the guests began to line up to thank Gittel for the hospitality. The Disciples, Mike, and Elisabeth loaded up in the SUVs and headed in different directions. Cering's warehouse wasn't far away. The warehouse acted as a reload for imports and exports coming into and leaving Jerusalem. Many aircraft could be seen and heard in the sky above Jerusalem. Israel had begun a bombing campaign in Iran, focusing on areas thought to contain weapons of mass destruction. Even though Iran tried to fend off some of the bombings with old F-14 warplanes, Israel was able to strike targets as it pleased in the first day of war. The airport in Tehran was destroyed.

Iran vowed to send troops through Iraq and Syria to attack Israel, and even though the US occupied much of Iraq, newly trained Iraqi security forces wanted nothing to do with Iran. Saudi Arabia denounced the actions of Israel, but their close relationship with the West prevented them from getting involved militarily. Jordan avoided involvement and requested insulation from the military campaigns between Israel and Iran. Although quietly, Jordan granted permission for the Israeli Air Force to fly through their air space at the beginning of military campaigns. Turkey had pro-West foreign relations, even though they denounced Israel publicly for bombing Iran. The Syrians and Lebanese hated Israel and would most certainly utilize their relationships with Hamas and Hezbollah to attack Israel with bombs and para-military trained at regional terrorist camps. Lebanon still suffered from the affects of the 2006 bombing raids from Israel after Hezbollah attacked Israel's northern border towns with small rockets. Israel had shown restraint for years and was tiring of countries in the area that supported terrorism and a jihad against the Jewish people of Israel. The US was a major ally of Israel. China denounced further US involvement in Middle Eastern affairs, but the US was undaunted and maintained their support for Israel and a peaceful Middle East.

Cering's company had a 150,000 square foot warehouse in an industrial park of Jerusalem. The company's name was Olive Branch and its business was to reload containers being shipped from the five major ports in Israel. When the Disciples arrived, they pulled into a large container yard at the back of the building. Cering and Matt left the vehicle, while Sesom, Amen, and Mike stayed behind to guard the SUV. Elisabeth remained in the backseat of the vehicle. Cering and Matt climbed a small set of steel stairs that took them to shipping and receiving. Cering rang a buzzer and a voice speaking Hebrew came over an intercom.

Cering spoke Hebrew in return and gave her name and employee number. A camera was watching their every move. After a few seconds, the door buzzed and allowed them access to the building. A man approached Cering and welcomed her.

"Ms. Kadesh." The shipping manager had a big smile.

"My name is Kemet," the man offered his hand to Matt.

"Nice to meet you, my name is Matt."

"What can I do for you Ms. Kadesh?"

"There should have been a package shipped from California that arrived at our warehouse a few days ago."

"Please follow me this way and we will check the log for will calls." As they walked through the warehouse, there were forklifts carrying pallets of product to steel racking. Several forklifts were unloading product from containers and placing it in a staging area to be received. They entered a door marked Will Calls and Kemet went to a computer located behind the counter. He began to type and located two crates from California in will call.

"Is your last name Hiatt?"

"It is."

"We have two crates for you in will call. I will instruct a driver to bring them to the dock. Looks like the package arrived two days ago by way of air. Is there anything else you're looking for?"

Matt knew Noah would come through, "No, that should be all."

"Would you like a refreshment?"

"No. We're good Kemet. Thank you for helping us," Cering smiled at Kemet. In some aspects, Kemet appeared to have a boyish crush on Cering.

As they left the office, Kemet kept up the conversation.

"How is your family?"

"Doing great. And yours?"

"My wife and I had our child two weeks ago. We welcomed a baby boy to our family. His name is Ashok."

"Congratulations. I hope that he is healthy and doing well, along with your wife of course."

"They are doing fine. You will find Will Call beyond the receiving doors; it's appropriately marked. Have a great day. Good to meet you Matt."

"You too Kemet," Kemet buzzed the exit for Cering and Matt and they returned to the SUV.

"Will Call is beyond receiving over there. There are two crates shipped in Matt's name. A driver is bringing them to the dock right now." Amen drove over to Will Call and backed up the SUV. A driver dropped one of the crates and went to retrieve the other. The crates were large and stamped with Delta Defense on them. They were too large to load in the SUV as containers; they would need to be unpacked on the dock and pieces loaded into the SUV.

Cering asked a spotter for help, "Could you bring a crowbar so we can open this?"

"Of course." The spotter went to get the tool and brought it back to Cering. By the time he arrived with the crowbar, the other crate was being dropped.

"Here you go."

"Thank you."

Matt jumped up on the dock and took the crowbar from Cering.

"Anyone have a knife?"

Sesom and Amen pulled out hunters' knives and held them up to Matt; they smiled at each other. Matt took Amen's knife and cut straps running along the crates. Matt wedged the crowbar between the first crate box and top, forcing the nails loose. Once he successfully removed the top, he began to dig through straw in the crate to find equipment. He pulled out a helmet first, a backpack, then the shoulder harness, gun, and mounting brackets. Matt continued to dig through straw until he knew the crate was empty. He took the crowbar and pried off the top of the second crate. As he dug through straw, he pulled out several ammunition belts designed specifically for the shoulder harness. Most of them were 50 caliber rounds, but Noah sent some small grenades for testing too. Matt remembered grenade testing was in the works, but he didn't know the Ammunition's Team at Delta had completed their project. The second crate contained a small envelope with software discs so Matt could load programs for the gun and have someone control the harness with a computer remotely. Sesom, Amen, Mike, Elisabeth and Cering loaded the back of the SUV. Matt began to pick up trash and place straw back into the crates.

"We'll get that for you. We'll recycle the material."

"Thank you." Matt jumped down from the dock and returned to the SUV. He gave the hunter's knife back to Amen.

"You know how to use that?" Amen was surprised by the technical nature of the gun.

"I know enough to use it." Matt was sifting though items in back of the vehicle. The SUV sped out of the container yard and headed back to Tel Aviv.

"Do you need to test it?" Sesom wanted to see the gun in action.

"No time. We'll have to load Talan's computer, equip the backpack with 50 caliber shells and grenades, and mount the gun to the harness. I'll need to activate voice recognition for the helmet, sight in a few targets, and place the gun on stand-by."

"Sounds complicated." Mike was impressed.

"When this weapon is active, Samil won't know what hit them in Gaza. We will bring Mary back safely." Matt squeezed Mike's shoulder.

"I know."

Amen telephoned security forces at the Grand Beach Hotel. Amen let them know he would be arriving with Disciples and a weapon that would need to be transported to Matt's room via containers or laundry carts. The ride back to the hotel was relatively quiet, due to a long morning and hearty lunch.

****

Matt skipped dinner as he loaded Talan's laptop with shoulder harness software and tested the weapon. The backpack was specially designed to load 50 caliber ammunition belts and small grenade straps. At Delta, the Ammunition's Team had spent months lightening the load of the backpack and ammunition for the cannon. By the time the pack was fully loaded with 500 rounds of 50 caliber bullets and 24 small grenades, it weighed only 48 pounds. The helmet had a microphone and ear bud hardwired on the right-hand side to pick up conversations and moderate decibel sounds. When the gun was fired, the microphone would cut off to protect the hearing of the operator. The helmet's shape was similar to that of a fighter pilot. Matt mounted the cannon to the harness and tested the LCD screen with head movements and acquiring targets. The software recognized his name and position with Delta. He put on all the equipment and ran though tests with the computer for close to 30 minutes. From the hotel room, the satellite feed from the LCD to the computer was clear and unobstructed.

Back at Delta, Noah was just beginning his day with a cup of coffee and a bagel. A message popped up on his computer that unit #12 was arming and targeting objects. Noah looked closely at the computer screen and saw the satellite feed was coming from Tel Aviv at the Grand Beach Hotel. He grabbed his coffee and switched the view to the LCD screen of the helmet. Noah pulled a microphone over to his mouth and clicked his computer mouse on a button.

"See you found the weapon!"

Matt hit the floor and the LCD feed revealed an image underneath Matt's bed, "Who are you?"

"It's me Matty, Noah." Noah began laughing.

"I programmed the helmet to receive audio from operations at Delta. I can see your hotel room and everything through the LCD. By the way, you might want to get up," Noah chuckled again.

"How are you Noah?"

"I'm well. You created quite a stir around here. Internal affairs and the Marine's Military Police have visited me on a few occasions."

"Do they know I'm alive?"

"They don't know anything. Between explosions, a couple dead at your townhome, and your Mustang missing, they don't know if you were killed by terrorists or disappeared. After Dan spoke with you he was livid, but when reports came back that something tragic may have happened to you, he became a little more sensitive."

"I'm sure it was just a little," Matt smiled at his appraisal of Dan. "How are you tracking my feed without getting caught?"

"A secure proxy server that is meant for very high ranking officials at Delta."

"How did you get access?"

"I created it."

Matt began laughing at Noah's abilities to work within and around a system.

"I've taken unit 12 offline with Delta Defense's tracking systems. Once you use the weapon in the field, it will be a matter of time before they find you. When they do, I hope you have a job waiting for me." Noah didn't appear worried and took a sip of coffee.

"Remember, you know nothing if they continue to question you." Matt wanted to protect his best friend at Delta Defense.

"Not far from the truth," Noah saw that Matt had a computer. "I see that you're linked."

"I am. The software loaded easily and is testing well."

"Good. All right Matt, I've got to run before people start showing up and asking questions. Stay safe out there."

"Thanks for everything you've done Noah. I owe you."

Noah joked, "When they throw me in prison for aiding and abetting, you can testify as a character witness for me."

"I will. Take care." Matt left the backpack on and loaded the helmet and cannon in a duffle bag. Talan's computer was placed on standby and put back in the computer briefcase. The time was 6:23 pm. The Disciples, Phil, Aaron, John, Mike and the kids, and Elisabeth were at the hotel dining room breaking bread. Security was extremely tight in the hotel given the circumstances and fact that Mary went missing earlier in the afternoon. Matt showed up at the dinner table.

"Did you dress comfortably?"

"I did, thanks to Kimi." Elisabeth had gone from praying at the Western Wall earlier in the morning to sitting down with complete strangers for dinner in Tel Aviv. Elisabeth was very much afraid, but Cering and Kimi made her feel at home and as if she was family to the Disciples. Cering had warned Elisabeth at lunch not to contact family members or run from the Disciples. If Elisabeth chose to run, she would be kidnapped by Samil and killed. Elisabeth had seen the Disciples, Mike, and Phil work to save Jewish worshippers at the Western Wall; in her heart, she knew they were good people.

Lucas came over to Matt, "I want you to have this," he took off a chain around his neck.

"I can't take that from you Lucas."

"You are not taking anything from me, I'm giving it to you. This is the statue of Christ in Rio de Janeiro. We call this Cristo Redentor in Brazil. Those who believe in Christ don't believe in luck or fate. We believe in God's will." Lucas smiled at Matt as he put the necklace around his neck.

"Thank you Lucas." Matt gave him a hug.

"Are you ready, Matt?" Sesom turned the conversation serious.

"I am."

"We will be on standby at Sde Dov in Tel Aviv with Black Hawk helicopters. Once you arrive at the border station at Hevel Aza, we will take off and fly patrol over the Mediterranean to the west of Gaza. Kimi finished stitching a transponder in the right tongue of these boots; you will need to wear them. If your GPS trackers are found and disabled, you will utilize the transponder in the tongue of your boot. Don't forget, if you run into problems at the border station, we have Israeli Defense snipers watching your every move. If they assassinate the border guards on the Palestinian side, we have replacements ready to take over the station. No one will know what happened."

"Sounds good. Can I get a piece of bread with some butter?" Matt took off his boots and put on the pair Sesom handed him. Matt felt the transponder in the tongue of the right boot.

Mike went to work and fixed some bread for his brother-in-law. Matt's nephew thought his military clothing and backpack were neat.

"Uncle Matt. That's a neat backpack. You look like my GI Joe." John was in awe.

"Thanks buddy. When you get a little older, I'll take you on a mission."

"Alright...cool," John grew a smile from ear-to-ear. Mike shook his head. He didn't know whether or not he wanted John to follow in his footsteps.

Elisabeth finished up some hot tea and got up from the table. Amen radioed for one of his Israeli Special Forces men to bring Matt's SUV to the front of the hotel. Amen had loaded a few handguns under the front seats, a new Tavor assault rifle between the seats, and a GPS tracking device attached to the frame of the vehicle. Amen didn't want to risk losing contact with his newest Disciple and their newfound companion.

"I left you an early Hanukkah gift between the seats. You'll like it," Amen gave Matt a nod.

"Thank you." Matt went to hug Mike, "I'll be back in a few with Mary. Cover me."

"You bet." Kimi elected to hang back and stay with the kids as Mike went on the Black Hawk missions with the Disciples. She knew that he wanted in on the action and an opportunity to save his wife from Samil. Elisabeth didn't know what to think of all the activity covering the past 12 hours. After all, the Disciples moved quickly and events were changing by the minute; she had never seen such chaos over a short period of time.

****

Matt and Elisabeth drove off into the darkness. Nobody trailed them, but GPS signals were being fed to Talan's computer. Talan could see that Matt was taking Highway 20 to Highway 4 south from Tel Aviv. All of the signals from Matt's position were being received clearly. Talan was an expert at communication and tracking devices, which were critical elements to the success of Disciples in missions and covert operations.

"How are you doing?" Matt was worried about Elisabeth and her emotional wellbeing.

"Okay." Elisabeth wasn't convincing.

"Don't worry, we won't let anything happen to you." A street light revealed a smile from Matt in Elisabeth's direction.

"What if we don't?" Matt cut Elisabeth off.

"We're not trading anyone. Our group doesn't negotiate with terrorists. If we trade now, we'll be trading for the rest of our lives. If we wipe them out and spoil their plans, they'll think twice about messing with our families and loved ones. These people have killed before and will kill again to upset our plans, there are no negotiations." Matt was speeding south. The time was 7:35 pm

Matt put in his earpiece, "Talan, do you copy?"

"I do. I have you on Highway 4 heading south. After you make it through the checkpoint at Hevel Aza, you will need to put your helmet on and send me a signal."

"Copy. Over."

As Matt drove, he noticed there was no moon and the sky was pitch. Stars began to break through the darkness as they moved farther away from Tel Aviv. Not much was said between Matt and Elisabeth, as they knew they were traveling into harms way without ground cover. Matt put his faith in Noah's ability to work out software bugs and produce an excellent field weapon. The time was 7:47 pm

"We're coming up on the border at Hevel Aza. Let me do the talking."

"No problem."

The border station wasn't busy. Not many Israelites would travel into Gaza at night, as the establishment was Palestinian and an Arabic settlement. The border stations were separated by one hundred yards between Israeli and Palestinian booths. Matt drove up beside a small booth at the Israeli border station. He rolled down the window and an Israeli border guard looked at his passports.

"Good luck," the border guard handed the passports back to Matt.

"Thanks." Matt drove the SUV to the next station at Hevel Aza that was Palestinian.

He handed the passports to the Palestinian guard.

"You are the American, no." The border guard continued to study the passports.

"Yes."

"And you have brought the woman with you?" The guard leaned down and looked inside the SUV.

"Yes."

"There will be a man one kilometer down the road on your right. He will have a sign giving direction. Nobody is following you?"

"No one."

"Continue on." The guard handed back the passports and smiled at Elisabeth. Matt pushed the accelerator and continued forward. As he pulled away from the Palestinian border station, Matt noticed the lights went out and the buildings went completely dark. Elisabeth noticed the station went black too.

"Looks like they just closed," Elisabeth said with a nervous laugh.

"Trust me, we're going to reopen that station before 9:00 o'clock." Matt continued into the darkness. At almost 1 kilometer, a man with a sign was standing on the right hand side of the road. He was holding up a sign that said, "Israel is Satan".

"That doesn't seem like much direction." Matt looked over at Elisabeth. He pulled up beside the man and rolled down Elisabeth's window. Before Matt could speak, the man alongside the road dropped his sign and displayed another underneath. The new sign said, "Turn right in 5 kilometers, stop at lake." The strange man picked up his other sign and displayed it once again, "Israel is Satan".

Matt looked over at Elisabeth, "Well that was interesting." Matt set the trip on the SUV to track his kilometers. The road became a little rougher as the SUV traveled from pavement to hard sand and rock. Elisabeth grabbed the handle above her door as she began to bounce around in her seat.

"Remind me to write the transportation department to complain about the roads," Matt chuckled.

"What?" Elisabeth couldn't hear what Matt said as items bounced around in the SUV.

"Never mind. Only 3 more kilometers of this." Matt punched the accelerator and tested the suspension of the vehicle. The backpack was cutting into his back as the vehicle bounced along the poorly maintained road. Boulders lined the road as Matt moved the vehicle back and forth, almost sliding from curve to curve as the odometer ticked higher. Trees began to pop up and Matt knew they must have been getting close to the lake.

"Do you see anything?"

"What?" Elisabeth was more focused on holding on than listening to Matt. Matt mashed on the breaks.

"Do you see anything?"

Elisabeth could hear Matt now, "No, not a thing."

"Good." Matt put the vehicle in park, shut off the lights, and went to the hatch in back. He opened up the back door and grabbed his helmet. Matt pulled out his ear bud and powered up the helmet before putting it on.

"Talan. Do you copy?"

"Yes. I can hear you but can't see anything."

"Hold on. Let me mount the cannon on the shoulder harness and put it on." Matt mounted the cannon, engaged the 50 caliber rounds and similar sized grenades from the backpack, and mounted the cannon to the harness. A firewire connection from the cannon to helmet allowed for quick communication between equipment and a remote user, in this case Talan. Once all the components were strung together, Talan would be able to see what Matt was looking at in the field. Little did Matt know that Noah was looking through the equipment as well.

"Is that better?" Matt was pulling the LCD screen over his left eye and listening through the ear bud in his right ear. The LCD screen automatically adjusted for night vision and Matt could see trees and the road he and Elisabeth traveled on. A flare went up into the night to his left, maybe one hundred yards from Matt's position.

"What's that?" Elisabeth said.

"They're getting a visual on our current location, there's bad guys throughout the desert watching us. They probably saw us stop." Matt looked through the LCD lens and could make out a few figures 200 meters away from his position, where the flare went up.

"Elisabeth."

"Yes."

"I need you to drive."

Elisabeth got out and went around the front of the SUV to the driver's side. She buckled up and waited for Matt to finish with his gear. Matt spoke into the headset.

"Eye Scan." A green laser scanned Matt's left eye.

"Hello Mr. Hiatt." Matt heard a familiar woman speak through his headset.

"Arm."

The cannon on Matt's shoulder came to life and began to follow his left eye movements. Matt felt the weapon arm and chamber a 50 mm round.

"Now we're in business. Talan, do you have a good read on my position?"

"I do. I'm also receiving a clear visual from the weapon too. I saw those guys in the distance, much like you did. I can also zoom in and capture their images on the computer and scan their identities."

"Did you find anything yet?"

"Just started."

"We're back on the road." Matt pulled out his favorite .45 and chambered a round. He lightly engaged the trigger and pointed the laser at the ground. He was ready to bring Mary back. Matt opened the door to the passenger side and looked at Elisabeth. The LCD was scanning potential targets.

"Don't point that thing at me!"

"Sorry." Matt didn't bother with the seat belt.

"You ready?"

"Do I look?" before Matt could finish the sentence Elisabeth pushed the accelerator to the floor and caught Matt off guard. The time was 8:00 pm

Elisabeth was speeding on the rocky road to an unknown rendezvous point somewhere by a lake. After driving for a couple minutes, Elisabeth and Matt saw headlights lined up in a parking area near a boat dock. There wasn't much cover in the area. Even though there were some shrubs and trees, they were scattered and didn't provide security for anyone. The lack of brush would work to Matt's advantage.

"What do you want me to do?" Elisabeth saw the headlights and began to slow down.

"Park right in front of them, about 25 meters away. Leave the lights on." Matt looked through the LCD. The lens automatically adjusted for the lights ahead of him. There were four vehicles with people inside each.

"Target gun." The LCD began a scan of the vehicles and people inside.

"Zoom." Matt began to zoom in on passengers inside the vehicles. Mary was in the vehicle second to the left in the back seat. He knew because she had a burlap sack over her head. Matt began a cadence that Elisabeth didn't understand.

"Lock, lock, lock, lock, lock, lock, lock, lock, lock." Each of the targets was minimized and sent to the top right corner of the LCD. Matt forgot how clear the picture was with the lens.

"What are you doing?" Elisabeth brought the vehicle to a stop.

"You'll see. Roll down your window and lay down in the front seat. Keep the lights on."

Elisabeth did as instructed and rolled down the window. She shut off the engine to the SUV. As she lay down, she could hear car doors opening and closing in the distance.

"Do you have the woman?" The accent was Middle Eastern.

Matt replied, "Do you have my sister?"

One of the men walked forward with Mary and removed the burlap sack from her head. He then shoved her head in front of a headlight.

The same voice echoed in the darkness, "Is this your sister?"

Matt spoke softly, "Fire." The cannon took care of the rest. The shoulder cannon delivered nine 50-caliber rounds successfully. Matt locked all of the rounds on the chest cavities of Samil. He knew that a 50-caliber bullet to the chest would be fatal, as the bullets would become wrecking balls upon entering a human body.

Matt took off running for his sister. Mary got up and began to run for Matt. As they met in front of the enemies' vehicles, small arms fire began to pierce the ground around them from a nearby hill. Matt pulled his .45 and began to shoot in the direction of the fire. He spoke into the helmet, "Grenades, target, lock, lock, fire." The grenades were the same diameter as a 50-caliber bullet and filled with a couple ounces of TNT packed tight. The minute the grenade shells struck a target they would detonate with a kill range of 10 meters.

Talan spoke into his earpiece to Disciples hovering over the Mediterranean in Black Hawk helicopters, "He's taking fire, provide air support." Sesom, Mike, Cering, and Li were in one of the helicopters, while Dorje, Ethan, Lucas, and Amen were in the other. The Black Hawk helicopters peeled off their current course and headed into Gaza. As they reached the shoreline, anti-aircraft artillery began to pepper the sky with bullets and tracers. Even though the Palestinian army had no idea of the Disciples' mission, they thought that Israel might be attacking their settlement. The Black Hawks didn't return fire as they maneuvered through the black sky. The Palestinian army was not their objective or enemy.

Matt and Mary made it back to the SUV. Elisabeth had started up the vehicle and was ready to leave Bayt Lahiya. Samil vehicles began to converge on the spot. Matt mowed down nine of their men. Small arms fire was still coming from three points around the SUV and getting closer. Matt got in the front passenger seat and Mary climbed in back.

"Step on it and roll up your window." Elisabeth crushed the pedal to the floorboard once again and drove in the direction she came from. Matt turned around and the cannon continued to follow his eye movement.

"Stay down." Matt rolled down his window and began to climb out the side of the SUV.

"What, I'm driving!" Elisabeth noticed there was a small truck directly in front of her firing at their position. Matt began to shoot his .45 at the truck and hit the gunman. The driver was on a head-on collision course with the SUV when the truck was blown from the road by a Black Hawk's AGM-114 Hellfire missile. Elisabeth drove right through the remaining carnage.

"That was close," Matt spoke into the headset.

"We have two Black Hawks covering your SUV, Matt. Mike is telling me that there are several enemy vehicles in the area converging on your position. Sesom says they will clear a path for you, but you shouldn't remain on the same road."

"Copy."

Matt climbed back in the vehicle and continued to bark orders. "We need to move off this road and head for the border station on a different route."

"Why?"

25 meters ahead of them, an Improvised Explosive Device detonated and Elisabeth turned left off the road onto the sand. She pushed the 4x4 button on the dashboard and geared down the SUV. They were now traveling across soft sand and were slowed by the weight of the SUV. Even though they still maintained a speed of 30-40 mph, smaller trucks would be able to catch them on sand with no problem.

"Keep the accelerator to the floor. Make sure you don't bottom out in the sand." Matt located the rear window control on the dashboard. He rolled down the rear window half way.

"Mary, cover the back."

Mary climbed over the rear seat to storage in the back. Matt yelled back at her, "Mary."

She looked in Matt's direction, "Take this," Matt held up the Tavor assault rifle that was between the front seats. Mary smiled at Matt, climbed over the seat, and grabbed the gun. Matt handed Mary a belt with five clips for the Tavor. Matt pointed at both his eyes and then pointed to the rear of the vehicle. She would need to cover the rear of the SUV. Five vehicles were within sight of Matt. He turned to Elisabeth and pointed to the sky.

"They will clear a path for us to the border. No matter what, just keep driving." Matt began to climb out his window.

"Where are you going?"

"I don't want to shoot you by accident," Matt gave a wink and a smile to Elisabeth and disappeared to the top of the SUV. He poked his head back through the passenger side window and startled Elisabeth.

"And try not to throw me off the top of the vehicle." Matt pulled a steel clip from his vest that was attached to a retractable pulley. He connected the clip to the storage rack on top of the SUV. Mary began to unload the Tavor on a truck that was closing in from behind. She took out the driver and the truck slowed to a stop. Mary pelted the engine and radiator, rendering the vehicle inoperable.

The Black Hawks were using their Hellfire missiles and Gatling guns to deter Samil from gaining a position in front of the SUV. Small trucks were flying over dunes and closing in on their vehicle. Matt knew that Mary would cover the rear of the vehicle; he would need to do the same for both sides of the SUV. To Matt's right, two trucks began to fire on the SUV and hit the rear quarter panel. The SUV repelled the small arms fire with no problem, even though Samil thought they were piercing the vehicle's side. Matt spoke into the helmet as he looked to his right.

"Grenades, target, lock, lock, fire." Two grenade shells pierced the rear of both small trucks and detonated around the gas tanks. Each left the ground as the tanks exploded and sent debris everywhere. Matt ducked as shrapnel from the explosions struck their SUV. One of the trucks to Matt's left had a Browning machine gun and opened fire on the SUV. Lexan on the windows repelled the machine gun fire and bullets ricocheted in several different directions. Matt plastered himself to the top of the SUV as Elisabeth continued to plow through the sand toward the border station. The Palestinian side was still pitch, but the Israeli side was lit up and a military convoy was waiting for them.

Matt locked on the truck with a Browning and fired two grenades at their position. One hit the front while the other grenade hit the back. The truck left the ground as it imploded from inside out with intense flames from the gas tank. Matt knew the remaining vehicles would change their weapons and opt for something more powerful. Mary was firing on three trucks to the rear and Matt had two more on each side of him. An RPG rocket flew over the top of the vehicle to the right and landed on the Israeli side of the border. Matt turned to his left and locked in on both trucks firing on the SUV with machine guns. "Rapid Fire Guns", Matt unleashed 50 caliber rounds on both trucks until he said, "Stop". The trucks were left disabled and all occupants dead. As Matt turned to the right, an RPG rocket struck the underside of the SUV. The SUV's right wheels left the ground and the vehicle began to tip to the left.

Matt's harness locked in place while the steel cable cinched against the pulley and clip attached to the SUV's top. Matt pushed his feet off the top of the roof and flung himself up as the SUV rolled over on its left side. As the vehicle came to an abrupt stop, Matt flew forward and hit the windshield at the front of the SUV. Talan could hear all the commotion through Matt's headset and began to call for him.

"Matt come in. Matt are you okay." Matt hit the windshield with force and was knocked out by the impact. Three remaining Samil trucks converged on the disabled SUV. Talan continued to call for Matt as Elisabeth and Mary climbed out of the SUV. Mary still had the Tavor assault rifle and began firing at the trucks; they stopped and returned her fire. Elisabeth and Mary got behind the SUV, where Matt was hanging from the rack upside down, almost touching the ground with his helmet. Elisabeth pulled the helmet from Matt's head.

"Matt. Wake up Matt. They're coming." Elisabeth was patting his cheeks and shaking his shoulders.

Mary continued to fire on the trucks, even though she was taking heavy fire. A Black Hawk helicopter roared over her head and came to a stop. 30 mm rounds began to emanate from a single barrel mounted below the helicopter's cockpit. The Black Hawk unleashed Hellfire missiles on the remaining trucks in the area. The trucks disappeared, almost as if they vaporized into the night.

"Put this thing down." Mike wanted to get to his wife and brother.

"No can do sir, brownout. You're going to have to rappel to the site."

Mike went to the side door of the modified S-70A. He already had a harness on and attached rappel guides to his body. Sesom assisted Mike with the cables and readied him for the jump.

"We're sitting at about 250 meters. They are just below us. Go!" Sesom didn't want to waste much time either.

Mike had rappelled numerous times in the past while working with Special Forces. He dropped with an M249 machine gun in his right hand and stabilized his drop with his left. The chopper still disturbed the ground at 250 meters and sand was flying in all directions. Mike made the drop in seven seconds. He saw Matt dangling from the SUV; Matt was coming out of his stupor.

"Hey buddy, you ready to get outta here?"

"Yeah, I think so." Matt was beginning to realize he was upside down hanging from the top of the SUV.

Mike turned to his wife and gave her a big hug. Mary was happy Mike made the trip.

"How are the kids?"

"Good. They didn't even realize you left for a few hours," Mike gave her a kiss as he held her long, dark hair.

"Excuse me. Can you guys take a break and help me down?" Matt was fully conscious.

"You bet," Mike grabbed hold of the pulley and released it from Matt's belt. Matt fell to the ground.

"Smooth landing." Matt brushed himself off and hugged Mike. His helmet was still dangling from the shoulder harness by the firewire connection. Dorje, Ethan, Lucas, and Amen were destroying Samil vehicles entering the area nearing Mike's position.

"What's the plan Sesom?" Mike spoke into his earpiece.

"We can't land. You must travel the 1000 meters on foot to the Israeli station. Don't worry about the Palestinian side."

"Ay Captain." Mike yelled into the earpiece to ensure Sesom could hear him.

"We need to head for the Israeli border on foot. Let's go." Mike led the charge into complete darkness with Mary by his side. Matt stayed close to Elisabeth; she appeared to handle the terrain fine by herself. When they were 150 meters from the SUV, Sesom's Black Hawk came roaring by to unload Hellfire missiles on the SUV. They made sure the SUV was completely destroyed and left burning in the sand. Amen's Black Hawk went for the Palestinian border station and opened up with a combination of Hellfire missiles and the 30 mm machine gun. If anyone were in the station, they wouldn't have survived the onslaught of artillery from the Black Hawk.

The trek across sand to the Israeli border station took ten minutes. Mike was pleased that the group didn't encounter further resistance from Samil. They met up with the Israeli convoy and loaded up into one of their Humvees. As they were leaving the area, Matt noticed rockets being launched from Gaza into Israel.

"What are those?" Matt was curious.

The Israeli driver responded, "Small rockets. They shoot them off all the time. The Americans referred to them as SCUDs during the first Gulf War. These missiles are far less advanced than SCUDs and rarely hit their targets. We still take precautions though and shoot many of them down with Patriot missiles."

The Palestinians didn't realize the covert operation carried out by the Disciples had nothing to do with the PLO, but was designed to rescue one individual from evil. Even though the campaign looked like Israel may be going on the offensive, realities were very different. The newspapers from Gaza would print that Israel had attacked Gaza unprovoked, and the Palestinians drove them from the border. As with many other complicated matters in the Middle East, Samil had worked to infiltrate several countries in this part of the world to bolster philosophies of evil. Israel, and other countries of the west, had become a scapegoat to perpetuate a bad guy in the Middle East. Mary's rescue would be reported as Israeli aggression, even though very few people knew the truth of the matter. Regardless, Mike, Matt, Mary, and Elisabeth were returning safely to Tel Aviv. Even in the midst of a war that had begun with Iran, small victories were always celebrated.

****

The Black Hawk helicopters peeled off and returned safely to base. Talan logged off the computer and retrieved a cup of hot tea. Kimi was reading stories to John and Rebecca as they began to close their eyes and fall asleep. As Mike, Matt, Mary, and Elisabeth crossed the desert of Israel, they noticed a build-up of Israeli forces to the south. Israel was sending troops to protect their borders and counter aggression from the Palestinians or groups working within Gaza. For the most part, Jews and Palestinians shared schools, worship, and other daily activities in their neighboring countries. Western papers and news agencies had a tendency to pit the sides against each other.

Matt removed the shoulder harness, helmet, and pack from his back.

"How is your head?" Mary was concerned about her brother.

"Thank goodness the windshield stopped it from becoming detached."

Mike saw an opportunity; "Mary always said you had the hardest head in the family."

"I think we just found that to be true."

Mike turned his attention toward Elisabeth, "Are you okay?"

"Yes. Not a typical day for me."

Matt said, "I don't know if that kinda day is typical for anyone."

The group could see the lights of Tel Aviv in the distance. Fighter planes were patrolling and an occasional rocket launched toward the East.

"What's the status of the war?" Matt knew that a campaign in the Middle East would draw many countries into the territory. Now that Israel was responding with force, many Islamic sects and governments would view this as a holy war. Israel wasn't concerned with perception and knew their fate would be determined by their ability to protect their homeland and prevent weapons of mass destruction from entering the country. Even though the leaders of several countries wouldn't admit it, many in the Muslin world didn't like rogue nations and hardnosed dictators.

"Great Britain, the United States, and Israel are attacking Iran with short-range and long-range missiles. The United States has moved 15,000 troops to the border of Iran and Iraq. Great Britain and Israel will be supporting special operations with a second wave of ground forces in the next couple days. Several other countries are determining what they want their role to be, or not be." The Israeli Defense soldier looked straight ahead as he updated Matt.

"I wonder what the Marines are thinking of your absence?" Mike knew the Marines would be looking for Matt.

"I'm not sure. But based on the use of this weapon, and possible surveillance at the Western Wall, they may already know my position."

"Will you go back?" Elisabeth was curious.

"Probably not. I'm not sure how to successfully explain the course of events over the past few weeks. The Marines won't be pleased that I acted on my own and left without notice.

The mess at my home doesn't help either. Hopefully the truth will play out over time."

"None of us can go back to the United States. Now that we're involved and vulnerable, we will have to remain far from home." Mike was disappointed, but excited about what the future would hold.

"Look here cowboy, we have two young children. You're not going to get all wrapped up in saving the world again." Mary countered Mike's testosterone.

"We may not have a choice, based on what Sesom has seen and said so far." Matt was beginning to believe their involvement might be a calling for something greater. "They had no issues kidnapping you, in front of the children, and holding you for ransom. Samil is determined to capture and kill Elisabeth for whatever reason."

Elisabeth had the look again. She didn't know who to trust and why the Disciples had journeyed so far to find her. Elisabeth knew the Disciples could trade her to Samil for a large sum of cash and be on their way. Why they hadn't done so already was a mystery to Elisabeth.

Matt turned his attention to Elisabeth and reiterated, "Don't worry, we're not negotiating with terrorists."

"This part of the world has heard that many times before from the United States," Elisabeth wanted to get her point across.

Matt said, "Fair enough, but we're not here representing the interests of our government. We're here to protect you and see what the future holds."

****

Dan showed up at Noah's door just after lunch.

"You have some explaining to do," Dan obviously found out about the use of the shoulder cannon and details of its use in Gaza.

"Is that so?" Noah knew that his dodging would aggravate Dan.

"Yes sir. Why was unit 12 deployed in Gaza? Can you explain intelligence showing pictures of Matt at the Western Wall yesterday? MPs are going to show up from the Marines any minute, I expect an explanation now!"

"Dan, our country is now involved, once again, in a Middle Eastern war. Rumor has it that the Department of Defense is going to order 200 shoulder cannon units from Delta Defense in the next week. At $500,000 apiece, our company stands to gross $100,000,000 in sales. The fact that Matt had a weapon and tested it in Gaza is beyond our control at this point. His activity at the Western Wall involved saving Jewish worshippers and establishing control at the site. I'm not sure what the Marines want with Matt, but we don't stand to gain a thing by sharing intelligence with Marine MPs."

"Didn't you see Matt activate the weapon and use it in Gaza?" Dan had papers in hand to support the facts.

"I did. Matt used the weapon on a reconnaissance mission to save his sister from kidnappers. Matt is involved in something personal that appears much bigger than a scuffle in the Middle East." Noah paused for a moment, "He appears to be working with an international coalition of covert operatives."

"What do you advise me to tell the Marine MPs?"

"Tell them what they want to hear. Advise them that Matt has a weapon and was scheduled to test it the week he disappeared. Share details and data of the weapon's success and let them know that we can produce several units for their operations overseas."

"What about the shipment to Tel Aviv of two containers from Delta Defense?"

"I believe the United States' government calls their cover-ups plausible deniability. In essence, staffers won't tell the President about several issues within the administration so he can play stupid if asked. My advice is that you play stupid. You can share whatever information you want with the Marines, but I believe stupid may be the best role for you at this time."

"You need to keep me informed!"

"I think it's best if I don't, that way you have plausible deniability," Noah winked at Dan.

Dan rolled up the papers and pointed them at Noah before he left the doorway. Noah went back to analyzing data of unit 12. The shoulder cannon had performed well for Matt in Gaza. From the retinal scan to the locking of targets, the 50 caliber bullets and grenades had struck their targets with great precision. The weapon's technology would allow greater flexibility for Special Operations in all divisions of the military. The $100,000,000 contract would allow Delta Defense more opportunities to develop weapons with allies overseas. Noah kicked back in his wheelchair and took a deep breath. Years of research and development had culminated in a successful testing of the shoulder cannon with live munitions.

****

Now all has been heard; here is the conclusion of the matter:
Fear God and keep his commandments, for this is the duty of all
mankind. For God will bring every deed into judgment,
including every hidden thing, whether it is good or evil.
Ecclesiastes 12:13-14

Matt passed out after returning to the Grand Beach Hotel. He
awoke to a world at war. Several theologians and visionaries
predicted the end of the world would begin in the Middle
East. From the United States involvement in Iraq over the
past two decades and recent campaigns in Afghanistan, the
territory was a hotbed of uncertainty. With Israel entering
the fray and launching attacks on Iran by air, the
connotations of a holy war were swirling through several
Arabic countries. Israel was done with negotiations and
restraint.

Matt went to the lobby. Cering and Kimi were having
breakfast with Elisabeth; Dorje and Li were playing a game of
chess at a table with two high back chairs. Amen was talking
to the Israeli security forces and updating them about the
mission last night. He didn't see Mike, Mary, or the kids.
Lucas was with Sesom at a table in the corner of the lobby;
they were speaking with a man and drinking coffee. Coffee
smelled like a good idea and Matt went to a small beverage
buffet that had some of the best Turkish coffee he'd ever
tasted. After doctoring a cup with sugar and cream, Matt
poured some coffee and stirred with a spoon. Sesom
motioned for Matt to join them at the table.

Sesom and Lucas stood up as Matt approached the table. The
stranger at the table stood up as well.

"Matt. This is Jonas. He has come to visit us from Rome."
Sesom smiled and placed his hand on Jonas's shoulder.

"Pleasure to meet you Mr. Hiatt."

"Good to meet you Jonas." Matt carefully sipped the hot
coffee.

"How is your head?" Sesom had observed Matt overnight to
ensure that he didn't suffer from a concussion.

"Dull headache, not bad. My helmet took the worst of it." Matt
turned his attention to Jonas, "Did Sesom say that you are
visiting from Rome?"

"Yes. On specific orders."

"Really. From whom?" Matt thought the orders would have
been from the Roman Army.

"The Vicar."

"Who's Vicar?"

Sesom began to laugh, "You don't know who the Vicar of
Christ is?" Sesom motioned for the men to sit down.

Matt began to piece together the conversation. "The Vicar of
Christ and Rome...you're here on the Pope's orders?"

"Yes sir."

Matt replied, "Wow. We're getting more attention than we
deserve. How did you get roped into this mess?"

"I work for the Pope as part of the Swiss Guard."

"You don't have one of those funny looking suits on though?" Sesom chuckled at Matt's observation.

"The tri-color is for show. Since the assassination attempt on Pope John Paul II's life in 1981, we wear all blue uniforms and street clothes to protect the Holy Father in public. We have many operatives that work in several countries throughout the world."

"Why did the Pope send you here?"

"Ever since Pope John Paul II's passing, we have been closely watching activities in the Middle East. When the Holy Father was 78, he began to journal some of his thoughts, dreams, and visions. We never publicized any of the documents because they would have been viewed as prophesying or pontificating. Although the Holy Father's body began to fail him, his mind was very strong up until his passing. In his writings, he predicted that God would incarnate himself once again for all people."

Matt sipped more of his coffee, "Can you share any details of his dreams and visions?"

"The Holy Father believed that a young girl would be born in the Holy Land and pave the way for the second advent of Christ."

Sesom interrupted, "The second advent is better known as the second coming to most."

Jonas continued, "The Holy Father believed that an incident at the Western Wall of Jerusalem would set in motion events that will change human history and bring the New Testament full circle. The Vatican believes the events of the past 24 hours confirm and usher in predictions of the Holy Father."

"So what does this mean to us?" Matt remembered the cross Lucas gave him and pulled it out. Lucas gave Matt a nod.

"We don't really know, but we'd like to have you visit the Vatican and speak with Pope Simplicius II."

"I do like the new Pope's name. What are you thinking Sesom?"

Sesom rubbed his beard; "Iran is vowing to bring every Muslim into this fight against Jews and Israel. They are denouncing any Muslim that doesn't rise up around the world and bring an end to Israel and Jewish rule. Iran has already claimed they possess nukes and will use them."

Lucas continued, "Weapons of mass destruction put us all at risk in Tel Aviv. We should leave as soon as possible to preserve the essence of your visions, Elisabeth's destiny, and our lives. Mike and Mary have brought young children to this country; we wouldn't want to see them perish at our expense because of indecision."

"That's true. How safe is the Vatican?"

"Very safe. We have called on a division of the Swiss Army to travel to the Vatican in the next 12 hours. 5,000 Swiss Army and our personal protectors of the Pope should provide more than enough security. A perimeter of five miles will be set-up around the Vatican. Only residents and Vatican personnel will be allowed to pass through checkpoints. Like many other intelligence agencies, we have received numerous reports of dirty bombs being deployed in several countries. While radical Muslims have called for jihads over the past decades, they weren't successful because Israel remained on the sidelines. Now that Israel has elected to go on the offensive with western allies, the rules of the game have changed. One thing is for sure, we are not safe in Israel."

"I've found that to be true since I arrived here." Matt laughed at his own comment. "Sesom, would we travel by boat?"

"We would take the Excalibur. John and Aaron have been on the boat since Mary's abduction. Platform welders have been mounting torpedo launchers, laser anti-aircraft cannons, and several 76 mm guns on the ship's deck. I hope they come with instruction manuals."

Amen overheard Sesom's conversation and came over to the table, "Sesom, the Israeli Defense Command is going to provide us with ten sailors for the Excalibur. These men are trained in torpedo launching, rifle and cannon fire, and evasive maneuvers with large battleships."

"How can we repay the Israeli Defense Command?" Sesom never took handouts.

"They're saying we already have by our actions at the Western Wall yesterday."

Sesom emphasized, "We were doing what's right. No debt should be repaid for doing what's right."

Amen wasn't in the mood to argue with Sesom, "It's settled Sesom. They have offered their assistance and we shall take it. They believe this to be right and we don't want to offend them." Amen merely turned Sesom's words around on him.

"Okay. Get with Captain Phil and work on sleeping arrangements and additional supplies for our new shipmates."

Amen pulled out his smart phone and dialed Phil as he walked away. Cering would handle additional supplies through her company and have them brought to the Excalibur. The Olive Branch was also acquiring munitions for new weapons being installed on the deck of the Excalibur. Sesom had discussed storing additional water with Cering and Phil in case of nuclear attacks on land. The Excalibur would retreat to high seas if a large-scale nuclear campaign developed between warring nations. Nuclear fall-out and radioactive dust would have a difficult time finding its way to the middle of the ocean. Ethan came over and took a seat with Lucas, Sesom, Matt, and Jonas.

Sesom introduced him as Jonas stood up, "Jonas, this is Ethan from Egypt. He has many family members spread throughout Egypt and the Mediterranean." Jonas extended his hand and welcomed Ethan to the table.

"Pleasure to meet you Ethan." Jonas shook Ethan's hand and returned to his seat.

Matt was curious to see if Jonas knew about Elisabeth's abortion and shunning by her own family. "Has Sesom shared the personal details of Elisabeth's journey over the past couple of years?"

"He has shared details of her pregnancy, abortion, and rejection by her own family. My understanding is that Elisabeth was forced into an abortion because of her parents' assumptions about a Jewish boyfriend and the consummation of their relationship. I'm not surprised, based on fractured relationships of Palestinian and Jewish people in this territory, that something like this has happened."

Matt continued, "Is the abortion a deal breaker?"

Jonas appeared a little confused, "What do you mean by deal breaker?"

"That we have missed our opportunity. That God, or whatever, was trying to communicate through people's dreams to pave the way for Revelation." Matt stopped and looked at Sesom, "That's the book isn't it? Revelation. When God rains on our parade and gives us a little humility." Sesom nodded his head to Matt; he didn't want to interrupt Jonas.

"Matt, there is a difference between thinking and all knowing. Sometimes humans elevate themselves to ideas of omniscience, even though they don't really know what will happen from one minute to the next. God has a plan, and his plan obviously involves this group of people. Pope John Paul's dreams dealt with an event at the Western Wall. He believed the event would trigger significant actions for the future of our world. Even though he had vivid dreams, he wasn't certain of their origin or timing. If we consider what has happened to Elisabeth, the Holy Father had no premonition with regard to her circumstance. Her abortion was a foregone conclusion, which culminated with your group looking for her at the most holy of Walls. The only recurring dream Pope John Paul documented was a world-changing event at the Western Wall. In the United States, I believe you would call the events a game-changer instead of a deal breaker."

"What specifically did he see?" Matt was curious to see how close his dreams were to the Holy Father.

"A woman at the Western Wall suffering and asking for forgiveness. She was alone, until a man came to her side. The man took her away from the Wall and washed her sin away with water. Even though the man was in great danger, he risked everything for the woman suffering at the Wall."

Matt was astonished, "What does it all mean?"

Jonas laughed, "Did you hear what I said about being all knowing? The Holy Father didn't know, but he felt that Jesus was speaking to him about the future. Pope John Paul II then began to document his dreams, visions, and thoughts with regard to the Western Wall. In the year 2000, Pope John Paul II visited the Western Wall and left two notes between the rocks. While one note is well documented, the other has been kept secret."

"What did the other note say?" Ethan was now caught up in the conversation.

"John Paul II left a note for Elisabeth. Wishing her peace at the Wall and letting her know that someone would be coming for her. The Holy Father even spelled her name correctly with an 's'. He forgave Elisabeth for her sins and wished her a blessed life as a child of God."

Nobody said a word at the table. The idea that Pope John Paul II had visited the Wall before September 11, 2001, the war in Afghanistan, the second Iraq War, deadly earthquakes in South America, China, Indonesia, two tsunamis that killed thousands, a hurricane that annihilated a gulf coast, sweeping political change in America, an uprising in Egypt; the Holy Father left a separate note for a young woman of Palestinian descent. Matt was beginning to comprehend Jonas's comment about being all knowing.

"What happened to the note?" Ethan was captivated by the story told by Jonas.

"It's with all the others, buried at the Mount of Olives in Jerusalem."

Matt continued with questions, "So how did you know about the note?"

"After the Holy Father's passing, his personal items were gathered up and placed in storage at the Vatican. While they were being archived, we discovered a journal he kept bedside. John Paul II recorded details of the notes he left at the Western Wall. What I'm telling you has remained a tight secret within the Vatican."

Matt stood up and began to pace near the table. "You're pretty quiet Sesom."

"This is our mission. This is what we have been called to do. The honor of meeting Pope Simplicius II is exciting in and of itself. To be part of something beyond our level of comprehension is overwhelming. Even though I was raised Muslim, I have deep respect and reverence for Christianity and Jesus Christ as a great prophet of God."

Lucas weighed in again, "We are not safe in Tel Aviv. Radicals launching a weapon of mass destruction on Jerusalem or Tel Aviv soil would leave us at great risk. When do you anticipate our departure?"

"It depends on the new equipment and how long it takes to wire the controls. Phil is overseeing the installation with John and Aaron. They are working with computer technicians from the Israeli Department of Defense. Once they are finished, we will leave for Rome. We will still have a 1600-

mile journey to Rome, a 2-½ day trip by Excalibur. I'll update the group this evening at dinner."

"Very well." Lucas thanked Jonas for his time and left the table.

"Jonas, you may want to consider traveling with us."

"Why is that?"

"A man infiltrated our group a few months ago. He ended up killing one of our Disciples, a dear friend of Ethan. He was working as an operative for Samil. Samil is the very venom of God and they are aware of our mission. They were responsible for kidnapping Matt's sister yesterday and the death of a fellow Canadian Disciple. Liam had met up with me in Italy and shared a vision that brought him to Italy. After a few months, Liam received news that his mother was ill and on her death bed in Canada. He went back to say his goodbyes and Samil ambushed his entire family. They even killed his mother in the hospital before she could pass. At that point, the Disciples determined that we should discontinue any contact with family members or friends. Just your being in the company of Disciples, puts you in danger. To be on the safe side, you should accompany us to Rome."

"On orders of the Holy Father, I have come to assist you in whatever way I can. If you would like me to join you on a voyage across the Mediterranean to Rome, I would be honored."

Sesom was relieved and looked at Matt, "In Jesus' time, the Disciples had to leave their families for safety reasons. Even though they believed their calling, they didn't want to subject family members to persecution. Jesus' father Joseph and the Magi, sent to Bethlehem on Herod's orders, had dreams that the King intended to kill Jesus. Those dreams convinced Joseph and Mary to flee Israel and stay in Egypt until Herod's death. Dreams and visions have played a role in God's work for thousands of years."

"Another Sunday school lesson?" Matt ribbed Sesom.

"Very important that you understand the nature of this mission. God has played a part in many cultures through Moses, Jesus, Mohammed, Buddha, and other prophets. Christianity is different in the sense that Jesus was a Messiah, based on several accounts of his apostles and enemies. The mere fact that Disciples became martyrs for their Father after his passing is proof enough that a resurrection, or some significant event occurred with Jesus. People won't die for something they don't believe in and haven't witnessed. Judas felt so strongly about his betrayal, he found a tree, hung himself, and burst into pieces on the Field of Blood."

"How did he burst into pieces?"

"You've seen a person decompose. The belly bloats and the body becomes swollen with gases and liquid. The rope hanging Judas likely broke under his weight and entrails spilled all over the ground."

Jonas interrupted, "Matt. You will have a chance to see our archives and many of the treasures contained within. People forget that Christianity is more than a thick book; it has left behind many artifacts that you can see and feel. The Dead Sea scrolls are being moved to the Vatican as we speak for protection. You will be able to see some very significant pieces of human history to reinforce your beliefs, whatever they may be."

"I lost interest several years ago when my school was attacked and my parents died during the attacks of 9/11. I became a free agent of religion. I didn't affiliate myself with any one belief."

Jonas understood, "Everyone's journey is different in life. Speaking with Pope Simplicius II and visiting the Vatican may help to mould a new perspective."

****

Conflict raged on in the Middle East. Day-by-day, the world was becoming more divided over the war. Indonesia, Syria, Lebanon, Iran, Pakistan, and Yemen vowed to bring an end to the reign of Jews in Israel. More moderate countries of Saudi Arabia, Egypt, Iraq, Jordan, and Turkey wanted stabilization in the area and knew that the Jewish nation of Israel would do everything in its power to maintain control in the territory. Several Muslim nations had been good neighbors to Israel for decades, and they didn't care much for jihadist and groups favoring terror in the region. Indonesia surprised the West with their allegiance to Muslim nations supporting a war with Israel. The Muslim population of Indonesia had turned the country against the west and backed their brothers in the Middle East supporting a jihad. The move had put China, Japan, and the Korean peninsula on alert and in a very difficult position with their neighbor. India remained a strong ally to the West and put Pakistan on notice to not get involved in a conflict.

Even after a few days, the world was watching the Middle East with baited breath. The territory had seen revolutions in support of democracy for the past couple years, but instability was a consequence of independence. Radical Muslims, Al Qaeda, the Taliban, and other fringe groups threatened the general population with violence and a civil war if countries supported pro-Western governments. The United States had been plagued by its own problems of greed and corruption. Politicians from both major parties had all but robbed the American people of their hard earned money and squandered the loot under the guise of banking reform and stimulus packages. The American people had begun a revolt of their own against an outdated, inefficient government. The Tea Party, with their set of radical beliefs, was taking the country back seat-by-seat in Congress. The

United States lacked leadership and amassed major credit card debt with their special interest backing, pet projects, and collective bargaining. Several Middle East countries, even moderate ones, saw the United States as a political form of corruption and greed.

A group called the Colonists had formed in the United States. They were calling for an end to the Federal Government and Federal Reserve. They believed the 50 states could manage themselves effectively and independently, taking ideas from the original 13 colonies. They pushed to maintain a President for the United States, but the role would be focused on military, organic economic growth, and international trade. The Colonists viewed the President as a Chief Economic Officer, and the goal was to maintain prosperity for the 50 states. The idea was catching on in the United States, as the Federal Government had run up a bar tab of trillions to finance a faulty government.

As the Disciples fortified Excalibur, planes were constantly flying overhead at Ashdod. Jonas elected to stay with the Disciples and assist them with supplies. Everything from dry foods, water, small and large ammunition, rocket launchers, torpedoes, a replacement SUV, and clothing was sorted and stored on the ship. Ten sailors had worked hard with Israeli Defense Command to equip the Excalibur with computers, communications, and storage for rockets and shells. The past couple of days had been filled with tests and welding on the ship. Loading the Excalibur with large guns, torpedo launchers, and laser guided anti-aircraft cannons required counterbalance weights and stabilization of the ship. While Captain Phil agreed to have additional security measures on the Excalibur, he didn't imagine that the modifications would make his vessel look like a modern day gunship.

Sesom was on the dock admiring the ship; "I don't think we have to worry about pirates anymore?"

Phil found humor in the statement, "Ya think?"

"How soon until we leave for Rome?"

"Israeli Defense should be wrapping up this afternoon. They are loading replacement gear in case computers fail or wiring becomes faulty. All of the weapons have been anchored with heavy bolts, welding, and steel girders. We've made room for the sailors and have plenty of supplies."

Matt was covered in grease and walked up to Sesom and Phil, "Torpedo launcher is done and tested. We have a 225 degree firing radius from the stern of the ship."

Phil was pleased, "How are the controls from second deck?"

"These guys are good. They have wired the satellite and motor controls to the deck. They will run independent satellite systems for air and sea. The configuration is cool." Matt had learned much about seafaring weapons over the past few days.

Sesom changed the subject, "Where is Elisabeth?"

"With Kimi, Cering, and Mary. They all went shopping in Tel Aviv. Elisabeth was in need of some clothes and Mary didn't have enough to last her. Amen and Lucas went with them."

Phil interjected, "When they return, we will need to load their SUV on Excalibur. When Israeli Defense completes their testing, this evening we will leave. Everyone will need to prepare for departure."

"I'm heading to the hotel to change and get packed."

"Let's break bread at 6:00 pm. We will invite our new shipmates. We'll have dinner at the hotel before we leave." Sesom was looking forward to visiting the Vatican once again.

"You bet." Matt went back to the ship to see if anybody else needed a ride. Israeli Defense forces escorted the Disciples from the Port to Tel Aviv and around the city. Amen had lectured Special Operations for allowing them to have Mary kidnapped. Because Amen was highly respected in the ranks of Israeli Defense, he was able to procure what he needed for the Disciples. Mary's kidnapping was unacceptable and Israeli Defense Command was critical to her return from the mission in Gaza. The Black Hawk helicopter pilots had flown precisely during their missions and received praise from the Disciples and Mike. Anyone associated with Israeli Defense and the Israeli Army had an enormous sense of pride. Mary's return to the Disciples and her husband was non-negotiable in their eyes; they would die for her safety and the success of their mission.

Li, Dorje, and Ethan joined Matt in a ride back to the Grand Beach Hotel. Talan stayed on the ship to ensure that his communications would sync with military upgrades from the Israeli Defense Department. All of the GPS, satellite systems, and warning systems would be monitored by Talan on the Excalibur. He would update Sesom and Phil as they determined a strategy for handling threats. Sailors from the Israeli Defense Department viewed Phil as their captain and would take orders from him; Talan's monitoring of activities would help Sesom determine a course of action against outside threats.

The Grand Beach Hotel was covered with security and reporters were forbidden to book rooms at the hotel. Cering had instructed hotel management to charge her for any rooms that could have been booked by reporters. She asked her employees to utilize the hotel and beach with all expenses paid by the Olive Branch. Cering also treated the Israeli Defense Department to suites at the hotel, which could be used by their family members and close friends.

"Matt." He heard the voice from behind him as he walked through the lobby.

"Yes." As Matt turned around he noticed Elisabeth was beckoning him. She was struggling with several shopping bags.

As Matt walked toward her, he blurted out, "Looks like it was a good day at the department store. Anything left?"

Elisabeth was embarrassed, "I know, it's a little much."

"Did you get me anything?"

"Did you want something?" Elisabeth took a more serious tone with Matt.

"No. I'm just kidding. Here, let me take the heavy ones." As Matt took the first bag, he dropped it to the ground as if it weighed a ton. He began to drag the bag along the marble floor of the hotel's lobby. Elisabeth looked at him and shook her head; she was smiling.

"I hope the elevator can handle this." Matt began to roar with laughter. "What room on the second floor?"

"200." The elevator doors shut as Matt hit number two on the control board.

"Isn't that a suite?" Matt was impressed Elisabeth had acquired a suite at the hotel.

"Cering has been so wonderful to me." The elevator doors opened on the second floor. Matt allowed Elisabeth to step out first and walk to her right. Suite 200 was located at the end of the hallway. There were Israeli Defense Forces positioned on the floor, with guards posted at the elevators and stairwells. The guards were exceptionally kind and accommodating, even though they carried Tavor assault rifles. Much like what Mary had used in the back of the SUV to eliminate the enemy, the Tavor assault rifle had become a weapon of choice for urban warfare.

"Good afternoon." Matt openly showed his appreciation and respect to the Israeli Defense Forces. Even though they failed to protect Mary during her abduction, Matt knew things like that could happen to any good Special Operation's division. For a second, he remembered the opportunity to eliminate Osama Bin Laden as an objective and his platoon was instructed to stand down.

Elisabeth utilized her key card to open the door. Suite 200 overlooked the Mediterranean with a beautiful beach view. Elisabeth couldn't wait to put down the bags and dropped them upon entering the kitchen. She asked Matt if he would like some tea as she went to the cupboards.

"I would." Matt took the bags back to the master bedroom. He came back to the kitchen and retrieved Elisabeth's bags as well. She put a kettle on the stove and began to boil water. Tea was a favorite of many European, North African, and Middle Eastern countries. Elisabeth had grown up drinking tea and enjoyed the aromas of different leaves. She was dressed in jeans with open toed sandals, a short-sleeved white blouse that had a small drawstring above her breasts, and her hair was pulled back in a ponytail. Elisabeth's blue eyes contrasted her olive skin; she was striking. After Matt's second trip to the master bedroom, he noticed her beauty as she carefully set the table with teacups, saucers, milk, sugar, and rugelach cookies. She was a very mature young woman who had experienced scorn from her family and guilt from her faith.

Elisabeth caught Matt staring at her, "Is everything okay?"

"Yes, it's fine. I'm sorry, I was in a daze."

"I'm making some Jerusalem mint tea. Very calming and refreshing to the body and soul."

"I've never tasted a Jerusalem mint tea."

"You're in for a treat." Elisabeth caught Matt looking at her again.

"What is it? Are you not comfortable in my company?" Elisabeth looked disappointed as she spoke to Matt.

"No. It's not that at all. In fact, it's just the opposite. I can't believe I'm in your presence. I'm having a difficult time comprehending how a woman I saw in a few dreams is preparing a mint tea for me in Tel Aviv. This is truly remarkable." Matt was in awe and took a seat at the kitchen table.

"Remarkable in a good way?" Elisabeth was still shaking off some insecurity.

"Oh yes. Except for some of that driving in Gaza." Matt began to chuckle as he eased tension in the room.

The kettle began to whistle as Elisabeth took cups from the table. She poured hot water into the cups allowing the tea to steep. The aroma of mint filled the kitchen. There was a knock at the door.

"I'll get it." Matt hopped up from the table and went to the door; he pulled out his .45. Cering was standing in the doorway; she was surprised to see Matt in Elisabeth's suite.

"Am I interrupting?" Cering gave Matt a little smile.

"What? No. Oh no. We're just having some tea, come in and join us."

"Hey Liz." Cering came into the kitchen, "Do you need some help?"

"No. Just finishing up. Have a seat, I'll get you a cup."

Elisabeth brought tea to the table. They began to doctor the tea with sugar and milk. Matt grabbed a rugelach cookie and dipped it in his tea. Cering laughed at his gesture.

"This isn't Dunkin' Donuts Matt." Cering remembered the franchise had tried to establish itself in Jerusalem at the beginning of the millennium and left after the fast food treat didn't catch on. Elisabeth giggled at Cering's observation.

"I miss Dunkin' Donuts back in the States. This tea is fantastic." Matt continued to shovel rugelach in his mouth as he poured another cup of tea. Elisabeth and Cering were amused by how Matt ate his afternoon snack.

"Sesom would like us to meet for dinner at 6:00 pm in the private dining hall. We will be leaving for Rome after dinner via the Excalibur. The ship is ready to sail and Sesom wants to leave as soon as possible."

"Why?" Elisabeth was sad about leaving Israel.

Matt began to talk with a mouth full of food, "We're not safe here. In fact, we couldn't be in a more dangerous place right now." The threat of nuclear holocaust or chemical weapons didn't curtail Matt's appetite. Two things Matt enjoyed about Israel were the food and the culture. "I'm going to miss this place too." Matt looked out the window at the beach and Mediterranean. "The people are great and very friendly. They also mean business when issues get serious. Those Tavor assault weapons are awesome too. Can you get us some of those Cering?"

"I'll see what I can do." Cering looked at Elisabeth and smiled while shaking her head.

Matt swallowed his food and looked at the women. "What? Those are some of the best modern weapons I've seen in years." Matt took a gulp of tea.

Cering continued, "Is there anything we can do for you before we leave this evening?"

"No. I believe I have everything I need. How far is the trip to Rome?"

"I believe it's two and half days. The Vatican is expecting us. Many countries and major cities are on high alert. The Vatican has been closed to the public and has a perimeter setup five miles around the Holy City. Only residents near the Vatican can get In and out of the area."

"Is this Samil in Rome too?" Elisabeth wanted to understand more about the people hunting her.

Cering wanted Elisabeth to understand the danger involved with Samil. "They are everywhere. Very well funded, connected, and armed to do plenty of damage worldwide. Samil has infiltrated some of the largest terrorist groups in the world. However, they lack leadership and don't trust each other. When you round up some of the most evil people on the planet, they don't show much care or concern for their counterparts. Seth, the man Ethan killed a few days ago, was a low-ranking official with Samil. His death will give them reason for revenge; yet leave them even more unorganized and confused."

"How did Ethan kill him?" Elisabeth was curious. She had never known mercenaries or people that killed others for a living.

"He choked him to death in a simple triangle hold while looking him in the eyes. Revenge for his killing one of our Disciples and Ethan's close friend. While we have specific beliefs and values, we look to exterminate any evil that we encounter, by any means necessary."

Elisabeth looked at Matt as he nodded his head and tilted it in the direction of Cering. "She's right. I have seen some gruesome stuff since serving in Special Operations for the US military. At the end of the day, we're not only protecting people's freedom, but also protecting them from evil dictators and people with misguided ideologies. I've fought against groups of people that have killed women and children, gassed their own citizens, and murdered people for just thinking differently. Fighting today is as much about good versus evil as it is about protecting democracy and eliminating dictators."

"What if I stay?" Elisabeth was curious to see if she had an option. Matt looked at Cering and took the lead.

"I'll share with you what Sesom shared with me. If you choose to stay, so will we. But understand the nature of this mission and the importance of your decision. You will put all of us at risk, but our objective will be to protect you. We have been brought to you through dreams and visions. All of us will be in great danger."

Elisabeth began to giggle, "God I love you. You're so serious and cute. I'm glad you found me. I didn't have any intentions of staying here anyway." Cering began to roar with laughter.

"What do you call it Matt? An Oscar? I shall nominate you for one."

Matt shook his head and rubbed his forehead. "You ladies are impossible. I've gotta go."

"No Matt. Don't go." Cering was still laughing at how Matt took the bait.

"I'm going to shower and get ready for our last supper in Israel." Matt winked and got up from the table.

"Are you sure you won't stay?" Elisabeth felt bad for Matt.

"No, really. It's time for me to go. Thank you for the tea and crumpets." Matt did a terrible impersonation with a British accent.

"C'mon Matt, stick around for awhile." Cering was still giggling.

"I'll see you tomorrow on the ship with a kendo stick. I hope you're ready!" Matt began to laugh as well.

"You're on."

"What's kendo?" Elisabeth didn't understand the conversation between Matt and Cering.

"You have a lot to learn." Matt was quick to answer as he made it to the suite door. "I'll see you in a couple hours." Elisabeth didn't want Matt to leave. She was enjoying his company and the time with him at the table. She made a pouty face as Matt closed the door behind him.

Matt approached the first Israeli Defense guard he saw. "Can I see that Tavor assault rifle?"

"Sir. I'm on strict orders." Matt interrupted the guard.

"Yeah, yeah, yeah. Let me just hold it and sight something in the scope. Please."

The guard discharged the magazine and emptied the chamber. "Mr. Hiatt, my weapon." The guard set the weapon on the floor and allowed Matt to pick it up.

"These are fantastic." Matt studied the weapon and pulled back the action on the Tavor.

"Ever had to use this in combat?" Matt redirected his right eye from the scope to the guard as he stood at attention.

"Yes. The Lebanon War of 2006 and recently Libya to eliminate members of a tyrannical regime."

"So you guys are the ones who pulled off that assassination?"

"I pulled the trigger sir. Please don't share those details with anyone as the operation is classified and sealed."

"I won't. Great job in Libya by the way." Matt set the Tavor back at the feet of the guard. "What's your name?"

"Captain Gideon."

"At ease Captain Gideon. Thanks for supporting us with your men and resources."

"We have a duty to Amen. He is highly regarded in the ranks of Israeli Defense. One of the best soldiers special forces have seen in recent history."

"Do you know him?"

"I do not. But my Major General does."

Matt pulled out a cell phone and dialed up Amen. Amen answered after 2 rings.

"Yes Matt."

"Can you do me a favor?"

"Absolutely. Just name it."

"Can you come to the second floor and meet up with Captain Gideon? I would like for him to join us at dinner this evening."

"Of course. Let me finish up with Sesom in the lobby and I'll be right up."

Matt hung up the phone. "Amen will be up shortly to ask you to dinner. We are pushing out this evening and I'd like you to join us. Are you the commanding officer in rank?"

"I am."

"Then put your First Lieutenant in charge and come join us at 6:00 pm. I insist." Matt smiled and offered his hand to Gideon.

"Thank you Mr. Hiatt. I would be honored to join you and Amen for supper." Matt gave Gideon a pat on the shoulder and continued on to his room. Matt was desperate for a nap. As he approached his room on the first floor, he heard a scratching at the door.

"Why that little..." Matt didn't finish his sentence.

"Did you miss me?" Scratches looked up at Matt as he entered the room. "Come here," Matt created a cradle with his arms and Scratches jumped into them. He took Scratches over to the king-sized bed and let her down. Matt set the alarm on his cell phone to ring 1 ½ hours later. Matt's head hit the pillow and he was out. Scratches bundled up at his side and began to close her eyes.

****

Gideon joined the Disciples for dinner at the hotel. Amen gave Gideon a toast and thanked the Israeli Defense Forces for their protection and their sailors. The meal included an assortment of Jewish foods including falafel and beef brisket. Desert included Arabica coffees, baklava, and different crepes. Phil, John, Aaron, and the Israeli Defense sailors joined the Disciples for dinner and affirmed their readiness to set sail that evening. The crew of Excalibur had worked hard to arm the ship with the assistance of the Israeli Defense Force. Jonas fit in well with the Disciples and enjoyed the company of the two children. Jonas had always wanted a family of his own, but committed himself to the Swiss Army and protection of the Holy Father. He held Rebecca as she slept in his arms. Jonas appreciated the irony of holding a peaceful child while the Middle East raged in war.

Sesom gave the Disciples, Elisabeth, Mike, Mary, their children, Jonas, and the crew of Excalibur orders to be at the ship in one hour. They would leave port at 9:30 pm and set sail for Rome across the Mediterranean. The Israeli Defense sailors on the Excalibur were ready to sail and had established quarters on the lower deck and hull. Phil was concerned about adding ten sailors to the ship, but he was surprised to find out how few supplies they traveled with and how efficient they were. In fact, Phil had never sailed with uniformed, military personnel on his ship, and he was surprised at how much respect he'd developed for the young men. John and Aaron were impressed by the professionalism and knowledge of sailors their age. Some of them had wives and children they were leaving behind in Israel. When asked about leaving their families behind, the sailors stated that they had been given a mission and they would see it through. The sailors, like many people around the world, were tired of all the fighting in their homeland and hoped their efforts would help bring peace. The sailors had no knowledge of the company they were in or the details of their mission. They had received orders from the Major General of the Israeli Defense Force. Nobody had ever received orders directly from the Major General, and they figured Amen's mission drew the attention of supreme ranking officials responsible for Israeli defense. The sailors were handpicked specifically for their special operations' training.

At 9:35 pm, Sesom ordered everyone to a toast at the Excalibur's bow. The toast was different this time around as several F-16 fighter planes were cruising above the Israeli coast. Off in the distance to the north, Matt noticed several tank battalions heading in the direction of Lebanon. Hezbollah had always been a menace to the north of Israel, even for the citizens of Lebanon, and threats of rockets with chemical weapons were becoming reality. Israeli Defense had already shot down over a dozen short-range missiles and a few of them were carrying mustard gas.

Sesom raised his glass of cider, "We set sail for the Vatican to understand our new place in this desperate world. For a year, we searched several countries and found Matt before Samil could. With his family, we embarked on a journey to understand the source of his dreams and nature of an unusual calling. At the most holy of places for Jews and Muslims, we found a beacon of hope praying at the Western Wall. Once again, we took action before Samil could spoil our plans. Even though Samil kidnapped one of ours and attempted barter, we ended their plans of deception and murder by taking the fight to them. I raise my glass to the brave men and women on this ship, for it is you who give me hope. God bless Israel and the Middle East." As Sesom finished the toast, an F-16 came overhead.

Everyone raised their glasses and watched the F-16 tail off to the southeast.

"Did you plan that?" Ethan spoke up after the jet engines roared away.

"Not at all. Let's hope it's a good sign for us and our travels."

"Probably not a good sign for where that jet was headed." Matt was quick to remind everyone of the war raging in the Middle East.

Elisabeth came to Matt and raised her glass, "Thank you for finding me and bringing hope."

"Finding you, yes. The hope thing, ask me after we visit the Vatican." Matt rattled her glass with his, "This is kosher cider, I'm sure of it."

"Your sister, Cering, and Kimi have been great. It's almost as if I've known them for years."

"That's only because you've shopped together in Tel Aviv." Matt began to chuckle. Another F-16 flew overhead close to the Port."

"Where do you think they're going?"

"To catch up with bombers over Jordan or Saudi Arabia. Saudi Arabia has always been a good ally behind the scenes. They have mastered speaking out of both sides of their mouths. While they support Islam and Arab countries, they don't care much for radical Islamic jihadists. They have always feared a rebellion in surrounding Arabic countries would lead to a dismantling of the region and relationships with the West and Asian countries." Matt took another sip of cider and continued.

"The dismantling has begun with radical dictators teaming up to see an end to Israel."

"Do you believe they will be successful?" Elisabeth evoked general concern.

"No. One thing I've learned about the Israeli Defense Forces and people of Israel is that they are very tough. I've served with members of the Israeli Special Forces; they are some of the toughest people I've served with in combat. Those people don't know how to lose. Since WWII and the genocide committed against millions of Jews, they have been relentless in their struggle against tyranny. Losing isn't an option. The only way Israel will fall is by a catastrophic event, like a weapon of mass destruction."

"The Jewish people have always been friendly to me."

"What happened to your boyfriend? He was Jewish, wasn't he?"

"After the termination of my pregnancy, we just couldn't continue on together. I believe, in the back of his mind, he always questioned my story and what happened."

Elisabeth took a more serious tone, "What do you believe?"

"With regard to?" Matt wanted Elisabeth to be more specific.

"In God, in a higher power, in a force greater than us."

"I believe in my family. I believe in Mike and what he stands for as a human being, he is a good man and treats my sister well. I believe in my friends and those that have covered my back in the middle of a firefight. When we were fleeing across Gaza, those men and women in the Black Hawks, those are the people that I believe in. If I didn't, I'd be dead several times over." Matt didn't answer Elisabeth's question.

"What about beyond that?"

"I struggle with what's beyond THAT." Matt emphasized the tail end of his sentence.

Elisabeth looked disappointed so Matt elaborated. "After coming back from my first tour in the Middle East and joining special operations, I spent a lot of time in coffee shops emailing friends and corresponding with people I met overseas. In the United States, many church groups and individuals meet at coffee houses for Bible study to discuss their opinions of the Old and New Testaments of the Christian Bible. Occasionally, I would recognize people sitting in with these groups and talking up a good game. Jesus this, Jesus that, almost as if they'd been a witness at the crucifixion. They would quote a verse in the Bible and discuss how it impacted their lives and their relationships." Matt took in some more cider, "Then I'd encounter the same people in society and they'd act like complete heathens. Yelling at checkout stands in the grocery stores, cutting in front of people to fill their gas, ripping off people through their businesses, and ignoring their own children. Some of these people were cheating on their spouses and playing politics within their own parochial schools. Really nasty stuff."

"Not everyone is like that though." Elisabeth was trying to focus on the good in the world.

"The problem is, I can't tell the difference. Did you ever hear about the Columbine High School massacre?"

"Yes. We discussed the tragedy in high school."

"Mary attended Columbine when the massacre occurred. The town was in an uproar about the response of police, SWAT, and rescue teams. The sheriff's department allegedly," Matt put up both his hands and made quotation marks with his fingers when saying allegedly, "covered up some of the information with regard to the killers' pasts. The boys were killers, but they were also very misguided in their beliefs. The Bible brigade came out and many people said the devil was directly responsible for the massacre. People were preaching at the school and crosses were erected to honor those who died in the tragedy, including the killers. Family members of the victims, close friends, and others denounced the crosses erected for the killers and began to vandalize them. Terrible things were written and the town became divided, which is likely what the boys wanted when they began their assault. I was turned off by the entire circus. People looking for an opportunity to push their religion, point a finger, or pass a plate. You know what I think?"

Elisabeth was intrigued by Matt's story and detail of the events, "No, I don't."

"At the end of the entire ordeal, there are parents that won't see their kids again. There was a teacher that left his family too early. Two kids gave their parents a legacy that they can't undo. Those who are left living carry the burden. 9-11 overshadowed Columbine and the Virginia Tech Massacre took violence to a whole new level on college campuses. At the end of it all, it's just death and destruction to terrorize people. No different than what happens in the Middle East.

There really is no purpose, even though people search high and low to find one."

"Do you believe life has no purpose then?"

"No, it has purpose. To rid the world of those that have no purpose." Matt started laughing.

"In all seriousness, I hope there is a God and that I have an opportunity to experience the company of my parents again. I'm not a big fan of the fairy tale endings and hypocrisy associated with organized religion today. Let's face it, when Jesus was crucified, it was violent. He was beaten, whipped, forced to carry his own cross, wore a crown of thorns, and hung on a fence post. The experience represents humanity today. There are very few that will talk the talk, walk the walk, and die for others to live. That's why I respect Jesus."

A tugboat brought the Excalibur from the shores of Ashdod to the deep seas of the Mediterranean. A harvest moon lit up the deck of the ship allowing Elisabeth to see all of Matt's expressions. Several Disciples went below to play cards with Israeli Defense soldiers. The soldiers were teaching Disciples how to play Whist, a very popular card game in Israel. The soldiers took a liking to the male Disciples and were enamored by the presence of Cering and Kimi. Phil sounded the horn for the tugboat as a sign of thanks.

Elisabeth cut to the chase, "Do you believe me Matt? Do you believe in my dreams, pregnancy, and termination of the pregnancy?"

"Why wouldn't I?"

"I don't know. I guess I'm finding the story hard to believe myself."

"You may not want to tell anyone else your feelings. You have a boat; I mean a battleship, of people who are willing to risk their lives to protect you. If you don't believe, then our efforts may be in vain."

"What do you mean by vain?"

"That we are making this journey for the wrong reasons."

"Why would God choose me though?"

"For the same reason he, she, it, whatever, chose my parents and sister to be part of tragic experiences. I've learned that I live on a very small planet in a very small galaxy. The universe is continuous and we don't even know of its ending or beginning. To think that my opinion, or an attempt at understanding why things happen makes any real difference in the world are beyond arrogance. I do what I believe is right. I believe being here with you is right where I should be."

Matt made Elisabeth feel safe. She was comfortable. Elisabeth faced the front of the ship and put her head on Matt's left shoulder. Matt put his arm around her. Sesom and Phil were leaning forward in the Captain's Bridge to see what Matt and Elisabeth were doing. When Matt put his arm around Elisabeth, Sesom leaned back and smiled.

"So are you a matchmaker too?" Phil began to laugh.

"I'm not sure if this is my destiny, but this is definitely a good sign."

"And why is that?"

"Those two have been chosen by a power greater than me." Sesom noticed that Kimi was walking up behind Matt and Elisabeth with a blanket. She put it around them and gave them both a hug.

"If there was room for one more, I'd climb in there with you." Kimi began to walk away.

"We'll make room." Elisabeth didn't want Kimi to feel left out.

"That's fine. You two look comfortable anyway." Kimi kept walking and disappeared into a doorway.

Matt and Elisabeth continued to chat away about their experiences with family, military, school, and other personal issues. Mike and Mary put the kids down and came to join them on the forecastle.

Mike lit up a cigar and began to puff away.

Matt turned to him and said, "You know that stuff will kill you."

"And trips into Gaza aboard a Black Hawk helicopter won't." Matt could see Mike wink at him through the smoke. The moon lit up the Mediterranean and forecastle of the Excalibur.

"You were pretty good out there old timer."

"Old timer. I was trying to make sure you didn't get my wife killed." Mike began to laugh.

"I had everything under control." Matt smiled.

"Especially that part when you were dangling from the SUV out cold."

"Who said I was knocked out?" Matt looked at Elisabeth. "You didn't tell them, did you?"

"Well they asked me what happened." Elisabeth raised her head from Matt's shoulder and looked him in the eye.

"Awwww man. Never give this guy any information. I'll never live it down. You did pretty good out there Mookie."

A storm was brewing to the north over open water. Lighting was licking the sea and thunder rolled in the darkness about 20 miles away. Captain Phil's voice came over the loudspeaker.

"Storm ahead. You guys may want to go below."

One thing about Captain Phil, he never had to ask twice to clear the deck. If he encouraged people to go below for a storm, they didn't hesitate. Captain Phil had seen plenty of storms over the decades on the high seas. Some of the most dangerous storms fell between seasons and winter was the toughest time of year on the ocean. Mike, Mary, and Elisabeth went down below and Matt joined Phil and Sesom on the bridge.

"We're heading into that?"

"You bet. It's not like we can go around it." Phil took a puff of a cigar and moved the stogie to the right hand side of his mouth. Sesom was smoking a cigar too.

"We're going to find out pretty quick how the Excalibur handles with a bunch of new equipment and steel reinforcements. If we begin to sink during the storm and swells, we'll know that we put too much equipment on the deck and below."

Sesom took a puff and blew smoke toward the ceiling while stroking his beard. "Matt, the trick to the high seas is to head right into the storm. If you try and run or move around a storm, the boat will be at greater risk in the swells. Captain Phil and I have sailed through 50-60 foot swells during storms. If you want to find out how strong nature is and how small we are, you've got the best seat in the house."

"I think I'll pass. I trust you. How long until we arrive in Rome?"

"About 2 days from now. We'll dock at the Port in Flumicino."

"Any pirates along the way?"

"Doubtful. The Mediterranean isn't favorable to pirates. They prefer to avoid military ships and other encounters with maritime police. Very few paths in and out of the Mediterranean. Countries like Italy and Egypt will blow pirates out of the water and use them for target practice."

"How do people know we're a friendly?"

"We constantly transmit our ship's information and communicate our position. Now that we have sophisticated satellites, we'll know who's in the air or on the water within about 50 miles of our location. Other ships will have their information broadcasted including their country of origin. The guys below are monitoring communication with other ships and planes. If they see or hear anything out of the ordinary, they'll radio Tel Aviv and have them run logistics. One of many upgrades we received for the Excalibur."

Sesom got serious, "Your American friends will eventually find us based on our means of travel."

"Do you have a plan for that?"

"Of course. The Marines will have a difficult time detaining you outside of the United States. In most cases, Cering and I are better connected than the US government. Over the past two decades, the United States has lost favor with several foreign countries and their leadership. While most people understand that doing business with the United States is necessary, many countries do everything they can to take advantage of US companies."

"That whole lipstick on a pig analogy." Phil began to laugh as he pulled the cigar out of his mouth.

"In other cases Matt, we have people on the inside at several different levels of the United States' military. We'll know when they're getting close."

"I had no idea." Matt seemed very surprised.

"Why would you? You've been raised to believe the United States is superior to other countries. In less than fifty years, the United States' military will no longer be the leader in the world. Other countries like India, China, and Russia will challenge the United States at several turns over the next century."

Rain began to bead on the windows of the Captain's Bridge. In a matter of seconds, the rain began to pound the windows. Captain Phil had wipers that cleared the rain and the three men could see the forecastle. Swells were beginning to crash into the front of the ship and spray the forecastle with saltwater. Phil could see the storm on his radar. He turned and utilized a compass to map out the storm on a table behind him.

"The next two hours will be a little rough. After that, smooth sailing." The phone rang and Phil picked it up.

"Yes...I see...two hours. Keep an eye on the equipment and communications." Phil hung up.

"The guys below received surge warnings with the storm; swells of 30-40 feet. I think they call those moguls in Colorado." Captain Phil gave Matt a push.

"You want to see some moguls? Let me know when you're ready. This is nothing." Matt began to laugh. "I'm going to turn in." Matt patted Captain Phil on the shoulder as John and Aaron entered the Bridge. They were ready to weather some of the storm inside.

"Goodnight Matt," Sesom spoke up as Matt disappeared through a doorway to the lower deck.

Matt yelled back as he was halfway down the stairs, "Goodnight guys."

****

Matt shared a room with Dorje. While several Disciples and Israeli Defense soldiers had retreated to the hull for some cards and other games, Matt was ready to call it a night. Dorje set up a hammock in the room to ride out the waves. Instead of listing with the ship, Dorje's weight would keep him from rocking back-and-forth or side-to-side. Dorje was fast asleep.

Matt grabbed his dopp kit and headed down the hall. As he walked down the hall, Matt could feel the waves crashing into the Excalibur and the ship began to rock a little. There were common bathrooms on each of the decks with toilets, sinks, and showers. Matt pulled out his toothbrush and wet it in the sink. He looked in the mirror and saw how tired he looked. Everyone on the Excalibur had worked hard to launch the vessel with new fortifications and supplies. The Excalibur took on the appearance of a gunship and several tons added to each deck would test the ship's wayfaring capabilities.

 Matt grabbed a cloth, wet it, and began to clean his face. He rubbed his eyes with his right thumb and finger. The warm washcloth felt good on Matt's face and he yawned while taking in a deep breath.

Matt talked to himself in the mirror, "A few weeks ago Los Angeles. Now I'm sailing the Mediterranean on my way to the Vatican."

He began to brush his teeth and held onto the vanity as the boat began to rock even more. Matt brought the towel around to his neck as he finished brushing his teeth. Another yawn worked its way up from Matt's chest as he grew more tired. A couple gulps of water and he packed up his dopp kit and headed back to his room. As the ship took on more waves and the storm engulfed the Excalibur, Matt could hear the creaks and squeaks of the steel ship. As Matt walked back into his room, he tossed the dopp kit in a dresser drawer and dropped onto his mattress. Dorje kept watch to ensure that the commotion was created by his roommate. After several years as a guard to the Dali Lama, Dorje took no sound or person for granted. Dorje closed his eyes once Matt settled in the small twin bed. Cering upgraded all the mattresses and bedding for the Excalibur. Matt was unusually comfortable given the circumstances of traveling by sea.

Matt focused on the ceiling and began to process the last couple days. He began to wonder how Elisabeth felt being with a group of strangers that, for all intents and purposes, were mercenaries, snipers, and Special Forces. Matt still had bumps and bruises from the recon mission in Gaza. He thought about Elisabeth driving and not panicking in the face of fear. She acted brave; she acted like a woman more mature than her years. Matt knew that she had experienced tough times and devastation with her own family. To be forced into an abortion with no say in the matter must have left Elisabeth scarred. According to Sesom and Amen, the child Elisabeth was carrying would have played an important role in the struggle of good versus evil. Sesom thought the child would usher in a new period of peace and prosperity, while Amen believed the child would serve as a beacon of hope and perhaps give rise to another Messiah. Some in the group believed that the Messiah had not been born yet, others believed that Jesus Christ would return in spirit to reclaim his people, while some Disciples believed Elisabeth was the chosen one to bring peace to the Middle East. With all kinds of interpretations, Matt didn't really know, or for that matter, care about what Elisabeth's destiny was with the group.

Matt had seen Elisabeth in dreams and knew that her life was meaningful, but he didn't want to speculate at how significant she would be in the future of a religion, a planet, or a people. The earth had experienced significant stressors and catastrophes over the past several years. From tsunamis to nuclear devastation, from terrorism to assassinations, and dictators focused on ending liberty and freedom for all, the world had become hell for many people. Even in the United States, the wealthy caused a collapse of economic markets that nearly ended the legitimacy of financial institutions and banking worldwide. Even though many retirees lost everything and were forced to return to the workplace, not one financial manager had been charged with a crime against humanity. The United States was becoming more entrenched in the battle of good versus evil than upholding the values of freedom and democracy. For that reason, Matt didn't feel bad about leaving the Marines to pursue a greater cause of humanity.

Matt had seen the hellish results first hand while on several deployments around the world. Elisabeth was a key to the future and Matt was anxious about the trip to the Vatican to understand his place in all this. Even though he wasn't religious and didn't pray, he witnessed the separation of good and evil in conflicts worldwide. Matt began to wonder if his involvement in these conflicts throughout the world were smaller campaigns of good versus evil building up to Revelation. Had Matt's parents died in vain? If it weren't for 9/11, would the United States have been exposed for its own greed and double standards? Matt had always struggled with a choice to pursue weapons of mass destruction in Iraq or completely ignore the Sudan. Matt had traveled to the Sudan and witnessed millions of people that were affected by infighting between rebels and the government. The United States turned its back on the Sudan to pursue oil interests in Iraq. The United States had also turned its back on

Afghanistan in a war with Russia. Matt's mind was wandering and found its way back to Elisabeth.

Elisabeth was a beautiful woman with a strong spirit. Matt was attracted to her, both physically and emotionally. All through Matt's high school and military career, he had never experienced a close relationship with a woman. Even though he'd been on double dates and out with groups of friends, Matt never felt an emotional attraction to another woman. Of course he had sexual attractions and desires for other women, but he never acted on them. He felt that he would be disrespecting a woman if he took her as an object of his lust, as opposed to becoming attracted to the whole person and then consummating the relationship. Matt couldn't believe he was still a virgin. At that thought, Matt rolled to his left and shut his eyes. He could feel the Excalibur listing 15-20 feet as he looked at the wall. Scratches came into the room and jumped on Matt's bed. She was purring as she approached Matt's head. Matt began to pet her as she settled in right next to his chest. Within seconds, Matt was in another world.

****

Financial markets tumbled in the midst of a third world war. The United States was involved in Iran, occupying Iraq, and undergoing a major party transformation in the homeland. Most citizens were fed up with big government and were abandoning the Republican and Democrat parties. To the world, a bipartisan government in the United States had ruined a prosperous nation. Political leaders had advanced their own wealth and prosperity at the expense of their people. The citizens were intent on taking their country back and were supportive of the Tea Party and the popular Colonist party. Millions of Americans wanted to dismantle the Federal government and maintain power at the state level. They called for a President to be elected with limited power, to be Commander in Chief and maintain a strong military. The President would also act as a CEO to promote economic growth. Outside of that, the President would no longer be responsible for Transportation, Treasury, Medicare, Medicaid, Social Security, or Homeland Security. The House would be abolished and the Senate would be maintained. Monetary cuts would be upwards of 75% for many Federal programs, with the other 25% being absorbed by the States. People were tired of funding bad government and bad programs. The plan made sense to citizens because States had to balance their budgets. The United States were in a last ditch effort to save their country and people.

The Excalibur was in a last ditch effort of its own. The Disciples had been called to the Vatican by Jonas to understand the nature of their journey. As a member of the Swiss Guard, Jonas knew a lot about the Vatican and the importance of the Holy City. Several mysteries were concealed within the Vatican that very few people had seen or heard. The Disciples would be given access to the Vatican and important artifacts of religious history in hopes of unraveling the mysteries of the Catholic Church and their quest.

Sesom and Phil worked with John and Aaron to keep the ship safe on the high seas of the Mediterranean. The front produced 40-foot waves and swells on all sides of the ship. Sesom and Phil continued to smoke cigars and tell stories from their past. Occasionally, John and Aaron would grab some coffee and join Sesom and Phil on the Captain's Bridge. The laughter continued throughout the evening, everyone else knew to stay below deck during the raging storm. Matt slept through the storm.

Deep within Matt's sleep, he began to dream. He was standing outside his townhome that had burned to the ground. He walked up on the rubble and looked at a pile of charred debris. He kneeled down to pick up a picture frame.

"There's nothing left Matty."

Matt turned around and his father was walking up on him. "Dad?"

"Yes Matthew, it's me." Matt's father was wearing a flight suit with a blue cap. "Hiatt" was stitched on the left pocket over his heart and on his cap.

"How is mom?"

"She's doing fine. We didn't anticipate losing our physical lives on September 11th and leaving our two children behind. However, your mother has been watching over you and Mary ever since." Matt's eyes began to mist.

"Boy, we really miss you guys." Matt uttered the words as his father placed a hand on his shoulder and squeezed.

"We miss you too Matt. Your life has purpose though and we are very proud of your accomplishments." Matt's dad smiled and continued, "Why don't you walk with me for a while?"

"I'd like that." Matt and his father began to walk down the street.

Matt's father looked at him, "You have made some new friends?"

"I have. They seem like really good people. Mike and Mary are with us too."

"How are my grandchildren?"

"Great. John and Rebecca seem to enjoy traveling and spending more time with Mike."

As they continued to walk, Matt noticed they were back in Littleton Colorado at his old house. "I'm sorry that I spent so much time working with the Air Force while you were a teenager. I should have been around more for you and Mary."

"It's okay dad. Mary and I understood your position was important to the Air Force and mom was always around to help us. We have no regrets."

"You and Mary experienced a lot at an early age. From the tragedy at Columbine to losing us in a plane crash on 9/11, you had to grow up quickly."

"And we did."

Matt turned around and he was at the Pentagon. Flames were everywhere and bodies were being pulled from the wreckage of an aircraft and the building's west block.

"Your mom and I didn't suffer. The accident happened so fast that we didn't have time to realize what was occurring. Our physical lives ended that day but our spiritual journey continued."

Matt was speechless. He couldn't believe what he was witnessing at the Pentagon.

Matt's father continued, "You are beginning a spiritual journey of your own?"

"I am, even though I've never been fond of church and organized religion. I've had a tough time believing in much of anything over the past decade."

Matt's father smiled, "Matty, the journey is much more relevant than the destination. Organized religion has its place in the world, but don't forget that Jesus loathed the hypocrisy of church during his time. Most of his teachings were done outdoors, away from buildings and temples."

"I loathe the hypocrisy today," Matt noticed his surroundings had changed once again. He was standing in St. Peter's Square in Vatican City. Thousands of people were listening to Pope Simplicius read scripture.

"Matt, he is a good man with a pure heart."

"So I've heard, I'm planning to meet him in a few days."

"I know." Matt's dad gave him a smile.

"You already know what's going to happen, don't you?"

"No. Freewill is still alive and well in the world today. However, take note of what Simplicius says about Elisabeth and her importance to your journey."

"My journey? What are you saying dad?"

"Matt, if I gave you the answers, life wouldn't be worth living. Some of this you must find out and decide on your own. I will be watching over and guiding you, but I will not intervene in your own physical experience. You could walk away from this group tomorrow, if you so choose. Your mom and I would love you no less. However, you understand what's at stake and how the world has sunk to depths not seen since Sodom and Gomorrah. People need to begin saving themselves and quit waiting for some made up superhero."

"Since when did you quote places in the Bible?" Matt found it humorous.

"Everything becomes clear once the physical journey ends and your spiritual journey begins. While authors of the Bible may have taken some creative liberties, the stories are relevant and have meaning for life. People get all wrapped up in the semantics of what was said, as opposed to applying scripture to their daily lives. Take note, the floor is cold and hard."

"What?" Matt was thrown from the bed and onto the cold steel floor of the lower deck. Scratches went flying too. Dorje awoke to see Matt on the floor and the cat scurrying to get out of the room.

"You may want to try hammock next time." Dorje started laughing.

"Not a bad idea." Matt picked up the comforter and pillow and stumbled back to his bunk, the ship was still listing. "I'm going to check out things up top." Matt looked at his watch; the time was 12:40 am Matt's running shoes and a pair of socks were nearby, he slipped them on and headed to the captain's bridge. Captain Phil and John were in the wheelhouse navigating the ship and monitoring controls. Sesom had turned in for the evening. Captain Phil turned to Matt.

"Couldn't sleep?"

"No. I ended up on the floor a few minutes ago. How are things?"

John answered, "Good. We've checked all modifications made to the Excalibur and the ship is holding together well. Israeli Defense continues to monitor our position and the status of the war in the Middle East. China made a surprise move and invaded Taiwan."

"Wow. They've been threatening to do that for decades. That's going to put a strain on relationships between the east and west."

"The Taiwanese are good people, they will surely fight to the finish to maintain their liberty." Captain Phil had carried cargo to and from the island.

"Big one portside." John was using binoculars to locate large waves. The boat rocked left to right as the wave smashed into the bow of the ship and flooded the forecastle with water.

"At least we don't have icebergs to worry about." Matt thought about the Titanic and how the ship was advertised as unsinkable.

"We'll be fine. We're still charging ahead at 23 knots and making fairly good time. Should be in Italy day after tomorrow in the afternoon." Captain Phil put the Excalibur on autopilot and came over to Matt. "You want a cup of coffee?"

"No thanks. I'll be up the rest of the night if I drink a cup now. You guys need any help from me?"

"No. We got it." Captain Phil poured himself a cup of coffee and went back to the wheel. "Only a few minutes of storm left before we pass through it." John came over to Matt.

"Matt. I'm really sorry about what happened to your sister back at the hotel. I feel responsible for her abduction." John had the look of a defeated man.

"Don't worry about it. Everything ended up working out fine. They didn't torture or rape her. Stuff like this happens all the time in the world. We just happened to be on the receiving end of it this time."

"Let me know how I can make it up to you." John was sincere about doing right by Matt and his family.

"Let's start by keeping me in bed for the next couple of hours. The steel floor isn't very forgiving." Matt disappeared into the doorway and returned to the lower deck. He could hear some other people were up and moving about their rooms. The seas were rough and sleeping had become difficult for many of them. As Matt entered the room, Dorje welcomed him.

"Everything good up top?"

"Yeah. Phil has it under control. Storm is still raging though. A few minutes more and we'll be through it."

"Would you like my hammock?"

"No thanks. I'll be fine." Matt lay back down and thought of the dream with his father. Odd that his father discussed spiritual journeys and referenced the Bible. His father wasn't a big talker on spiritual matters while he was alive. The family went to church and worshipped on most Sundays, but they didn't pray before meals or discuss the spiritual significance of their decisions. His dad seemed at peace though and smiled throughout their conversations. Matt thought to himself, "I wonder why mom wasn't in the dream too? If anything, she discussed matters of religion more frequently than dad." The dream was puzzling to Matt but seemed very lucid, like he was actually there with his dad.

"Weird." Matt whispered to himself.

"What?" Dorje responded.

"Oh nothing, just having some random thoughts."

"Nothing random. Life have purpose. Your dream have purpose. Sure you don't want Tibetan hammock for rest of morning?"

"I'm sure." Matt thought Dorje's observation about dreams was weird, almost as if he'd known he'd had one.

****

When Matt woke up, the rocking had stopped. He could hear engines humming through the thick steel walls. Passengers of Excalibur were treated to a beautiful morning. The sun was up, there were very few clouds in the sky, and the sea was calm. The main deck was drying out and plenty of gulls had found their way to the ship. A few smaller albatrosses had also managed to find the deck of the Excalibur and took refuge. Captain Phil loved birds, but never fed them. The only time birds would receive a treat from the Excalibur was when they fished from the ship and cut bait.

The next day and a half were glorious on the Mediterranean. Mike took John fishing and showed him how to bait a hook and throw a line. John loved to reel the line in for his dad and sometimes they were able to catch Sea bass or Grouper. Captain Phil would slow the boat down while John was fishing. Mary and Rebecca spent a lot of time on deck watching birds and looking for wild dolphins. Rebecca also enjoyed the lap pool and hot tub on the lower deck. The Disciples took turns cooking and many of them liked preparing meals for their adopted family. They broke bread and occasionally sipped wine from Captain Phil's cellar. Sesom didn't drink, but he would imbibe in a glass of wine for the taste and aroma. Israeli Defense sailors also cooked and joined in the fun with wine and spirits. Long work and preparation on the Excalibur paid off and everyone respected Phil's ship.

Cering and Kimi enjoyed training Mary and Elisabeth in combat and martial arts. Disciples and sailors would spar with Mary and Elisabeth to work on counterattacks and self-defense. Many sailors had been trained in martial arts and fought with Cering and Kimi. They had never encountered women as tough as men, women that could beat them into submission. The sailors were learning techniques from Cering and Kimi as well. With kendo sticks and nun chucks, somebody was always training on the mats or sparring with a partner. Amen and Sesom would spar a couple times a day. They were two of the toughest men on the ship and challenged each other the most. Even though they would show mercy, there were many times their fighting took on the nature of a real battle. They trained hard and had the bumps to prove it. Matt could also hold his own with Amen and Sesom. While Matt's techniques were different, his results were unmatched in hand-to-hand combat. Matt had been a bruiser since high school and could endure an amazing amount of pain before he began to feel the effects. John and Aaron were also becoming skilled in martial arts, kendo, and other eastern fighting techniques.

The Excalibur ferried its way around Italy and through the Strait of Messina. There were plenty of boats and people fishing from bridges, shorelines, and small vessels. The Disciples were happy to see land again and little John was excited to see all of the activity on the Mediterranean. He would point to the fisherman and get excited when they reeled in fish or threw out nets. The Mediterranean was home to some of the best fishing and boating in the world.

"I can't wait to have some Italian food." Ethan loved Italian culture, mostly the food.

"Me too. Especially at the Vatican." Lucas's booming voice could be heard throughout the forecastle.

"Sicily is portside. Home of some of the most notorious crime families that immigrated to the United States." Jonas had spent some time in Sicily.

"You talkin' to me?" Mike was doing his best Italian voice and imitating Tony Montana in Scarface. The other Disciples got a kick out of his impersonation.

"I think Scarface was Cuban Mike." Matt began laughing with the Disciples. "You might want to work on the godfather and *swearing on your grandchildren's eyes.*" Matt threw in his own Sicilian accent at the end of the sentence.

Captain Phil came over the ship's radio and announced they would be in port in five and a half hours and all hands were to begin preparing the ship for docking. They would leave the SUVs on the ship as the Swiss Guard was providing an escort to the Vatican City. The Disciples would be heavily armed and Jonas was fine with the group carrying heavy artillery to the Vatican. John, Aaron, Mike, Mary, Elisabeth, Israeli Defense sailors and the Disciples began to prepare the Excalibur for arrival. The Excalibur hugged the coastline and took in the sights of Salerno and Napoli. Flumicino was a busy port and the Swiss Guard awaited the Excalibur's arrival. Security was tight as Phil guided the ship into the dock. The Israeli Defense sailors put the weapons' system on stand-by and went to the deck to help with the ship's arrival. The sailors would hang back with Phil, John, and Aaron to secure the ship and check supplies. The Excalibur would need to be guarded because of the weaponry that had been installed.

Once in port, the Disciples loaded up with gear and joined Mike, Mary, Elisabeth, Jonas, and the children. Matt had his 1911 .45 loaded with one in the chamber. Mike carried a 9mm and the rest of the Disciples packed semi-automatic and automatic weapons for the short trip. The Swiss Guard had a caravan of seven vehicles to transport their guests to Vatican City. The ride was a quick 15 minutes from Flumicino. The caravan was allowed through checkpoints to maintain the safety of Disciples and Swiss Guard. Matt was surprised that St. Peter's Square looked identical to his dream; Matt hadn't shared the details of his dream with Mary yet. The caravan pulled up to the Apostolic Palace and parked in front of some beautiful columns. Because St. Peter's Square was empty, Vatican City looked enormously vast.

Mary stepped out of a vehicle, "Wow, this is amazing."

Mike had been to the Vatican, but it had been packed with tourists. "Amazing yes. I can't believe how empty it is." John jumped out and began to run around St. Peter's Square. Mike continued, "How many kids in the world get to do that?" Mary gave Mike a smile.

As Jonas stepped out he answered, "None. Vatican City has been closed to the public since the war started and threats came in by the hundreds. The Holy Father is a symbol of many things, including the strength and power of Christianity worldwide. Many radical groups would prefer to see his Holiness dead."

Lucas and Li grabbed bags from the back of their SUV. "Can you believe this?" Lucas's voice echoed through the Square.

"No." Li looked up at the buildings and around the square. He had never seen anything like Vatican City.

Ethan walked by and observed, "The Sistine Chapel is right there, inside St. Peter's Basilica."

Cering had been to the Vatican numerous times; this was Kimi's first. "I can't believe we are going to meet Pope Simplicius II." Kimi could hardly contain her excitement as she took in St. Peter's Basilica.

"I hear that he is a man of humility with humble roots."
Cering grabbed her bag and followed Jonas. "Come on,"
Cering motioned her head for Kimi to follow. Cering put her
arm around Elisabeth and continued behind Jonas into the
Apostolic Palace.

Sesom had exited an SUV and walked to the center of St.
Peter's Square. He stood there, taking in the serenity while
turning full circle to view everything. The sun shone on his
face and he couldn't hold back a smile. Sesom had been in the
square once before for a mass. He couldn't believe how
peaceful the Vatican was without people. He closed his eyes
for a moment and prayed to God. Sesom jogged back to the
vehicle and grabbed his bag. As they entered Clementine Hall,
the Disciples couldn't believe the ornate details of the
sculptures and decorative marble. The hallway corridors
were equally beautiful with large ceilings and marble
carvings.

"We shall meet in the dining room and share a meal with
Pope Simplicius II. You will stay on the 3rd floor with his
Holiness. When your friends arrive from the ship, they will
be housed on the 2nd floor. We have room for the sailors from
the Israeli Defense Force, please let them know." Jonas
continued to speak as he walked up stairs. When they
reached the 3rd floor, Jonas instructed the Disciples,
Elisabeth, Mike, and Mary to find a room and make
themselves comfortable.

Jonas left the guests with some parting instructions, "You're
free to visit anywhere in the city. The only stipulation is that
you must be escorted by a senior officer of the Swiss Army."
Jonas continued down the corridor in the direction of the
Papal Apartment. "The meal will be served at 6:00 pm in the
dining room."

****

Sesom rounded up everyone at 5:45 pm to walk as a group to the dining room. Many of the Disciples had ventured out to see the Sistine Chapel, St. Peter's Basilica, and the museum. Matt, Mike, Mary and the kids went to the museum and library. Elisabeth stayed with Cering and Kimi and they spent time chatting in the courtyard outside the Apostolic Library. Sesom toured the Vatican with Jonas and discussed several unique treasures and secrets kept within. They all received an amazing history lesson and saw some of the finest works by Michelangelo, all within a couple of hours.

Phil, Aaron, John, and a few Israeli Defense sailors joined the other guests for dinner. Mike and Mary left the kids with some members of the Vatican staff. The Apostolic Palace had several cooks and wait staff that helped entertain guests of Pope Simplicius II. At Lucas's request, the cooks were preparing a fine Italian meal for their guests, chicken filled tortellini with a white alfredo sauce. Ciabatta and a salad were also prepared for the meal with some fresh asparagus. The guests could choose between wine, water, and cold or hot teas. Pope Simplicius II entered the room through the kitchen doors. He was carrying a new loaf of ciabatta. Many people didn't realize the Pope had entered the room. He was wearing a long, black robe.

"More bread sir." Pope Simplicius II asked Matt first.

"Sure." Matt had no idea who was serving him. Simplicius broke a piece of the bread from the loaf and set it on Matt's plate. Matt thought it was odd the server wasn't using tongs.

"I'll take that from you." A staff person came over and took the bread from the Pope.

"I can't finish serving my guests?"

"No your Eminence." The woman was defiant about having the Pope take his seat. Matt turned and stood up. "I'm sorry. My name is Matt and I had no idea."

"How would you? Good to meet you Matt." The Holy Father took Matt's hand and gave him a hug. "Jonas has told me much about you."

The Holy Father went around the table and took time with each of his guests. He also shook Jonas's hand and gave him a hug. "Thanks for bringing this wonderful group to the Vatican." Simplicius was very relaxed. A man in his mid-fifties, he was one of the youngest Popes to become the Bishop of Rome. He was a good-looking man. Almost as if the Pope could be the executive of a large, successful company. Simplicius wanted to make sure his guests were comfortable and receiving good treatment.

"How are your rooms?"

"Very comfortable. Thank you for having us as your guests." Sesom spoke for the group.

"You're welcome, it's my pleasure. I brought something from the museum, but before we get to that, I'd like Sesom to lead us in prayer."

Sesom said a heartfelt prayer focusing on God's will and bringing peace to a violent world. While Sesom wasn't much of a religious person, his spiritual power was unique and obvious to those he met. He blessed the meal and asked for God to guide Pope Simplicius with his decisions.

"Thank you Sesom. Now for a little surprise." Simplicius pulled a letter out of his robe and asked Elisabeth to read it. The letter was passed down the table until it reached Elisabeth. The letter had been folded over twice and was written in Italian. Elisabeth took one look at it and said, "My Italian isn't very good, is there someone else that would like to read the letter?" Ethan was seated next to Elisabeth and volunteered.

He read the note in Italian first and then began his translation.

"I hope this note finds you well Elisabeth. Your journey to the Western Wall comes with much sadness and regret." Elisabeth's eyes began to tear up. Ethan continued, "You are not alone and someone will come for you. He comes from the West and his name means most high. Your sins are forgiven and you will have a blessed life." The letter and its contents visibly upset Elisabeth. She couldn't believe such an important person in history took time to write her a letter. Pope John Paul II had no idea of who she was or when she would visit the Wall. Ethan began to pass the letter in the direction of Simplicius.

"No. That letter was written for Elisabeth and shall remain with her." The letter was passed back to Elisabeth and she put the paper in front of her on the table.

"You have been on an interesting journey that's only beginning. Jonas told me that Sesom has led the group through the deaths of two friends, an attack by pirates, and the kidnapping of Mary." Simplicius broke some bread and dipped it in some fresh tomato soup made with tomatoes from the Papal Garden.

"More importantly, he has protected Matt and Elisabeth from the evils of Samil and their attempts to destroy them. It's an honor to be in your presence." Simplicius motioned for everyone to begin sharing the meal.

"Samil is an uncommon term in mainstream society and only understood by those who study religion and religious history. In a nutshell, Samil represents much of the evil in our world today. Not just everyday evils, but world changing events. The beginning of wars, assassination of leaders, the prevention and disruption of Christianity, and other worldly religions for that matter. Samil is not guided by a spirit, but a principle of evil that supports commerce, power, terrorism, and encourages smaller nations to take what they want from good people. Is it the work of the devil?" Simplicius looked around the room.

"Yes." He continued, "Is it a devil in the sense of fire and brimstone and what is portrayed in the Bible?"

Simplicius answered his own question, "No."

"Whether or not people have lost their way, deny what's written in the Bible, or turn their backs on God, the result is still the same over time...evil."

"We are at a crossroads in our world. While the earth becomes more and more secular, there is a breakdown of values and morals in society. The biggest misconception about what's happening worldwide?" Once again Simplicius looked around the room and crossed his hands.

"That it's not a holy war. That we're not in a period of good versus evil." Simplicius took a sip of wine. "From near economic collapse worldwide to the overthrow of evil dictators in Northern Africa, I'm here to tell you that we are in a holy war. Not one against organized religions and different tribes of the Middle East, but against those who have power and abuse it to terrorize and suppress people throughout the world." The Vatican staff began to serve salads to their guests.

"I believe over the next three decades, we will see a dramatic change in the way people see the world, the way people view God, and the way human beings treat each other. In essence, the preparation for the second coming of Christ will be empirical. Each of you have been called, including the sailors of your ship, to take a message to the world and fight against the evils of Samil."

Pope Simplicius took a few bites of salad. He wanted to share his thoughts with the group, but he was more interested in gaining feedback from such a diverse group of people.

"Please, share your thoughts with me." Simplicius encouraged his guests.

Amen was first to speak up, "We have seen the evils you speak of. Samil has already infiltrated our group and murdered two of our brothers. We have retaliated with greater force and eliminated several Samil. I ask for your forgiveness as we have killed many men and will likely kill many more."

"The Apostle Paul wrote passages about war and not to pay back evil for evil. Matthew also made reference to those who live by the sword will surely die by the sword when soldiers came to take Jesus from the Garden of Gethsemane." Simplicius took a bite of salad. "However, the Roman Catholic Church recognizes that any injustice that promotes economic or social inequality must be overcome to promote peace and avoid war at all costs. According to Old Testament writings, we have a God that does his work through prophets and holy wars. Therefore Amen, you are forgiven, and in the eyes of this Pope doing God's work." The dinner was being served and Lucas got excited, clapping his hands together once and rubbing them together.

"Has it been a while since you've had Italian food Lucas?"

"Real Italian food, yes."

"Well dig in and enjoy the meal." Simplicius thanked his staff for serving the meal.

Cering continued with a question, "Do you believe this war will spread throughout the world?"

"It has and will continue to spread to many parts of the world. China has made a bold move to invade their brothers to the east. Taiwan has pledged to fight China until every last drop of Taiwanese blood is spilled. I have visited Taiwan, and those people are very serious about protecting their liberties. Korea or Japan may involve themselves in a campaign against Indonesia. With a large Muslim population, some of which has turned radical, Indonesia may become very important to India, Japan, and South Korea. North Korea has already pledged to strike South Korea with weapons of mass destruction. Looking at our planet objectively, I'm not certain there could be a worse situation facing us now."

Mike thought of his children and asked another question, "What will bring us back, what will bring peace to this planet right now?"

Simplicius thought for a moment before answering, "A trillion dollar question. This group is a good starting point. All of you have been chosen. Elisabeth is one of few people to have been visited by a Holy Spirit in over 2000 years, and the spirit was likely Mary. Many people don't understand that once Jesus' ascension occurred, God's work was done. He had forgiven us, plain and simple. Stories were told and gospels eventually written to guide mankind on a new journey. I doubt the Prince of Peace would be proud of our work over the past millennia." Simplicius paused to eat some tortellini and sip some wine.

"With that said, man has found his way into this mess and will surely need to find his way out. Nobody knows with great detail what the second coming will look like, but the return of our Lord will be upon us before we realize it."

"What do you believe the second coming will look like?" Mary was curious.

"You're looking at it. Uncontrolled wars by dictators and ruthless leaders. Squandering the wealth of billions of people at the hands of a few. Even some of the more literal interpretations of Revelation in the Bible about the forces of evil being destroyed and obliterated are relevant. Satan walks amongst us, and he is about to make his move."

There was silence in the room. The Disciples, Mike, Mary, and Elisabeth knew big things were happening around the world. The cascading effect of evil over the past several decades was uncontrolled and largely unpunished. Matt thought about how the United States was a power of respect and influence from World War II until the mid-eighties. From that point on, the country had been plagued with substandard leadership and a complete breakdown of values nationwide. Matt thought about some of his friends in the Marines and how they'd fought together in several different campaigns to preserve those very values. He worried about the United States and how they would handle the conflicts worldwide.

"Any good news Pope Simplicius?" Jonas wanted to lighten the tone. Some Disciples began laughing.

"Of course there's good news, 27 books of it in the New Testament. I don't want anybody to think for a minute that the Vatican or its leadership has lost hope. This is a time of great significance and many people are counting on Christians, Muslims, Buddhists, and other peaceful religions to rise up against evil worldwide."

Simplicius continued to enjoy his meal and the conversation grew lighter in the room. He discussed books, the recent move of the Shroud of Turin and Dead Sea Scrolls to the Vatican library. He continued to talk about how the Catholic Church hadn't made a decision on the Shroud's legitimacy, but the cloth was an impressive artifact. Simplicius encouraged his guests to take in the many sites of the Vatican while it remained closed. He was also discouraged that the Vatican was closed to the very people it aimed to serve, but the risk of keeping it open was too great. Servers brought out an assortment of cannoli with a variety of chocolate sauces. Lucas was still excited and ate everything in site. Matt caught a whiff of the coffee and couldn't resist the dessert.

"After we finish the meal, I would love to have Sesom, Matt, and Elisabeth join me in my apartment."

"Absolutely." Sesom knew that Simplicius would offer more information about Matt and Elisabeth in private; he was surprised that the Pope invited him as well.

"Jonas will take everyone else on a more private tour of the Shroud, Dead Sea Scrolls, and some of the Papal tombs. I'm sure he will surprise you with a trinket or two in the library."

When the dinner concluded, Simplicius thanked the staff
once again. The Disciples, Mike, Mary, and Elisabeth also
thanked the staff and ventured into the kitchen to thank the
cooks. Lucas was especially appreciative of the great meal.
Matt, Elisabeth, and Sesom walked with Simplicius to the 3rd
floor. Even though there was an elevator, Simplicius
preferred the exercise, especially after a rich meal that ended
with cannoli. There were several chairs to choose from and
Simplicius offered his guests coffee. Sesom and Matt wanted
another cup, Elisabeth refused. While Simplicius went to
brew the coffee, Elisabeth began to look over the catalog of
books in the library. She pulled down the Canterbury Tales.
Matt noticed her beauty again. She was in a white dress with
a black belt. Her hair was down, even though Cering had
French braided it for Elisabeth while they were in the
Apostolic Courtyard together. She smiled as she read a few
lines of Chaucer's old tale. As she flipped though pages, she
noticed that Matt was staring at her.

"Would you like to read this?"

"No thanks. Sorry, I was staring."

"It's okay. This all seems like a fairytale of its own."

Before Matt could expand on her fairytale comment,
Simplicius returned with coffee.

"Please, have a seat and make yourselves comfortable." After
sharing the coffee with Sesom and Matt, Simplicius took a
seat in a green chair with a high back near the bookshelves.

"Quite a collection of books." Elisabeth was very impressed.

"I love reading. On a gloomy day, I'll visit this chair and spend
a day with books. Sometimes I'll read the Bible, sometimes

I'll read fiction by American authors, and other days I'll revisit some of the great comedies and tragedies written by Shakespeare."

Matt said, "Shakespeare has always been a favorite of mine. I probably saw more plays in the park than the number I read in high school. Shakespeare in the Park was always a favorite of many students at Columbine. In many cases, we passed literature with the help of Shakespeare in the Park. Back then, I enjoyed Othello and As You Like It."

"A little sweet and sour with your Shakespearean tastes. As You Like It was one of his better comedies in my opinion. Touchtone was a great clown. I could discuss Shakespeare all night, but I'd like to change the subject." Simplicius waited for affirmation.

"Sure," Matt obliged.

"Jonas has briefed me on your story, backgrounds, and the reasons for your visit. We have reason to believe that you've been called by God to prepare the world for the second coming of our Father. From the notes John Paul II left to the visions you've experienced of each other, there is a higher power at work in your lives." Simplicius took a sip of coffee and inhaled the aroma.

"We also have reason to believe that the world as we know it will come to an end. Not like in the movies, but through significant events that will alter our way of life and pit good versus evil. While we experience good versus evil in everyday life, the changes will be significant and have begun with the war in the Middle East. I am aware of your story Elisabeth, and know that your heart is heavy based on choices that were made for you. There is no doubt in my mind that you were visited by Mary, mother of Jesus, and blessed in the womb. I believe your story, I understand your pain and suffering."

"Why me though?"

"You represent two opposing forces. Not necessarily good and evil, but people who oppose each other until death in the Middle East. Your pregnancy may be viewed as reconciliation between the two, an alignment of Islam and Judaism, an attempt at the reconciliation of principles that have divided important nations for thousands of years. Really hard to say."

"But my pregnancy was terminated. I no longer carry a child." Elisabeth was saddened by the thought of changing God's will through her parents' decision to end the pregnancy.

"There are other ways to become pregnant." Simplicius looked at Matt.

"I'm glad he looked in your direction." Sesom began to laugh.

"What are you saying Simplicius?" Matt was surprised by the inference.

"You haven't figured out your calling yet Mr. Hiatt?"

"No. Not yet."

"Your seed shall fertilize Elisabeth's womb. You began to experience dreams about the time of Elisabeth's abortion. Very similar to Newton's laws of movement, one action creates an equal and opposing reaction."

"Seems more coincidental to me." Matt dodged the inference.

"A coincidence. A coincidence that you had visions of Elisabeth at the Western Wall and other places after her abortion? That you traveled halfway around the world with this man, a man whose name has significant meaning when spelled in reverse. In this life Matt, there are very few things that happen by chance or coincidence. Life does not end with one abortion, but can begin anew with one birth. You don't really believe that you're just along for the ride?" Sesom rubbed his beard and gave Matt a look of confidence while shaking his head in the affirmative.

Elisabeth began to giggle with a nervous laugh.

"What's so funny?" Matt was on the defensive.

"Maybe that's why you were staring." Elisabeth went from giggling to laughing. Matt began to laugh as well; he knew that Elisabeth caught him staring on a few occasions. There was an attraction between Matt and Elisabeth, but they had not considered their attraction in a physical way. Their bond was even closer based on some of the dreams they shared for each other. Something was different about their relationship, almost as if they had been made for each other.

"But Father, I've had an abortion and made a terrible decision with regard to my body."

"Forgiveness is something that transcends physical or emotional sins. The decision involving an abortion was predetermined by your parents; therefore, Pope John Paul II knew of the sin and forgave you before the pregnancy started."

Matt was confused, "Hold on a minute. You're telling me that the mother of Jesus visited this woman in spirit, fertilized her womb, only to have Elisabeth's parents force her to have an abortion and ruin everything?"

"Yes."

"So why bother?"

"Free will." Pope Simplicius was quick to answer.

"What do you mean by free will?"

"Ever since the crucifixion of Christ and the forgiveness of our sins, humanity has been blessed with free will. We can make our own decisions. At any time, you could leave this place and not look back. Elisabeth could choose not to believe me and walk out the door. You have free will to make your own decisions." Pope Simplicius took another sip of coffee and continued.

"Just because we have free will doesn't mean the Holy Spirit will turn its back on us. The Holy Spirit will always try and guide humanity in the right direction. Elisabeth's abortion was not of her own will and she's asked for forgiveness. Why dwell on the past? The Holy Spirit is calling on this group of people to protect Elisabeth's well-being and pregnancy. The dreams, the Western Wall, and other signs have been overwhelming. With that said, you can choose not to be part of this experience. That doesn't mean the Holy Spirit will turn its back on humanity. If that was the case, Revelation would be a foregone conclusion and evil would prevail over good."

Matt didn't know what to think. The words of Pope Simplicius made sense. From Columbine, to the deaths of Robert and Dorothy Hiatt on 9/11, to confronting a ruthless enemy on the battlefields at home and abroad, Matt had seen evil at work over the past decade. In reality, he was a perfect candidate to be called for a higher purpose. Matt hadn't lost hope, he had found the good in others in a terrible world, and most importantly he had fought to uphold the liberties and freedoms of others. Matt directed his attention toward Sesom.

"What do you think Sesom? I trust your judgment."

"We are in the presence of a holy man. One who knows more about the historical events of Christianity, Islam, Buddhism, Hinduism, and other major religions worldwide than most other people on the globe. I'm Muslim by birthright, but I've always respected the teachings and parables of the Christian New Testament. I respect what Pope Simplicius says. He has visions beyond my understanding. Much like you, I would lay down my life for him." Sesom was all business.

"Thank you Sesom. Your birthright can be traced back to Moses with biblical significance and transcendence. You are a child of Abraham and have been well chosen to represent this group of people." Matt hadn't considered what Sesom's name spelled backwards.

"You're a descendant of Moses?"

"I am."

"Wow." Matt didn't know what else to say.

"The Holy Spirit didn't die with Jesus or the first Disciples. There is a presence amongst us in spirit and flesh that dates back thousands of years. There is not much difference between the traditions of Judaism, Christianity, and Islam. Radical people make the differences seem much more significant than they really are." Sesom sat back in his chair and relaxed.

"The reference I made at dinner, the one about Satan making his move." Simplicius took a more serious tone. "The move will be made in the United States inside your government."

"What do you mean?" Matt appeared confused.

"We have very reliable intelligence that your Vice President is corrupt. While your President is a good man and has worked well with other world leaders, the Vice President is a bad man with bad intentions."

"How bad?" Sesom was drawn into the conversation.

"The Vice President of the United States aims to have the President assassinated as soon as possible. Not only to assume power, but to change the course of the United States' government forever. The Vice President is Samil, and he wants to usher in a period of evil dictatorships at home and abroad." Simplicius got up and went to the window.

"Where did the intelligence come from?"

"Turkey of all places. We have had our fair share of problems with the Turkish government and our stance on European Union integration. Pope John Paul II supported integration of Turkey into the EU, and Pope Benedict XVI had a different opinion of the country entering the EU. The Vatican has been very involved in Turkey ever since and has worked hard to have a better understanding of Islamic culture in Turkey. While making strides in our relationship, an Ambassador to Italy approached the Swiss Army to share highly sensitive information about these assassination plans for the President of the United States. The information was received three months ago and was handed over to the CIA. I'm not sure if the CIA did anything with the information, but the

Ambassador to Italy died shortly after sharing the information. Even though the Ambassador was young and healthy, he died of a heart attack. The sequence of events was suspicious."

"What were the plans?" Matt said.

"According to intelligence, there were Syrian operatives inquiring about trained Turkish paramilitary to carry out the orders of an assassination. The Ambassador stated that the United States was very much involved in the plans. The United States was offering large sums of money through the Syrian operatives to recruit a dozen Turkish paramilitary to carry out the plans. The plan was to assassinate the President of the United States and then have the group take their own lives; making it look like radical Islam was responsible for the attack." Simplicius looked out the window and sipped more coffee.

"Your President is a very popular man. He has been respectable since taking office." Sesom's voice carried through the library.

"I know. His popularity rating is over 60 percent and people like him. Why would the United States be involved in a plot to assassinate him?" Matt couldn't put the details together.

Simplicius provided the answer, "Your Vice President is a bad man. The United States have been fairly corrupt for the past couple of decades. From financial bailouts to wars in the Middle East, many countries have been very suspicious of the United States."

"The Vice President and Secretary of State served together in Afghanistan. I wouldn't be surprised if they were well connected in the Middle East." Matt was beginning to see the bigger picture. "What can we do?"

"There isn't much you can do. While countries have always shared intelligence with each other, implicating people within a government involved in a coup will be dismissed with contempt. The problems in the United States are internal and don't involve the international community, at least not yet."

"I know some people in the CIA, I served with them on some missions. I might be able to speak with their commanding officers and share details of our conversation." Matt had forgotten about how he left the United States.

"Matt, you are a wanted man in your own country. The government won't listen to a fugitive and someone that went AWOL from the Marines. Regardless of who your contacts may be, we must only trust each other. You must not make contact with people from your past." Sesom had a serious tone.

"So what can we do?"

"We could depart for the States and utilize other means to contact the President. Or we could lay low and see what happens next." Sesom was exploring options.

"You are welcome to stay here and search out your destiny. We have plenty of Swiss Guards and Army to protect the Vatican." Simplicius came back from the window and took a seat near Sesom. Elisabeth took Simplicius' place at the window and looked out over St. Peter's Square. She could see guards in the distance.

"I'm not very good at sitting around and waiting for things to happen. I believe we should make them happen." Matt was showing his impatience.

"You must make them happen with Elisabeth." Simplicius gave Matt one of those looks that embarrassed him. Elisabeth turned red as well. Simplicius continued, "Your offspring will usher in a new world order and prepare us for the second coming of our Messiah. Elisabeth has been blessed and you have been chosen, a child is in your future."

"I still have a hard time believing this." Matt was defiant.

"I don't." Elisabeth spoke up from the window and affirmed what Simplicius said. "I am from the Holy Land and have witnessed many mysteries since I was a child. When Mary visited me, I felt safe and secure in her presence. She wasn't forceful, she wasn't overbearing, and she spoke with me as if I was her own daughter. When my parents forced me to have an abortion, I became depressed and saddened by the circumstances. But I never lost hope." Elisabeth's face lit up. "I have made decisions that I'm not proud of, but I hold out hope that what Simplicius says is the truth and our destiny." Elisabeth looked directly at Matt. Matt didn't know what to say, Elisabeth's statements shocked him.

Silence settled in the library. Sesom and Matt sipped their coffee while Simplicius relaxed back in his chair. Simplicius was fine with silence; he knew that thinking brought about silence.

"We must return to the States and try to protect the President." Matt made up his mind.

"The President has hundreds of men and women protecting him on a daily basis. What makes you think we will have any success warning the President about hearsay coming out of Turkey by way of the Vatican?"

"I don't know. I haven't thought it through yet."

"Do you realize how many threats are made against the President of the United States per day?"

"About 40," Matt knew the details.

"What makes you think that our story will be any different from the number of threats the President receives in a day, month, or year?"

"We have two highly decorated servicemen in our group. If I can't get through, maybe Mike can. He is very well connected with commanding officers and Special Operations. They've been wanting him to return to service for the past several years."

Sesom rubbed his beard and looked at Simplicius, "He is a testy little minion, isn't he?"

Simplicius began to laugh, "Testy, yes; minion, no. Matt's been trained too well to be considered a testy minion."

"I understand what you are saying Matt, but consider the risks. If the Marines should pick you up, we will have a very difficult time rescuing you. Not only that, but your involvement is very clear to Samil and the people trying to kill you and your family. Once again, you will put us in harms way if you choose to return to the United States."

"What about the President? Is he not in harms way already? According to Simplicius, there is a coup d'état about to occur within his own government."

Simplicius interrupted Matt's thought, "There are plenty of horrible things that happen in the world everyday. Close to 20,000 children die each day from hunger. Another 20,000 people die from the affects of poverty. When the Vatican released very sensitive information to the CIA from the Turkish Ambassador to Italy, he died a very suspicious death. The United States' government is likely involved at multiple levels in the plans for your President."

"Shouldn't we do something? Shouldn't we try Simplicius?" Matt was becoming frustrated with the pontiff.

"You are doing something. You have found your calling and rescued Elisabeth from evil. When Jesus went to Gethsemane, he anticipated deception and death. Jesus knew that his life was coming to an end, but he struggled with a betrayal at the hands of his own Disciple. At many times in history, we have seen men become enraged with envy and kill their leaders. Just before the birth of Jesus, Brutus plotted and successfully killed Caesar in collusion with other Roman Senators. Conspiracy and coups have occurred all throughout history. Some of these events were meant to happen." Simplicius sat forward in his chair.

"You tell me Matt. Knowing the circumstances, should you try and save the President's life?"

"Yes." Matt was firm and began pacing the library.

"Then you shall go back to the United States and try to prevent the coup." Simplicius looked at Sesom, they were both thinking the same thing.

Elisabeth looked out the window. The sky was becoming darker as the sun set over the Mediterranean to the west.

Elisabeth forgot about the war, where she was, and what was being discussed in the library. She focused on the beauty of the sunset and shadowing from the buildings nearby. A golden hue was cast over her body as she stood near the window. Matt stopped pacing and noticed a glow from Elisabeth's direction. The golden rays of the sun shone through the window and illuminated Elisabeth's white dress. She was glowing. Sesom noticed Elisabeth at the window too.

"Remember Matt, there are more people involved in this than you. Think of the bigger picture."

"I'm thinking of a country and all of the citizens of the United States." Matt pulled his attention away from Elisabeth.

"Then it's decided. We shall set sail for the United States and try to make contact with the President. You will stay here with Elisabeth though."

"But I was…" Sesom interrupted Matt.

"You are not going Matt. You will stay here with Elisabeth, Mary, your nephew and niece. We will not be taking them. Mike can assist us with strategies and communication, but you will not make the trip." Sesom had made up his mind.

"Fair enough. I would like us to try and prevent this travesty from happening." Matt began to relax a little.

The room became quiet again. Elisabeth kept her place at the window. Matt took a seat and finished his coffee with Simplicius and Sesom. They discussed matters of the current war and what the Italian Army was doing to protect its homeland through coordination with the Swiss Army. Simplicius shared his feelings about war and how many civilian casualties he believed would result from global conflict. War had become part of modern day culture since countries developed the capabilities to sail or fly and deploy bombs upon each other. Simplicius knew that the world must usher in a new era of peace, and he believed that would only come through Revelation and great devastation.

Matt joined in the conversation as Elisabeth took a seat near Simplicius. Matt was saddened by the thought that the world seemed to lack a moral compass and children were exposed to hunger, war, sex, and other sensitive issues at such an early age. Many parents had inadvertently abandoned parenting to try and stay ahead with bills and groceries. As the inner cities of the United States became more depressed and impoverished, Matt always questioned why the military efforts were focused on rebuilding on foreign soil. He felt like the military would be better served assisting with the reorganization efforts in Detroit, New York, or some of the hard hit areas of California and Florida.

Phil had taken the young sailors under his wing and treated them with great respect and dignity. He knew they were being asked to leave their families and might never see them again. Phil was a perfect father figure for the deckhands of the Excalibur. They all respected Phil and trusted his judgment as a captain on the high seas.

"Matt, what if Mike doesn't want to leave his family and return to the States?" Sesom was still trying to talk Matt out of the decision to return to the United States.

"He will. The President is his Commander in Chief. He won't sit back while his own party plans a coup d'état. Mike has put his life on the line for his country and the President before, he will again. I would."

"Then you shall talk to him and we will leave in two days. Like I said before, you will not be taking this trip with us to the United States. Too much is at risk. You will stay here with Elisabeth, Mary, and the children."

"Fair enough." Matt thanked Simplicius for the fine meal and excused himself from the group. He wanted to find Mike and discuss the problems abroad. Sesom and Elisabeth stayed with Simplicius and discussed family, friends, and current affairs.

Matt found Mike and Mary in their room. John and Rebecca were asleep and their exhausted parents were out on the veranda sipping coffee. Matt discussed the Turkish intelligence with Mike while Mary listened intently. Mike wasn't surprised that a coup was planned inside the United States' government. Mike had seen and heard intelligence about other countries becoming involved in a coup to overthrow the United States' government. Details were always sketchy and based more on hearsay than hard facts.

"Will you be making the trip?" Mike was curious.

"No. I'll hang back to watch Elisabeth, Mary, and the kids." Matt appeared disappointed that he wouldn't be able to join the Disciples on this operation.

"I don't know Matt. Maybe hanging back isn't such a bad idea. Over 8,000 Secret Service, countless CIA, and a strong military protect the President; that will be challenging to navigate through, at best. Not to forget the added complications of military and other sources you must avoid. Remember, you are a wanted man." Mary squeezed Mike's hand and looked him in the eye.

"It's an inside job Mike. The Vice President is involved with the operation." Matt was persistent.

"That's what bothers me. How are we supposed to get close enough to the President to warn him about his own staff?"

"You'll have to work through the Vice Chairman of the Joint Chiefs of Staff and hopefully gain an audience with the Defense Secretary." Matt knew the military was the only option to warn the President, and fortunately Mike knew one of the Four Star Generals in the army.

"Very risky. I can contact General Gilmore once I return to the US, but I'm not sure if he'll have any luck with the Joint Chiefs."

"Does this mean you're going?" Mary sounded disappointed.

"I have to try. I would feel terrible if something happened and I didn't even try to warn the President. The war is continuing to get worse and I have to try for their sake." Mike motioned to the bedroom where John and Rebecca were sleeping.

"But Mike, we left New Jersey at the same time Matt's home was raided. The military will surely be suspicious of Matt's whereabouts and why we left abruptly. They may think that you're involved with Matt's disappearance." Mary shared her concerns.

"Regardless of what they believe, I need to let General Gilmore know the truth and about things we've experienced over the past couple of weeks." Mike continued to build his resolve; "I will meet with Sesom tomorrow morning and make arrangements for our departure. You will hang back with Mary and the kids." Mike's last sentence sounded more like an order than a statement.

"I will."

****

The morning came with rain and cold weather. Matt went to the window to scan St. Peter's Square. Other than a few birds, the Square was quiet. Scratches kept guard perched on the windowsill peering out the window.

"Go get 'em Scratches." Matt encouraged his cat to catch the birds. Scratches would meow and chatter at the fowl. Matt went to the kitchen and pulled some coffee out of the pantry. Morning coffee had become a ritual for those traveling on the Excalibur. The Vatican had single cup dispensers and a variety of flavors from around Europe and South Africa. Matt pulled a cinnamon pastry flavor from the box and set it in the coffee maker. Within seconds, the aroma of cinnamon filled the air.

Matt went to the fridge and grabbed the milk. He put some in a dish for Scratches; suddenly her attention was redirected from the birds to the milk. She came over and began to lap up the beverage. Matt finished doctoring his cup and headed downstairs to the dining room. He could hear commotion coming from the dining room. Elisabeth was the first to approach Matt.

"Bad news from the United States." Elisabeth had the look of fear.

"What happened?"

"Dirty bombs in New Hampshire. The President was in Concord when several bombs went off. Even though he escaped the first explosion, the second and third bombs were direct hits. Al Qaeda has claimed responsibility."

"Al Qaeda?"

"Yes Matt, they have claimed responsibility." Matt blew past Elisabeth and went to Sesom.

"What's going on?" Sesom was sitting with Mike, Lucas, Amen, Ethan, and Jonas.

"Dirty bombs in the United States, a couple in the vicinity of the President."

"Did he survive?" For the first time Matt looked worried.

"We don't know?" Mike joined in the conversation.

"The dirty bombs were more sophisticated than what we would normally see from Al Qaeda. Even though they claimed responsibility, the assassination attempt seems far-fetched for Al Qaeda." Amen continued the analysis.

"How many bombs were there?"

"Three in Concord, two in Los Angeles, one in New York, and one in Miami. Whoever planned these attacks focused on the location the US President was going to visit. The other bombs seem more like a diversion from the real target." Amen had received much of his intelligence from the sailors on Excalibur.

"The sailors are receiving updates from Tel Aviv about what's happening in the United States. They are feeding us information as they receive it." Sesom sipped some coffee.

Mike continued, "The U.S. government is being very quiet about the status of the President. No leaks. No media. Only speculation being reported from news agencies at this point."

"Several hundreds are reported dead or dying from the attacks. The kill zone was several blocks for each bomb." Ethan weighed in.

"I don't understand," Matt took a seat. "Al Qaeda? Many Al Qaeda leaders were angry that Osama Bin Laden carried out the attacks of 9/11, which brought the wrath of the US overseas. Why would they want to make the same mistake twice?"

"They wouldn't." Mike's tone softened as Mary and Elisabeth entered the dining room together. Cering came over and took a seat by Sesom.

"It's part of a coup within our own country," Mike looked at Matt. "Based on what you told me and Amen has shared with me this morning, the Ambassador from Turkey was aware of the plans for an overthrow of our government."

"But how?" Matt was astonished.

"Syria was fishing around their border with Turkey. They found some Turkish paramilitary that would carry out an attack on the President of the United States and other cities in the US for a price. They needed the Turks for their knowledge and connections with weaponry. The United States approached a group of Syrians while they were on an envoy to the Middle East. The Secretary of State is likely involved with funding the operation, although none of the money will be traced back to your government." Amen was well connected and understood how mercenaries worked in the Middle East.

Sesom continued, "A group of Turks and Syrians crossed the border between Mexico and the United States four to five weeks ago. From there, it's hard to say what happened, but they hit their target in Concord. Their own devices killed the Turks and Syrians involved with the bombings. This made the operation appear like crazed suicide bombers seeking revenge against the US carried out the mission. When in reality, the operation was meticulously planned and funded with the help of the United States' government."

Mike interrupted Sesom, "I heard rumblings and rumors about the United States being involved in a coup with its own government a few years back. The whole story seemed farfetched and pretty unremarkable in the field. Most of special ops thought the story originated with Al Qaeda or Taliban as propaganda. I can't believe the intel was true?"

"The border between the US and Mexico has always been an area of concern for the Federal government. When the Department of Homeland Security hired contractors to begin building a border fence, the contractors had illegals on the payroll. The illegals created weaknesses in the fence by not pouring concrete in some spots and not finishing welds at critical seams in the joints. They documented their work well and let other immigrants know about the less secure areas of the fence." Matt wasn't surprised by a breach at the US-Mexico border.

All of the women came over and the group was seated for breakfast. Several Israeli sailors were joining the Disciples for breakfast.

Mary spoke up, "Has the mission to the US been cancelled?"

"Yes, we no longer have a mission in the United States." Sesom was surprised events were changing so quickly.

"Sesom, what are we to believe of the news that Al Qaeda was involved in the bombings?" Kimi asked.

"We are not to believe the announcements, and our knowledge and conversations shall remain in this room." The staff of the Vatican began to pour coffee and juices while serving pastries.

Kimi wasn't satisfied with Sesom's answer, "So, what are we to believe then?"

"We have shared information with Simplicius, Suzie, and several sources in the United States. We have reason to believe that the United States is undergoing a coup d'état orchestrated by the Vice President. Vice President Crevan designed an elaborate plot to involve paramilitary from Syria and Turkey to carry out the assassination of President Palmer." Sesom sipped more of his coffee.

Cering continued Sesom's train of thought, "So Al Qaeda was framed to carry out the assassination as a diversion away from the United States' government and those really involved."

"Exactly."

"News agencies have not confirmed the survival or death of the President." Cering said.

"And they won't. Not until the government develops a plan of succession for the office." Matt remembered reading about the chaos and speculation surrounding the assassination of John F. Kennedy in Dallas. The government rushed to swear in Lyndon Johnson on Air Force One shortly after JFK's death. As speculation grew and conspiracy groups began to theorize the assassination was all part of a major plot, Lyndon Johnson was criticized for his haste to assume office.

"So what to do Sesom?" Dorje drank some juice being poured by the staff.

"Sometimes it's best to do nothing in instances like this. We have found Matt and his family, recovered Elisabeth, and are in the company of Jonas and his protectors from the Swiss Army."

Mike began to question Sesom, "And what happens when dirty bombs go off in or around the Vatican? Our very presence in this holy place puts them at great risk."

"I am concerned about that as well. There is no doubt that Samil is tracking our movements, and now that Vice President Crevan is calling the shots, he will have the Central Intelligence Agency looking for us." Sesom did not eat ham or bacon, so the chef prepared him a steak for breakfast.

Amen knew how the game worked and added, "They will peg us as a hostile group involved with the assassination of President Palmer and the killings at Matt's townhome. An elaborate story will be concocted tying us to the Syrian group that carried out the operation. We will become some of the most hated and hunted people in the world."

"Oh no." Elisabeth was beginning to understand the significance of President Palmer's assassination.

"Oh yes. The White House Press has more influence than any other cabinet position in the government. They can spin things however they want and have the national media follow suit." Mike summed up all of Washington's press fairly well.

Amen shared some Israeli intelligence; "The United States is preparing to strike Iran, Syria, and Pakistan very hard. The

U.S. military hasn't ruled out the use of nukes. The government will use the dirty bomb attacks and Al Qaeda's claims of responsibility against the Middle East as propaganda legitimizing their retaliation. The paramilitary from Syria and Turkey that carried out the attacks have been given asylum in Russia. The bombers' families are well taken care of and have been removed from the Middle East. The Israeli military will pull back when the US obliterates these areas. Israel will look to exterminate Hezbollah and Hamas in the short-term."

"Genocide?" Cering had a tone of sadness in her voice.

"In that region, absolutely." Amen was quick to answer.

"The Jews will take back all of Israel and move the Palestinians north to Lebanon and Syria, or what's left of them. They will claim Jerusalem once again and look forward to the coming of their Messiah." Sesom shared his views on the war and future.

"My parents and family." Elisabeth whispered as she began to realize the magnitude of what was happening.

"Iran will be hit very hard by the West in the next couple of days. They won't allow Iran to launch weapons of mass destruction against Israel or friendly Arab countries. Iran understands that they will be destroyed and will do everything in their power to launch a preemptive strike against the West. Russia will be a crucial partner in all of this. If they side with Iran and other volatile countries in the region, a long drawn out war will ensue." Ethan weighed in on the conversation with his thoughts.

Jonas was listening to the conversation going back and forth at the table. The Swiss Army gathered intelligence for the

Vatican and corroborated much of what the Israeli Defense Department was finding. There were several meltdowns occurring all over the world, but the most troubling spots were located in the United States, Taiwan, and Indonesia. China's bold move to attack Taiwan was for opportunistic reasons only because the West had over allocated resources to the Middle East and South Korea. By now, all of the Disciples and sailors had joined the table and were eating breakfast.

"There is somewhere safe we can go on the seas." Captain Phil spoke up.

"Are we going to run?" Ethan countered.

"More like hiding. Based on reports that are coming in from Israeli Defense Forces, we would be wise to do what Mike suggests. Sooner or later Samil, or whatever, will catch up with us and we don't want to put innocent people in harms way." Phil scratched his head.

Jonas interrupted, "You are welcome to stay as long as you wish. We have fortified our positions around Vatican City."

Sesom cut in, "Thank you Jonas, but I believe Phil is right. These people are crazy enough to fly planes into buildings with large payloads and gas their own people. They will find a way to attack Vatican City and Rome if they believe we are here. We can't allow that." Jonas remained silent.

"And what do you propose Phil?" Sesom redirected.

"We leave day after tomorrow and continue transmitting our signal. The bad guys will see that we are leaving the Vatican. As we cross the Strait of Gibraltar at the southern tip of Spain, we go dark and head for South America. The Israeli

Defense Force will still track our position through an encrypted signal." Phil had thought through several details.

"We are heading for Brazil?" Lucas appeared excited.

"Farther south."

"Antarctica?" Lucas asked with curiosity.

"Not quite that far; the Falkland Islands off the southeast coast of South America. I know some folks from England that will provide cover and keep us safe, at least until the earth cools. Very few people, even fewer problems." Phil had sailed around South America several times and formed strong relationships with people on the Falkland Islands.

"I have been there before." Lucas shook his head in affirmation.

"There are two large islands and several smaller islands. Outside of fishing and sheep herding, not much else happens. I doubt they would be a target of anyone, unless Argentina decides to invade again." Phil chuckled at his last thought.

"I've always wanted to herd sheep." Matt's sarcasm filled the room.

"You can't even take care of a cat!" Cering chimed in. Elisabeth and the rest chuckled at the inference.

Everyone at the table was filling up on pottage, breads, and breakfast meats. The kitchen was preparing omelettes made to order for the group. In some cases, the sailors ordered two omelettes. Fresh vegetables were taken from the Papal Garden.

Several Disciples still couldn't believe they were staying at the Vatican. Even during breakfast, the guests would admire artwork and sculptures adorning the dining hall. While Rebecca stayed with Mary on her lap, John acted and ate like one of the boys. John was just happy to be with his father. He listened intently to the conversations, even though he didn't understand them.

"How many days?" Sesom knew the trip would be long.

"Eleven, in rough seas too. October is a tough time to be on the Atlantic."

"Great." Li put his head down and lost his appetite.

"The Atlantic won't be that bad Li. How long do cowboys have to ride bulls in a rodeo?" Phil caught Li's attention.

"What?" Li didn't understand what Phil was saying.

"You've seen bull riding. How long does a cowboy have to stay on a bull before the ride is over?"

"I have no idea." Li sat back in his chair.

"Eight seconds." Phil made a point, but no one understood it. Phil sipped some coffee and continued.

"The Excalibur will be lucky to see eight days of bad seas in that eleven day stretch. Eight days versus eight seconds." Phil nodded and continued with his coffee. Sesom began to laugh. Li turned white as a ghost.

"Cering."

"Yes Sesom."

"Please purchase plenty of oils and Dramamine for the trip." Sesom smiled at Phil.

"Absolutely." Cering smiled too.

Sesom turned to Li, "You should have your sea legs in three to four days."

Li offered up sarcasm, "I'd prefer eight seconds." The table laughed at Li's comment.

Matt sat across the table from Elisabeth and thought about what Simplicius said. Elisabeth was a beautiful young woman with an exotic look about her. Matt had not fallen for her yet, but he was attracted to her beauty, mind, and confidence. Elisabeth acted bravely in Gaza and Matt admired that quality in a woman.

"What do you think?" Matt caught Elisabeth's attention.

"Let's take a walk." Elisabeth was ready for some fresh air.

Matt grabbed his cup of coffee and escorted Elisabeth to St. Peter's Square. Swiss Guards were in the square and on every rooftop of the Vatican. Elisabeth was used to seeing armed guards in public places.

"What do *you* think?" Elisabeth directed the question back at Matt.

"I think this is a beautiful place and I'm with a great group of people." Matt paused for a second.

"What do you think about what Simplicius said?" Elisabeth was pushing Matt to understand their relationship.

"When you were standing by the window last night as the sun was setting, I saw beauty like I'd never seen before. Even though I've been staring on occasion, I felt a connection between us that I can't explain." Matt couldn't believe he was speaking so openly.

"Thank you. I'm glad you find me pretty." Elisabeth spoke with the innocence of a schoolgirl.

"I didn't say pretty, I said beautiful." Matt stopped and placed his right hand on Elisabeth's shoulder. "I've never felt this way about a woman. I've never even had a girlfriend. I was always too busy with sports and the military."

"Really?"

"Really." Matt appeared guilty of something he hadn't done. Elisabeth smiled and leaned into Matt. She gave him a kiss on the lips and threw her arms around him. Captain Phil, Sesom, Amen, Cering, Dorje, Kimi, Li, Lucas, Talan, and Ethan were standing in one of the archways watching Matt and Elisabeth kiss for the first time. Matt brought his hands up to Elisabeth's cheeks as he continued to kiss her.

"What do you think boss?" Lucas directed the question at Sesom.

"I think life happens for a reason and that reason happens to be in the center of St. Peter's Square." Sesom folded his arms and smiled.

"Think we have room for one more?" Cering also folded her arms and smiled at Sesom.

"We will make room!" Sesom nodded his head in affirmation.

Captain Phil asked, "We still leaving day after tomorrow?"

"Bright and early." Sesom turned and went through the door that led the Disciples back to the dining room. Mike and Mary were chatting with Jonas and some of the Israeli Defense sailors. Rebecca was asleep in Mary's arms and John was sitting on the lap of one of the sailors.

"Everything okay?" Jonas noticed the group returning to the dining room.

"Better than okay. We are ready to see the Dead Sea Scrolls and the Ark of the Covenant." Sesom winked at Jonas.

"The Dead Sea Scrolls we can do. The Ark of the Covenant is still located somewhere in the United Kingdom or South Africa." Jonas spoke as he left his seat.

"Jonas. You understand my bloodline. I'm very much aware of where the Ark of the Covenant rests. There are reasons people are not allowed to enter the Archives of the Vatican. One of them is the Ark. I would like to witness the most tightly held secret the Vatican has to offer. I would like to see the tablets of Moses."

"Let's start with the Scrolls." Jonas didn't acknowledge Sesom's demand.

"As you like it Jonas." Sesom patted his newfound friend on the back. The Disciples followed Jonas as he took the group toward the library. Matt and Elisabeth remained in St. Peter's Square. Dark clouds began to form to the north, reminding them of a change in season and darker days ahead.